**Confronting Income
Inequality in Japan**

Confronting Income Inequality in Japan

A Comparative Analysis of Causes, Consequences, and Reform

Toshiaki Tachibanaki

The MIT Press
Cambridge, Massachusetts
London, England

MIT Press books may be purchased at special quantity discounts for business or sales promotional use. For information, please email special_sales@mitpress.mit.edu or write to Special Sales Department, The MIT Press, 55 Hayward Street, Cambridge, MA 02142.

This book was set in Palatino on 3B2 by Asco Typesetters, Hong Kong.
Printed and bound in the United States of America.

Library of Congress Cataloging-in-Publication Data

Tachibanaki, Toshiaki, 1943–
Confronting income inequality in Japan : a comparative analysis of causes, consequences, and reform / Toshiaki Tachibanaki.
    p.   cm.
Includes bibliographical references and index
ISBN 0-262-20158-5 (alk. paper)
1. Income distribution—Japan. 2. Income distribution—OCED countries. 3. Japan—Economic conditions—1945– 4. Japan—Economic policy—21st century. 5. Japan—Social policy—21st century. I. Title.
HC465.I5T3   2006
339.2′2′0952—dc22   200505462

10 9 8 7 6 5 4 3 2 1

Contents

Preface

There is concern being voiced in Japan about the mounting inequality of income distribution. It is about what equality, or rather *inequality*, engenders. In particular, it is alleged that the high inequality of income has led to loss of equal opportunity. The purpose of this book is to scope out the truths behind these worries. It is also an attempt at various policy recommendations that might restore equity and economic efficiency.

Some seven years ago I published a small nonacademic book in Japanese that had similar aims. The book was well received by readers and the media. It encouraged economists and the larger public to debate the issue of high inequality in Japan. My hope for this English-language edition is to bring the debate to the outside world because high inequality of income has become a global issue as well.

This English-language edition, however, is more than a translation from the Japanese edition. It is an entirely new edition, rewritten from beginning to end. I have several reasons for enlarging the English-language edition:

First is the position of Japan in the world. Internationally Japan is at once a highly industrialized country and a relative late player. It is an Asian country whose culture differs from that of the West but a democratic country despite its traditional society, which is much as it was before the war. These and other features of Japan provide us with unique base for international comparisons.

Second is the academic orientation of the book. Unlike the Japanese edition, a large number of relevant scholarly works are noted to support the discussions. Besides this literature in economics, the literature in ethics, philosophy, political science, and sociology is included where appropriate to the understanding of inequality.

Third is the demand, in this more academic English edition, for rigorous distinctions to be made between equality of opportunity and equality of outcome, between equality of opportunity in education and equality of opportunity in occupational attainment within the hierarchies in organizations, between welfare states and nonwelfare states, and between income distribution and economic growth. To these are added discussions on the importance of native ability, and the cubic hypothesis concept is introduced to illustrate the movement of high income inequalities.

Fourth is the allowance for changes occurring in Japan in the interval of years since the publication of the Japanese edition. The criticisms and debates on income inequalities have led to developments that had to be included in the English-language edition.

Japan today is at a crossroad. Japan's period of economic prosperity has come to an end, and there is a need to revitalize the economy and halt the drift toward higher inequality. Some specialists have argued that the rising inequality is unavoidable and is due to a cycle that will help Japan regain its economic strength. I do not subscribe to this view, as will be clear from the points I make in this book. I leave it to readers to judge whether or not I am right.

1   Rising Higher Income Inequality in Japan and Elsewhere

The general belief about Japanese society, both internally and internationally, is that it is oriented toward social equality. Social equality is believed to be at the core of Japan's very efficient production system, and that in response to Japanese society's emphasis on equality, every worker has a strong incentive to work.

The features of Japan that have long been recognized as representative of its equality are as follows: First, income and wealth gaps are narrower in Japan than in other advanced industrialized countries. Second, no significant numbers of individuals or families are extremely rich or extremely poor. In other words, the great majority of the Japanese people are economically in the middle class. Third, the education, occupation, and income of an individual's parents do not matter in the determination of a professional career—nor in schooling, employment, or wages. Equality in opportunity is assured at least in intergenerational social mobility. Fourth, several economic indicators such as the growth rate and the employment rate have been strong, by which one usually infers that economic prosperity is being sustained. Today we have serious reservations about the truth of any of these features. Since the early 1990s Japan's once superb economic performance has declined, and today, at the start of the 2000s, Japan has yet to recover from over ten years of recession.

In this book I show how the significant inequalities that have emerged in Japan are impinging on the economic and social lives of the people. I trace the changes over time and make international comparisons. My historical discussion examines the economic and social lives of the Japanese over the past hundred years or so, back to the Meiji Restoration. By this longer perspective I believe that it is possible to understand better the nature of Japan's modern society, and the vigorous energy burst it received from postwar social and economic reforms. For the latter reason I consider at length the policy recommendations by the US occupation in the late 1940s that altered the stratification of Japanese society and began the drive toward equality.

The international comparisons made are with advanced and industrialized countries because Japan belongs to such a group of countries. Japan, however, is unique among these prosperous countries in that the culture is Asian, and not of the so-called Euro-American variety. All other countries of this group have Euro-American traditions. Another unique feature regarding Japan is that its economic development has been very different from that of Europe and North America.

However, international comparisons are never easy, especially where measures of income and wealth inequality are involved. Wealth figures are nearly impossible to compare. The reason is that in definitions of income and wealth the sampling and the measures used differ greatly among countries. It is nearly impossible to obtain reliable international comparative data unless it is due to group effort by the concerned countries' experts on income and statistics, as in the famous Luxembourg project.

As a single author unable to commit to such a painstaking comparative analysis, I do not pretend to have gathered and adjusted the statistics for Japan. Because I must depend on published studies, I consider only those that provide reliable adjusted measures of income, and similarly for the comparable international data I use to support my arguments.

Critical to comparing inequality in Japan with that in other advanced and industrialized countries are the concepts of inequality of opportunity and inequality of outcome (consequence). I do not overlook the fact that value judgments on issues pertaining to inequality and different cultural and religious factors must be considered in international comparisons, besides the economic development and political processes that are vital to understanding any income redistribution policy.

Further I pay attention to the spread of economic inequality. Economic inequality is not limited to measures of income and wealth distribution; there are issues of intergenerational transfers of educational and occupational opportunities to consider, as well as the advantages of native ability, family lifestyles, business and government policies, the effects of both tax policies and social security programs, and so forth. I show that these factors are important because we should not fail to lose sight of the result, which is the unequal distribution of income.

1.1 Toward Inequality in Income Distribution

Changes in Japan over Time

Income is the main indicator used in Japan for assessing the economic condition of individuals and households. The two other indicators of economic well-being are wealth and consumption.

Why is income the main indicator? There are two explanations. First, in Japan nearly all people receive a monthly income. Besides wages for employees, pension payments to retired people are considered to be monthly income. In other words, most individuals know their economic position by their monthly or annual incomes. Income, of course, is of very large concern to people as can easily be learned from idle talk. Second, statistics on income are more reliable than those on wealth and consumption. The measurement of wealth is unavoidably difficult, and that of consumption requires monthly household account books. So any collection of data on consumption is bound to introduce significant measurement errors.

Although data on income are not free from measurement errors, the reliability of income data is much higher than that of wealth. Thus, to the two reasons given above, there might be added a third reason why income is the preferred economic measurement. That is that many studies, not only in Japan but also internationally, draw on income distribution for inferences about affluence relative to statistical data on wealth and consumption, and so on.

The primary statistical source in Japan used for income data is the *Income Re-distribution Survey* published by the Ministry of Welfare and Labor. This source has been published for more than forty years and is valuable for studying time-series changes in the income distributions. Another useful feature is that the income data collected by the Survey includes nearly all the different samples of the heterogeneous occupations of Japan.

There are several other statistical sources that provide data on income distribution in Japan. Among these, the *Households Expenditure Survey* appears annually, the *National Survey of Family Income and Expenditure* every five years, and the *Wage Structure Survey* annually. The first two of these sources contain a sampling bias, and the last source gives only wage figures of employees who work at firms numbering more than ten workers. So it is hard to say that these three sources are representative of Japanese households. The advantage of the *Income Re-distribution Survey*, for our purpose, is that its more comprehensive

Table 1.1
Inequalities of income distribution in Japan

Year	Gini coefficients	
	Primary income	Redistributed income
1962	0.390	0.344
1967	0.375	0.328
1972	0.354	0.314
1975	0.375	0.346
1978	0.365	0.338
1981	0.349	0.314
1984	0.398	0.343
1987	0.405	0.338
1990	0.433	0.364
1993	0.439	0.365
1996	0.441	0.361
1999	0.472	0.381
2002	0.498	0.381

Source: Ministry of Welfare and Labor, *Income Redistribution Survey.*

sampling serves to show the pervasiveness of income inequality in Japan.

Nevertheless, our reliance on the *Income Re-distribution Survey* should not imply that the other surveys mentioned above are useless. These surveys do provide different interesting and valuable data on income distribution. Therefore we will return to these surveys from time to time and examine how results based on the *Income Re-distribution Survey* sometimes differ from those based on other surveys. The reader should understand that the *Income Re-distribution Survey* allows one to obtain a wide picture of income distribution over a long period of time.

Shown in table 1.1 are the Gini coefficients of the inequality results for primary income and redistributed income based on the *Income Re-distribution Survey*. The Gini coefficient is the usual index used to understand the issue of inequality. It takes zero value when complete equality is achieved, and it takes unity when perfect inequality is achieved. Thus the higher the coefficient is, the higher is the inequality. There are a number of other inequality measures used in the academic world such as the SCV (squared coefficient of variation), the MLD (mean log derivation), the Atkinson measure, the Dalton measure, and the Theil measure. Studies that adopt these measures do so in the interest of obtaining more precise inequality estimates. The results in table 1.1 are based on the Gini coefficient, which is, again, because the Gini is the most widely used measure.

The difference between primary income and redistributed income is important. Primary income is the income before tax and social insurance payments are subtracted; redistributed income is the income transfers in the form of social insurance and social security benefits to needy households and retired individuals. Redistributed income is thus more appropriate than primary income as a measurement of income inequality. This is because redistributed income shows more exactly what a household has to live on.

Table 1.1 shows simply the primary and redistributed income measurements for Japan. Other comparisons may use several definitions of income and redistributed income in accord with the social insurance benefits. For example, the *Income Re-distribution Survey* considers after-tax income, post–social insurance contributions, and post–social security benefits. The various ways of interpreting income will be examined later when we evaluate the taxation and social security contributions to income redistribution policies.

The important evidence in table 1.1 is the inequality of redistributed income. Note the significant upward trend that occurred in the 1980s and 1990s. The difference between the lowest inequality, 0.314 in 1981, and the highest one, 0.381 in 1999 and 2002, is 0.067. This is an alarmingly large difference, and it is indicative of the large increase in inequality.

Of course, some of the large variations in table 1.1 can be explained by changes in the economy. For instance, the substantial increase in the Gini coefficient, of 0.02, between 1996 and 1999/2002 corresponds to the deepening of the recent recession, when the unemployed and low-wage earners joined the ranks of the poor. The small decline in inequality in the 1960s and 1970s was due to fairly equal income distribution in these two decades. Note that these trends are also reflected in the primary income figures. That is, a small decrease in income inequality occurs in the 1960s and 1970s, and a significant increase in the 1980s and 1990s.

Overall, however, the already high income inequality observed in the table appears to have been rising higher. In the remaining part of this book we will consider the causes of this inequality and the effects on the daily lives of the Japanese. We will also examine the changes in Japanese society and economy.

International Comparison
An international comparison of inequality calls for data on other
advanced and industrialized countries that work on the same market
principles as Japan and include democratic decision making. Japan
belongs to a group of advanced, industrialized Euro-American countries that are understood further to be closely allied in terms of prosperity through industrialization. However, while such an international
comparison can yield significant results, it should not be forgotten that
Japan is not a Euro-American country.

It is, as I mentioned earlier, almost impossible to obtain international
income data that are strictly comparable. In international comparisons
of income, problems can arise in the sampling, measurements, definitions of incomes, and so forth. The most dependable source is that
produced by the Luxembourg Income Studies (LIS) group. The Luxembourg project has collected comparable statistical data on income from
many countries. Japan refused to participate in this project. Thus no international comparison in terms of the LIS data is available for Japan.
We will nevertheless take the imperfect data for Japan, make some
adjustments, and accept that the data are not fully consistent with the
LIS attempt.

A rough comparison of the state of international income distribution
is presented in tables 1.2 and 1.3. Table 1.2 gives the latest data, and
table 1.3 the 1980s data. These data come from a study by the OECD

Table 1.2
Comparison of income distribution in Japan and in other advanced countries

Country	Gini	Country	Gini
Denmark	0.225	Canada	0.301
Sweden	0.243	Spain	0.303
Netherlands	0.251	Ireland	0.304
Austria	0.252	Australia	0.305
Finland	0.261	Japan	0.314
Norway	0.261	United Kingdom	0.326
Switzerland	0.267	New Zealand	0.337
Belgium	0.272	United States	0.337
France	0.273	Italy	0.347
Germany	0.277	Portugal	0.356

Source: OECD (2004), *Income Distribution and Poverty in OECD Countries in the Second
Half of the 1990s.*
Note: An adjustment was made for household size by using an equivalent scale for data
on disposable income.

(table 1.2), and from studies by Atkinson et al. (1995) and by Shirahase (2001) (table 1.3).

As table 1.2 shows, Japan belongs to a group of OECD countries with the highest level of income inequalities. Note that Japan ranks sixth among these OECD countries. The statistical source for Japan used in the OECD study is the *Income Re-distribution Survey*. Since the reliability of this statistical source is good, it can be concluded that Japan's income inequality is currently among the highest of the advanced and industrialized countries.

Nishizaki et al. (1998) attempted to correct the sampling bias of the *National Survey* based on the *Income Re-distribution Survey's* population figures, and they proceeded to estimate the Gini coefficient using the adjusted samples. Their results are reported in panel A of table 1.3. Clearly, the increases in the inequality of income distribution in Japan were high, although they were lower than in the United Kingdom and the United States in the 1980s.

Table 1.3
Income distributions in Japan and other advanced countries in the 1980s

Country	A. Adjustment by population size		B. Adjustment by household size			
	Year	Gini coefficient	Year	Gini coefficient	Year	Gini coefficient
Japan	1984	0.291				
	1989	0.301	1980s	0.293	1990s	0.319
Australia	1985	0.320				
Belgium	1988	0.235				
Finland	1987	0.210				
France	1984	0.372				
Germany	1984	0.250				
Italy	1986	0.310				
Netherlands	1987	0.268				
Norway	1986	0.234				
Sweden	1987	0.220	1980s	0.221	1990s	0.220
United Kingdom	1988	0.350	1980s	0.296	1990s	0.345
United States	1986	0.341	1980s	0.335	1990s	0.367

Sources: Panel A: Nishigaki et al. (1998) for Japan and Atkinson (1995) for the other countries. Panel B: Shirahase (2001). These Gini coefficients were averaged for the 1980s and 1990s.
Note: An adjustment was made for household size by using an equivalent scale for data on disposable income.

Panel B gives estimates from Shirahase (2002), who used the *Income Re-distribution Survey* for Japan and made careful adjustments using an equivalent scale (i.e., adjustment by family members). The data for Japan indicate its income inequality to be lower than in the United Kingdom and the United States, where income inequality has been rising drastically, and much higher in inequality than in Sweden, an icon of equality among the Scandinavian countries.

From the rough international comparison attempted here there can be concluded that income inequality in Japan is currently quite high. Japan's level of income inequality is moreover nearly equivalent to that of several European countries with the highest levels of income inequality, and it is much higher than that of the Scandinavian countries, where equality of income distribution is a norm.

It may be interesting to see how this present international picture of income inequality compares with the past, since the data in tables 1.2 and 1.3 are fairly recent from the 1980s and 1990s. In table 1.4 we have the international data for the 1960s and 1970s from an OECD study. This study was challenged by a number of national authorities. One such challenge came from the French government, since France performed the worst in showing the highest level of income inequality among the OECD countries.

The Japanese government, however, used the OECD study to popularize the myth that Japan belongs to a group of countries with the

Table 1.4
Income distributions in advanced countries in the 1960s and 1970s

Country	Year	Gini coefficient
France	1970	0.414
Italy	1969	0.398
(West) Germany	1973	0.383
United States	1972	0.381
Spain	1973	0.355
Canada	1969	0.354
Netherlands	1967	0.354
United Kingdom	1973	0.318
Japan	1969	0.316
Australia	1966	0.312
Norway	1970	0.307
Sweden	1972	0.302

Source: Sawyer (1976).
Note: Incomes were not adjusted by an equivalent income scale.

most equally distributed income. As table 1.4 shows, the income inequality in Japan was one of the lowest, and almost equivalent to countries like Norway and Sweden. The impact of this finding was at least
great in Japan, and it was pronounced throughout Japan by news
media as "Japan is a country of equality."

The international OECD comparison, and the general impression
about the rules generally observed in the social and economic existence
of the Japanese, such as lifetime employment, seniority system, and
equal treatment of children at schools and of employees at professional
activities, led most Japanese to believe that their society is equality oriented. We will return to this belief and examine it more closely later.

The results appearing in tables 1.2 and 1.3, of course, reinforced the
good feeling about income distribution in Japan. They proved in the
late 1990s that Japan did not belong with the country group with
the lowest inequality. Still it is not entirely clear what the relative rank
of Japan was internationally among the advanced countries. Japan
appeared to be considerably more unequal than average, or just below
the highest inequalities of the United Kingdom and the United States.
The bottom line, however, cannot be ignored: income inequality in Japan has not stayed low. Today the inequality is high and rising higher,
and the same is true for other advanced and industrialized countries.

The findings in tables 1.2 and 1.3 combined with that of table 1.1
show the high income inequality over the past twenty years to be
based only on the income differentials. The subsequent discussions
will show disparities due to wealth to be prevalent in educational and
occupational attainment, in hiring of workers and their promotions,
and in a people's mentality that accepts the loss of both opportunity
and outcome.

1.2   What Is the Income Distribution in Other Types of Countries?

Capitalist versus Socialist World

The preceding comparison of income distributions consisted of only
the group of industrialized countries to which Japan belongs. It may
be interesting to see how the income distribution in Japan compares
with the income distributions of socialist countries and also of developing countries. The reasons for such comparisons are as follows: First, it
is useful to see how the market-oriented income distributions of capitalist countries, of which Japan is one, differ from the income distributions of the socialist countries. Second, right before the rapid economic
growth in the 1960s and 1970s Japan's economy was close to that of a

Table 1.5
Comparison of income inequalities in socialist and capitalist countries in the 1980s

Country	Wages	Income
Australia	High	High
Canada	Middle	Middle
Czechoslovakia*	Very low	—
(West) Germany	Middle	Middle
(East) Germany*	—	Low
Hungary*	Very low	Low
Sweden	Low	Low
United States	High	High

Source: Gottschalk et al. (1997).
Notes: High, middle, and low refer to the Gini coefficient values. More precisely, high means that the Gini is higher than 0.3, middle between 0.26 and 0.3, and low between 0.2 and 0.25; very low is then lower than 0.2. Former socialist countries are indicated by an asterisk (*).

developing country, and this lasted for nearly fifteen years after the Second World War.

Table 1.5 shows the income distributions in some formerly communist countries compared with those in some capitalist countries. Note that the income inequalities were very low in the formerly communist Czechoslovakia (before separation), East Germany (before unification), and Hungary and that these low levels are only slightly below that of Sweden, which is a welfare state.

Another observation in table 1.5 can be made about the income differences between East and West Germany. Although the two countries had at one time a common language and culture, the shift to income inequalities is clearly due to the different economic systems experienced in the twentieth century, namely the communist East and capitalist West.

There are the usual reasons for the differences in income inequalities between planned and market economies. First, there is the sharp contrast in ideologies. The communist ideology takes an egalitarian view of all workers, whereas the capitalist ideology makes a distinction in value among the different contributions of capitalists, managers, and laborers. Second, the centralized economy makes it feasible to allocate common wages to workers. Wages are not controlled in the decentralized capitalist economy and are left to individual firms to establish based on the expected performances of workers. Several capitalist countries like West Germany (before unification) and Sweden have

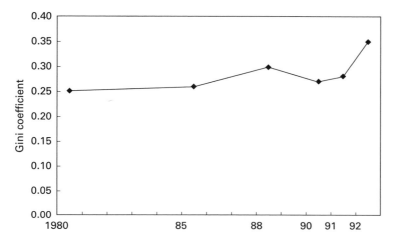

Figure 1.1
Gini coefficients recorded for the income distribution in Russia after the 1989 reforms.
Source: Doyle (1996)

tried some form of centralized wage control. The experimentation with centralized wage setting was not so large as to provide these countries with uniform wages as in the formerly communist countries.

Russia and the formerly communist countries of Eastern Europe, on the other hand, experienced a complete transformation in 1980s and early 1990s when their planned economies were displaced by market economies. Figure 1.1 shows the Gini coefficients for the income distribution in Russia from 1980 to 1992. The decentralization through economic and social reforms started in late 1991. As the figure shows, there was a drastic increase in the Gini coefficient in 1992 when the changes to introduce a market economy were first implemented. The subsequent experiences of these countries with high income inequalities provide solid proof of the differences between market and planned economies: a market or capitalist economy is likely to have higher income inequalities than a centralized or planned economy.

The theoretical differences between the market and centralized economies in wage distribution and in other areas, of course, contributed to the high tension that existed between the capitalist West and the communist East. In recent times most centralized economies have disappeared as the eastern European countries emerging from communist control have chosen to adopt market economies. Even in China, which holds an influential and powerful position among the remaining communist countries, the economy is frequently referred to as a communistic market economy, which is an amalgam of a market economy and a planned economy.

Advanced Countries versus Developing Countries

Our next objective is to compare advanced and developing countries. We examine two regions for this purpose, the Asian continent and the entire three American continents. Today Japan is the most advanced country on the Asian continent. One could eventually add South Korea, Singapore, and Taiwan, which are presently only semi-industrialized countries. The same holds true for Brazil, Mexico, and a few other semi-industrialized countries of the American continents.

How do the income distributions in the countries of these regions compare? Table 1.6 shows these differences in terms of the Gini and Theil coefficients of income distribution. Excluded are China and the formerly communist countries. Note that the Asian inequality in income distribution was lower than that of the rest of the world in the 1960s, 1970s, and 1980s. For Japan, at least, this has changed. The equal distribution in income that was characteristic of Asian past was due to the great majority of Asian countries being developing countries. The egalitarian nature of these societies was probably also due to certain

Table 1.6
Comparison of income inequalities in Asia and rest of the world

Year	Gini coefficients		Theil coefficients	
	Rest of world	Asia	Rest of world	Asia
1962	0.65	0.53	0.78	0.51
1964	0.65	0.55	0.78	0.54
1966	0.66	0.58	0.81	0.62
1968	0.66	0.60	0.81	0.68
1970	0.66	0.61	0.80	0.72
1972	0.67	0.63	0.81	0.77
1974	0.67	0.63	0.82	0.78
1976	0.67	0.63	0.81	0.78
1978	0.67	0.63	0.82	0.78
1980	0.67	0.64	0.82	0.81
1982	0.67	0.65	0.83	0.83
1985	0.67	0.64	0.83	0.80

Source: Yoshida (1997).
Notes: Asia excludes China, and the rest of the world excludes former socialist countries.

Asian religious and cultural traditions. Table 1.7 shows the estimated Gini coefficients for households in a number of Asian countries. As is evident from the Gini coefficients, the income distributions differ considerably from country to country, but they remain fairly the same over time.

Taken together, the results in tables 1.6 and 1.7 cannot be simply explained as due to income inequality being generally low in Asia, since the differences in the income distributions of these countries are large. A better explanation may be that each country has its own history and particular phase of economic development, just as its culture and language do not represent Asia as a whole.

The case for the developing countries of the Americas is presented in table 1.8. Note that the Gini coefficients show great income inequality in these countries. The income inequality among these developing countries is also considerably higher than among Asian countries. Note that the income share of the bottom 20 percent of the population is below 5 percent, which is at the poverty level. Nevertheless, it is not right to categorize the entire American Southern Hemisphere as having high income inequality because *all* the countries in the region are in the process of developing industrially. However, compared to the relatively equal distributions of income in the developing countries of Asia, the countries of the Americas have higher income inequality.

We can arrive at the following conclusion about developing countries compared to advanced countries: the income inequalities in

Table 1.7
Income inequality in Asian countries

Country	Year	Gini coeffi- cient	Year	Gini coeffi- cient	Year	Gini coeffi- cient	Year	Gini coeffi- cient	Year	Gini coeffi- cient
Korea			1965	0.34			1985	0.39	1989	0.43
Taiwan							1980	0.36	1990	0.36
Philippines			1961	0.48	1971	0.37			1991	0.47
Malaysia	1957	0.45			1976	0.52	1987	0.46		
Indonesia							1981	0.35	1987	0.33
Thailand							1981	0.43	1992	0.52

Source: Mizoguchi and Matsuda (1997).
Notes: The estimated income inequalities are based on various statistical sources of each country. This table presents only a small selection of the statistics in order to give a rough idea of the income distribution in Asia.

Table 1.8
Income distribution in the American Southern Hemisphere, 1989

	Gini coefficient	Share of bottom 20%
Brazil	0.63	2.1
Chile	0.57	2.1
Costa Rica	0.46	4.0
Dominica Republic	0.50	4.2
Guatemala	0.59	2.2
Honduras	0.59	2.8
Jamaica	0.44	5.1
Mexico	0.52	3.9
Panama	0.57	2.0
Venezuela	0.44	4.8

Source: Psacharopolos et al. (1995).

developing countries are, in general, higher than that in advanced countries. The features of inequality, however, considerably differ by region, as in Asia and in the Americas.

1.3   Wealth Distribution

International Comparison

For a long time the Japanese people had reason to believe that their distribution of wealth was fairly equal. Most households had modest assets, largely real assets that were valued slightly below the so-called average. Why "below"? This is because the wealth distribution was skewed. There were no extremely wealthy families, as in America. There were no extremely wealthy CEOs of large firms, movie stars, professional sport players, best-seller writers, real estate magnates, stockholders, and so on. The number of wealthy people in Japan was very small. They were the exceptions, and ordinary people did not pay attention to them. See Tachibanaki and Mori (2005) for more on the rich in Japan.

As shown in table 1.9, the Japanese people's understanding of their equal wealth distribution is supported by the international Gini coefficients. The higher share of wealth in the represented countries is due to the top 5 percent wealth holders. These data are from the 1980s because international data collections of wealth distribution are not attempted frequently and take a long time to amass. For this reason we have to wait a few more years to see the results of the 1990s' mea-

Table 1.9
Comparison of wealth distribution in advanced countries

Country	Year	Gini coefficient	Share of top 5%
Japan	1981[b]	0.58	
	1984[b]	0.52	25
United States	1983[a]	0.77	54
	1983[b]	0.79	56
	1988[b]	0.76	
France	1986[a]	0.71	43
West Germany	1988[b]	0.70	
Canada	1984[b]	0.69	38
Australia	1986[b]		41

Source: Wolff (1996).
Note: The higher the share of the top 5%, the higher is the wealth inequality.
a. Gross wealth.
b. Net wealth.

surements of wealth. Table 1.9 nevertheless gives a useful profile of wealth inequalities in the advanced countries.

Clearly, in the 1980s the wealth inequality in Japan as expressed by the Gini coefficients was considerably lower than in other advanced countries. This accords well with our knowledge of Japan's history in the early 1980s, since in this period the wealth of the people was fairly equally distributed.

What jumps out in table 1.9, however, is the very high inequality in wealth distribution in the United States. The US Gini coefficient is the highest, and more important, the share of the top 5 percent wealth holders is 50 percent of the national wealth. An exceptionally large portion of the wealth (over 50 percent) is concentrated in a very small number of wealthy households (about 5 percent) in the United States. Skewed wealth is an unvarying feature of US society, because the majority of the people consent to it.

Changes in Japan over Time
Wealth distribution in Japan changed drastically in the second half of the 1980s. This was the time of Japan's bubble economy. In these years real estate prices soared. The prices tripled and quadrupled the equity value of homeownership, and launched the discrepant wealth distribution.

Table 1.10 shows the effect of the bubble economy on wealth distribution. Where two sets of figures are given, the first is the author's

Table 1.10
Changes of inequality in real assets over high-growth period

		1983	1984	1985	1986	1987	1988	1989	1990
Tachibanaki	(A)			0.428	0.452	0.548	0.525		
	(B)			0.752	0.762	0.804	0.794		
EPA	(A)	0.467	0.433	0.434	0.441	0.482	0.535	0.520	0.516
	(B)	0.668	0.668	0.668	0.672	0.704	0.734	0.726	0.723

Source: Tachibanaki (1989, 1996b).
Notes: Tachibanaki refers to the name of the investigation, and EPA refers to the Economic Planning Agency (a government agency). (A) signifies only homeowners, and (B) signifes homeowners and renters.

own estimate, and the second is the government's estimate. The distinction is between households that own their homes and those that do not. Sample A shows the Gini coefficient for households that own their homes and sample B for homeowners and renters combined.

Sample A's Gini coefficient is clearly higher, and thus more unequally distributed for all households besides those that own their homes. This is characteristic of both samples A and B. The reason is in large part due to the fact that the households that do not own their homes (those who rent) are least concerned about their real assets.

Second, samples A and B also show the Gini coefficients to start their rise in 1985, at around the time the bubble economy began to form, and likewise they reach their highest levels in 1987 and 1988. The amount of increase is 0.1 for sample A (i.e., for households that own their homes), and 0.04 and 0.06 for sample B (i.e., for all households combined). These increases enlarge in the next two to three years. The correspondingly gap that occurs in wealth distribution is large.

The media seized the polarization of haves and have-nots as a sign of the times, and in bold headlines called for readers to express their intolerances. The bubble economy did not last very long, however. By 1989, or 1990, the prices of real estate started a sharp decline, and the bubble economy burst soon after.

For the households that owned their homes and enjoyed home equity, their extreme wealth now felt like it had been dreamed. The economy edged into a serious recession from which it has yet to emerge. The only good thing about the burst of the bubble is that the fall in real estate prices has evened out the very high inequality of wealth. Japan's return to a modest inequality in wealth distribution after the bubble's burst will be discussed next.

1.4   The Slow-Growth Economy

End of the Bubble Economy and Subsequent Serious Recession

The end of the bubble economy also meant years of slow growth for the Japanese economy. More recently there have been periods of no growth, or even negative growth economy. The zero growth has had an enormous impact on the daily lives of ordinary people in many fields. The unemployment rate is high, and the losses of income have hit the people hard.

The recession that has now lasted for over ten years is the first serious recession to be experienced by the Japanese since the end of the Second World War. A large number of firms, among them financial firms, have declared bankruptcy, and most banks have carried non-performing financial bonds and assets. The rate of unemployment is nearly 5.0 percent, a record high since the war. It is an interesting question why the Japanese economy is in so serious a recession, and has been unable to recover for so many years. Open discussion on policy reforms to induce recovery appears to be necessary. Because the main purpose of this book is to examine inequality, we will abstain from further observations on this interesting point. We can only admit the effects of the present recession that intersect with the inequality-related issues.

The zero increase in household income caused most Japanese people to lower their living standards. The households of the large number of unemployed have had to adjust to the decreases in household incomes, but so have the majority of people. This is a new experience for Japan's postwar history, where for more than fifty years the growth rate of the economy had always been positive. The recession is therefore on the minds of many Japanese people.

How do the Japanese see their living standards improving in the future? Most economists in Japan have led the people to believe that an eventual positive turn in the economy will bring a growth rate of 2 to 3 percent. I have a more cautious outlook. I do not believe that a growth rate of more than 0.5 to 1.0 percent is possible in the near future for Japan. There are several reasons for this. First, because Japan's standard of living is relatively high, people who have suffered income losses must be willing to make sacrifices and work harder to meet the high living standards. Second, the pursuit of a high growth by an industrially rich country like Japan will come at a cost to the natural environments of developing countries and will likely widen the income differentials there. I know quite well that this opinion belongs to a minority, and thus will elaborate on it later.

Similarly troubling is the deflation of prices, where currently the rate of the increase in nominal price levels is negative, something like minus 1.0 percent. One school of thought argues that the deflation cannot be criticized too strongly because it helps lower the very high general price levels in Japan, compared with those of other advanced countries. The other school of thought argues for an inflation-targeting policy to help ease the serious recession. The pro-deflation school admits that it is important to rescue the Japanese economy but prefers policies other than inflation targeting. Their view of the merit of decreasing prices in Japan is countered the inflation-targeting school's view of deflation as an evil. I tend to support deflation because I believe that it can help raise the real living standard of Japanese people, although it may be also necessary to adopt other measures to recover from the recession.

A Dispute on Shares
The slow-growth or negative-growth economy has not reduced but worsened the income inequality. The reason is that the no growth means a stagnant gross national income. The zero growth shares of the economy are allocated to individual households as distributions of income. Because capacity does not increase, the value of each allocated individual share is null. Only the individuals with the strongest voice or power obtain the highest shares.

This outcome can be easily understood by a fictitious example. Suppose several brothers and sisters, all very young, have a single cake to divide among them. If the cake is large in size, the children do not quarrel because they all will probably enjoy a large slice of cake. If the cake's size is small, they will likely start to argue over the size of each slice because one or two children may have to accept a smaller slice. As is usual, the physically weaker or less aggressive child will have to accept a smaller share of cake.

Something like this happens at the national economy level. Rich people or aggressive individuals manage to obtain larger shares (i.e., household incomes) than poor or less aggressive individuals when the economy does not grow. This is because the rich and economically strong individuals will push for a larger allocation of ever-decreasing total capacity. Income inequality thus tends to enlarge when the growth rate of the economy is zero or low as powerful individuals gain over powerless individuals unless the government commits to a strong redistribution policy.

Who are the powerful and powerless in a population? This question is important to the issue of income distribution. Some representative examples are men versus women, capable (productive) persons versus less capable persons, educated persons versus less educated persons, workers employed in larger firms versus workers employed in smaller firms, households with huge equity versus households with little or no equity. The effects of such characteristics as gender, capability, education, firm size, and wealth will be examined later when we investigate income distribution.

The point to remember from the preceding descriptions is that a weakening economy worsens income distribution, as has been observed during recent serious recession in Japan.

Equity versus Efficiency

The slowed economic growth has therefore widened the breach between equity and efficiency. Distribution of income is associated with equity, and the growth of the economy is associated with efficiency. Because with low or no economic growth, the income gap becomes larger, the drop in equity is inevitable. Similarly, because efficiency is positively related to equity, lowered efficiency should bring a corresponding decline in equity.

Economic theory nevertheless suggests that this relationship operates inversely. That is, efficiency and equity are traded off in the real world. Okun (1975) undertook to examine the veracity of this trade-off. If we interpret high growth economy as a symbol of efficiency, and low income inequality as a symbol of equity, economic theory normally infers a negating relationship between the two circumstances. If we desire more efficiency, we have to sacrifice some equity, and we have to sacrifice some efficiency to achieve more equity.

Why does economic theory presume such a trade-off between efficiency and equity? The one clear explanation that we consider is the following relationship between the macroeconomy and income distribution. We can regard equity as a higher degree of equality in after-tax income distribution, and understand efficiency as a higher growth rate of the macroeconomy. Higher equality in after-tax income distribution requires a considerably higher progressive tax rate on income. This means a higher tax rate for rich people, and a lower tax rate for poor people. A high progressive income tax could lower the incentive for rich people to remain in the labor market and/or discourage the intensity of their work effort, and at the same time decrease the savings rate of rich people. In general, a reduction in labor supply and/or work intensity of the rich affects productivity negatively at the macroeconomic level, and a fall in savings rate can further lower the funds available in the market for capital accumulation. In turn, the adverse effects on labor and capital will lower the growth rate of the macroeconomy, and thus be detrimental to economic growth (i.e., efficiency). This is the delicate balance confronting the trade-off between equity and efficiency.

Critics of the welfare state, in which the government must levy higher average income taxes with a higher progressive marginal tax rate, often use this trade-off argument to defend the efficiency of a free market economy, as we will see later in this chapter. Whether or not the criticism of a particular welfare state makes sense, however, depends on the elasticity of labor supply and of savings arising from the income tax rate. In welfare states where the elasticity is very high, the growth rate of the economy can be seriously impaired. In those states where it is very low or negligible, the adverse effect can be minor, and not be a serious detriment to efficiency. Therefore it is critical to assign elasticity values to labor and savings in determining the trade-off between efficiency and equity.

As I will argue later, the numerical values of both labor supply elasticity and savings elasticity in Japan are very low in general, implying that the degree of trade-off between efficiency and equity is at a minimal level. Consequently it should be possible to raise income and social security taxes with a higher progressive tax rate that keeps a certain degree of equity in income distribution, one that does not compromise efficiency and the Japanese macroeconomy.

The general mood in Japan, however, does not endorse this view. The Japanese people favor reductions in both average tax burden and the progressive marginal tax rate, even though this policy has led to more inequality in income distribution. In fact the government's tax policy was adopted some twenty years ago, in the 1980s, and was based on the so-called supply-side economics of the Thatcher government in the United Kingdom and the Reagan administration in the United States. Even these countries now strongly believe that the trade-off in the equity and efficiency relationship should be carefully observed. I will give more attention to this issue later.

Effect of Income Distribution on Economic Growth

So far we have been concerned mainly with the effect of economic growth (i.e., efficiency) on income distribution (i.e., equity). There is, of course, yet to consider the effect of income distribution on economic growth. It may be useful to review this effect. Income distribution is often studied in relation to economic development. More precisely, unequal income distribution is found to be the natural outcome in the developing countries undergoing strong industrialization processes and is thus associated with high economic growth. In developing countries, however, strong industrialization is the primary goal. The important Kuznets hypothesis of an inverted-U economic growth is based on this fact, that during intensive industrialization income inequality is highest at the earliest stage.

Japan, however, is already highly industrialized. The effect of unequal income distribution on economic growth is discussed here for two reasons. First, the results of other economic studies can serve as a starting point for seeing the inequality as a factor in economic development (the history of the economic development of Japan is deferred to the next chapter). Second, from the differences in income distribution among advanced countries, developing countries, and former socialist countries, the causes of the inequality can be understood.

A large number of studies that analyze income distribution during economic growth apply the two-sector model, which focuses on the agricultural sector (traditional sector) and the industrial sector (modern sector). Some important investigations of differences in incomes between these two sectors come from De Janvry and Sadoulet (1983), Murphy, Shleifer, and Vishny (1989), Eswarn and Kotwal (1993), and Bourguignon (1990), but these studies are largely concerned with changes in the demand for products (i.e., agricultural products and industrial products).

The study by De Janvry and Sadoulet (1983) proposed that when industrial products are luxury goods, a high inequality in income distribution can lead to stronger industrialization, and likewise, when a middle-income people feed the demand for industrial products, a high equality can result from stronger industrialization. The difference in the savings rates in the two-sector model is what matters. If the savings rate of the industrial sector is higher than that of the agricultural sector, the high inequality will strengthen industrialization because larger savings are available for investments.

Murphy, Shleifer, and Vishny (1989) investigated the role of the demand for industrial products. In times of high income inequality, most demand is only for agricultural products, and thus strong industrialization is not feasible. Equality in income distribution is therefore desirable for economic growth, and any redistribution policy should promote high demand for industrial products.

Eswarn and Kotwal (1993) focused on the ability of an export-led economy to achieve strong industrialization. Exports can be used to accomplish fairly equal income distribution because an export-led developing economy does not lower the demand for industrial products, even if income transfers from the rich to the poor are made. In third-world countries poor tenants must depend on income transfers from rich landowners, and there is little in the way of international trade. Opening a country to international trade can work better than land reforms to achieve equity and strong industrialization.

Bourguignon (1990) rejected the Kuznets inverted-U hypothesis. In his view, high income inequality occurs during economic growth because the price elasticity of agricultural demand is higher and the income elasticity lower. Bourguignon (1990) argued that economic growth could lead to equity in income distribution only if there is low price elasticity of agricultural products and high income elasticity to enable the purchase of those products.

All the studies mentioned so far were interested in analyzing the effects of demand for agricultural and industrial products on the relationship between equity in income distribution and economic growth (or development). The more recent interest is on the supply side, namely on human capital investments such as education, on technological advances, and on rising or falling financial and capital markets. Each of these subjects will be addressed briefly because they help us understand why many advanced countries suffer from the growing income disparity.

The accepted analytical tool for investigating the role of human capital investment is the endogenous growth model. The idea of an endogenous growth model originated from work by Romer (1986) and Lucas (1988). Later several theoretical studies, such as those by Glomm and Ravikumar (1992), Perrotti (1993), and Galor and Zeira (1993), explored the relationship between education and economic growth.

The important result by Glomm and Ravikumar (1992) is singled out first because of the positive effect observed for education financed by public funds. Glomm and Ravikumar found education often to lessen the income inequality in a growth economy. Education financed by private funds was also positive when the marginal productivity of human capital (i.e., education) was decreasing, while it was negative when the marginal productivity was increasing. The distinction between decreasing and increasing marginal productivity appeared at different stages of economic growth, and also at the different levels of income inequality. Glomm and Ravikumar's results suggest that public education is more apt to reduce income inequality when income is distributed unequally, and private education is more apt to increase the growth of the economy when income is distributed equally.

Perrotti (1993) argued for strong income redistribution policies from the rich to the poor so that government can invest in raising the education of the poor to achieve higher economic growth; this view thus addresses the externality of education. Alesina and Rodrik (1994) drew a similar conclusion from a median voter model they used to determine an income tax rate. They found that income inequality has a negative effect on the growth rate of the macroeconomy.

Benabou (1996a), Aghion and Howitt (1998), and Persson and Tabellini (1994) extended the theoretical analysis to several other policy issues using cross-sectional country data. Their main line of argument is that a high income inequality is detrimental to a high growth economy because of capital market imperfections. They all agree on income redistribution as the desirable means of promoting economic growth of the macroeconomy and, at the same time, evening out the income inequality.

There are two other phenomena that are likely to breach the connection between income inequality and economic growth. These are technological innovation and misallocations of labor. In the case of technological innovation, it is the direction of the change that is important—that is, whether the technological innovation favors skilled workers or less skilled workers. In early days of the literature on economic growth there were three types of technological innovations investigated: (1) innovation biased toward capital augmentation (Solow neutral), (2) neutral (Hicks neutral) innovation, and (3) innovation biased toward labor augmentation (Harrod neutral). Today most attention is being paid to technological innovation that is biased toward skilled workers over less skilled workers. While this is mere

common sense, Aghion and Howitt (1998) showed that recent technological innovations favor skilled workers and thus have widened the
wage differentials between skilled and less skilled workers that are
prevalent in most industrialized countries.

The misallocation of endogenous human resources involves two sectors. A misallocation occurs when simultaneously in an economy one
sector has less physical capital but a large number of skilled workers
and another sector has more physical capital but a large number of
less skilled workers. Because the misallocation will equalize the wage
differentials in the two sectors, there will be a negative effect on the
growth of the economy. Acemogle (1997) analyzed this type of income
inequality due to misallocation. He found that where there exist high
income disparities due to misallocation of human resources, the economy experiences a slow growth rate.

In sum, the economics literature takes the relationship between income distribution and economic growth and argues for a trade-off between efficiency and equity. The consensus appears to be that the
lower the income inequality, the higher is the economic growth. In this
regard the allocation of human resources involving skilled and less
skilled workers is critical.

1.5   Recovery of US Economy in the 1990s and Some Complementary Effects

US Experience of High Inequality

In the late 1990s and early 2000s as the Japanese economy experienced
a serious recession, the US economy experienced a boom. In these
years, until the start of 2001 when its economy began to flag, the
United States was an economic world winner. The high growth of the
economy and low unemployment had, by the end of the 1990s, wiped
out the government deficit. The economy of Europe, in contrast, except
for the United Kingdom was weak in performance.

Why did the UK and the US economies fare so well? I will tender
three explanations. First, the strong deregulation and privatization
policies in these countries had already revitalized their troubled
economies. Second, a restructuring had effectively eliminated low-
productivity industries and enabled the information technology industries to rise, and the service industries to perform better. Third, the
supply-side economics worked to decrease the income tax burdens of
households and the corporate tax burdens of enterprises and thus to

increase consumption and investments. These are all policies that were initiated by the Thatcher and the Reagan governments in the 1980s and were regarded as neo-conservative economic ideas. The Nakasone administration in Japan adopted the same policies to a lesser extent, and they worked marginally well. This is why I refer to this line of neo-conservatism by the three administrations Reagan–Thatcher–Nakasone that dominated the economic and political world of the 1980s.

Economic policies in the United Kingdom and the United States in the 1980s emphasized economic efficiency through the market mechanism. If we accept the argument of a trade-off between efficiency and equity, as was noted previously, it may be no surprise that the outcome in both the United Kingdom and the United States was high inequality of income and wealth distribution.

A good many academic studies and the popular press reported on the strong shift in these two countries toward inequality in incomes, wages, wealth, and so on. Among the popular publications (which I mention together here because unlike academic works I do not cite them throughout the text) are Harrison and Blueston (1988) and Luttwak (1999) on the US economy, and Hutton (1996) on the UK economy. To these it is useful to add Kelsey (1997) on the New Zealand economy where a deregulation policy was also widely applied. The particular focus was on wage (i.e., earnings) inequality for some obvious reasons. First, the most dramatic increase was observed in wage inequalities. Second, the data on wages are relatively abundant and more reliable compared to data on income and wealth. Third, economic measures is well prepared to handle wage differences, but income and wealth differences are more complicated to access. Government taxation and social insurance data may be relevant to an analysis of income distribution, but wealth holding can be influenced by "luck," which has not been accounted for in economic theory.

As a matter of fact, in the United States the increase in inequality started in the late 1970s and continued until the 1990s. We will consider, first, what happened to income inequality. As figure 1.2 shows, there were great differences in incomes between the 1960s and the 1980s, the two critical periods of high growth when income increased by five quintiles. In the 1960s, already the highest increase in income, 60 percent, was observed by the first quintile (i.e., the poorest quintile), and nearly the same amount of increase, 40 percent, was achieved for the other four quintiles including the top 5 percent. In the 1980s,

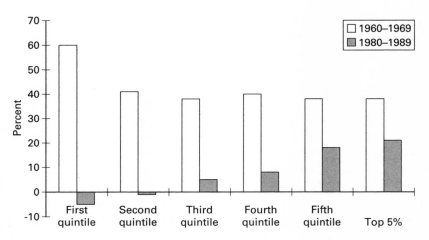

Figure 1.2
Growth of household incomes in the United States by income class. Source: Klasen (1994)

however, a fall in income is recorded by the first quintile, and the growth rate rose considerably with income, implying that higher income earners enjoyed a higher increase in income than lower income earners. This figure clearly indicates that income inequality increased dramatically in the 1980s when compared to the 1960s.

Atkinson (1995, p. 97) reports the increase in the Gini coefficient in the United States from 1980 to 1992 to be about 0.09, which is fairly large. Similarly the Gini coefficient for the United Kingdom from 1977 to 1991 rose by 10 percentage points. So both countries experienced dramatic inequality in the 1980s and 1990s. I have already discussed the Japanese experience in the latter period. Two other countries that followed the US/UK suit were Australia and Canada. Two books, Gottschalk, Gustafsson, and Palmer (1997) and Cohen, Piketty, and Saint-Paul (2002), provide comparative studies on the income distributions and some general issues in these countries written by different native specialists.

Causes of Inequality
Why had the income distributions deteriorated so greatly in the advanced countries? There are many causes of income inequalities to consider, but they differ from country to country. Nevertheless, it is possible to find at least three phenomena that are common to all countries. The first is increased wage (i.e., earnings) inequalities. The second

is high rates of return to real and financial assets due partly to the bubble economies. The third is government policies, and changes in family structures, that encourage the inequalities. Each cause will be more fully addressed at various points in this book.

As was noted previously, the most attention has been given to earnings inequalities (or dispersion of income). Deere (2001), for example, reports that the average wage differential between college and high school graduates has increased from 45 percent to 66 percent since 1967, and that the differentials between wages at the 90th and 10th percentiles of wage distribution have increased by 35 percentage points relative to the median wage.

There is a strong consensus that among the many reasons for the earnings inequalities is the widening wages disparities in the supply–demand for skilled workers and unskilled workers, and/or for the educated workers and less educated workers (e.g., see the studies by Levy, and Murnane 1992, Katz and Murphy 1992, Gottschalk 1997, Johnson 1997, and Topel 1997). The reasoning is that the demand for a skilled and educated work force increased enormously compared to that for the unskilled and uneducated worker, and that the supply for these workers was not met adequately. The market mechanism naturally encouraged the increase in wages for a class of workers as a consequence.

Why had the demand for skilled and educated workers increased? The main explanation is technological change. Employment became biased toward skilled and educated workers with the automation of industries and the introduction of information and system technologies in the 1980s and 1990s, particularly in the United States. Because the supply of these workers is limited, competition has raised wages of these workers. Some theoretical justifications for this phenomenon were argued previously. However, for the stock of unskilled and uneducated workers, the wages for the available jobs have remained very low. Further, in the low productivity industries, these workers are mostly unskilled immigrants who among the abundant numbers arriving from developing countries were fortunate to find employment as part-time or contract workers. In other words, the sufficient supply of workers for low wage jobs in advanced countries like the United States is the reason for a sharp decline in wages paid to unskilled workers.

Another explanation for the wide wage disparities in advanced countries comes from international trade. The globalization of the US economy in the 1990s encouraged many manufacturing industries to move their plants to low-wage developing countries in South America and Asia. The tradable goods are produced in the low-wage countries where the skilled workers hired come from the high-wage advanced country. The increased openness of economies thus accounts for another contribution to the wage inequalities between skilled and unskilled workers.

On the strength of the argument that the supply and demand for skill and education are responsible for the widening earnings dispersion, it should be possible to come up with policy to curb the increasing inequality. That is, government could intervene to raise the level of skills and education of the unskilled and less educated workers. Alternatively, the wage equalities denied these workers could be left to correction by natural market forces without public policy intervention.

An interesting observation is due to Atkinson (1997). He concluded from a series of studies on income distribution by Aghion and Bolton (1992) and Galor and Zeira (1993) that the market mechanism does not work well to raise the skills and education levels of unskilled and less educated people. The reason is that the poor, or children of poor families, cannot easily borrow funds from the financial market because of capital market imperfections. If there were no borrowing constraints, poor families could invest in formal training and more schooling. Over the long term this borrowing constraint due to capital market imperfections achieves equilibrium composed of two groups with different capital and assets. In the richer group are the skilled and educated workers and in the poor group are the unskilled and less educated workers. The poor cannot move up to a higher level because of the capital constraints they face.

Besides the capital market imperfection just mentioned there is the lack of will on the part of government to spend on training or educating the less skilled worker. The US evidence considered by Topel (1997) suggests government disinterest in more public spending on human capital investment, such as to provide more opportunity for training and formal education to children of poor families. A more recent study by Kosters (2001) suggests the US government policies to have shifted instead to more inequality in expenditures on education.

In some European countries, notably Denmark, Finland, and Sweden, considerable public funds are invested in the education and training of workers. Thanks to the large number skilled and educated workers, these countries have been successful in promoting high-technology industries. Again, these Scandinavian countries are well-known welfare states, whereas both Japan and the United States are not. Government intervention in public education and training is the difference between the welfare state, which invests heavily in education, and the nonwelfare state, which does not. This difference will be discussed fully later in this book.

Wage Inequality Let us return to the issue of wage dispersion. It is important to understand the institutional factors behind wage dispersion in addition to the demand–supply for skill and education, and the international trade factor. Labor market and industrial relations are affected by regulations and deregulations of the public sector. Whenever the government in power changes, wage dispersion is affected. Fortin and Lemieux (1997), for example, argued that the wage gap in the United States has been widened by three types of changes: (1) fall in the real value of the minimum wage (i.e., lowering the minimum wage), (2) fall in unionization (i.e., deunionization), and (3) deregulation of industries.

The system used to establish wages can vary, for example, as centralized wage-setting versus decentralized wage-setting, or corporatism versus competition. Both the United States and Japan belong to decentralized competitive type of wage-setting, while many Northern European countries belong to centralized corporative type of wage-setting. Decentralized wage-setting tends to induce wider wage gaps, whereas the centralized type tends to reduce the wage gap. These subjects will be examined later, after we first compare (1) international wage inequalities and (2) past and present wage and income inequalities in the United States and Japan.

Since 1970 there have been two schools of thought on wage inequality. One school sees the United States as the most extreme case in which the wage inequalities are largest among the advanced countries, and increasing more rapidly than in the other countries. More recently Gottschalk (1997) and Gottschalk and Smeeding (1997) have subscribed to this view. Figure 1.3 shows the huge wage gap in the United States of the 1990s continuing to widen. Peracchi (2001), however, uses the LIS database and reaches a different conclusion whereby the general US trend does not appear so extreme in comparison to that of most other countries during the same period. By this view, the most advanced countries, among which is the United States, experience similar trends.

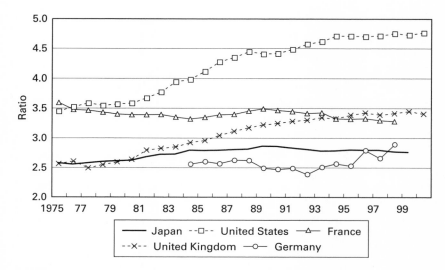

Figure 1.3
Comparison of wage inequalities worldwide based on a ratio of ninth and first decile figures for each country. Source: OECD, CDE (http://www.oecd.org/scripts/cde/)

My understanding of the two different views is as follows: First, I see the difference as being that one school is concerned with wage inequalities in the aggregate while the other is concerned with wage inequalities by gender, age class, and education (for a comprehensive study of the latter, see Tachibanaki 1997). Because wage inequalities can be considered from either perspective, both schools must be right. Second, I believe it is necessary to add the United Kingdom to the list of the countries with very large wage inequalities, in particular regarding the rate of the increase in the wage inequalities. Third, I support the finding by Gottschalk (1990) that Japan, which experienced small but positive changes in wage inequality, should belong to the second group of the Nordic countries, the Netherlands, France, and Italy. I will examine the Japanese case later more comprehensively.

Goldin and Katz (2001) studied the wage inequalities in the United States over the past century. They compared the first half with the second half of the twentieth century and concluded that the first half experienced narrowing inequality and the second half experienced widening inequality. Skill differentials were low, so was education in the first half-century, as might be expected. The astonishing result is that the great concentration of wages in the first half-century was not fully canceled by the great divergences of wages in the second half, especially over the past thirty years. The United States, which had been an equality-driven country up through the first half of the twentieth century, turned out to be an inequality-driven country after 1970.

This is in strong contrast to Japan. As will be discussed in chapter 2, the Japanese society before the Second World War was a very unequal society not only in wages and income dispersions but also in all aspects of social life such as education, occupation, gender, and the parent-child relationship. After the war Japan changed remarkably as it adopted highly equality oriented principles due to the US occupation. Japanese society succeeded in becoming equal to a great extent, although its direction has altered in recent years. Why have both the United States and Japan taken such different directions in inequality in the two half-centuries? This interesting difference is will be addressed later in this book.

Poverty   A variable that cannot be ignored in our analysis of inequality is the growth of poverty. Poverty is difficult to interpret and measure internationally. The definition of poverty differs from country to country. Also poverty can be described in different ways, by income or by consumption, by treatment of family members, and so on.

Here, to show the rate of poverty in Japan, the United States, and other advanced countries, we adopt the studies by OECD (2004). The definition of poverty is given by a household whose household income is lower than the 50 percent of the median income in all households. This definition is common to the EC countries, and thus the figures for North America and Japan may be different from the national income source of these countries. A minimum adjustment, however, to the EC definition is made for these countries in table 1.11.

As this table shows, the US poverty rate is very high, at 17.0 percent. There are two countries, namely Mexico and Turkey, where the poverty rates are very high as well. However, because these countries are regarded as semi-industrialized countries, the US poverty rate is the highest among advanced countries.

One could concede that despite showing a very high poverty rate, the living standard of the poor American people is not so low compared to that of other countries, even if they are in poverty by definition. A careful study would be needed to show that the average income in the United States is higher than that in other countries where the poverty rate is lower.

Table 1.11
Poverty rates in OECD countries (in percent)

Mexico	20.3	Germany	10.0
United States	17.0	Austria	9.3
Turkey	15.9	Poland	8.2
Ireland	15.4	Hungary	8.1
Japan	15.3	Belgium	7.8
Portugal	13.7	France	7.0
Greece	13.5	Switzerland	6.7
Italy	12.0	Finland	6.4
Australia	11.9	Norway	6.3
Spain	11.5	Netherlands	6.0
United Kingdom	11.4	Sweden	5.3
New Zealand	10.4	Czech Republic	4.4
Canada	10.3	Denmark	4.3
Total	10.7		

Source: OECD (2004), *Income Distribution and Poverty in OECD Countries in the Second Half of the 1990s.*

The high poverty rate noted for Japan in table 1.11 is alarming. The 15.3 percent poverty rate in the late 1990s rose from between 7 and 8 percent in the 1980s. The poverty rate in Japan today ranks third highest among the advanced countries, with Mexico and Turkey excluded for the reason given above. So over the past decade poverty in Japan increased by around 10 percentage points. The poverty rate is further not showing any signs of abating, and this is one of many indications that Japan is moving toward higher inequality, as will be discussed in chapter 6.

Equality of Opportunity versus Equality of Outcome
How is the increasing inequality in incomes and, in particular, wages in times of economic prosperity evaluated by American people? As will be argued later, there is a group of philosophical writers, among them social theorists like Rawls and Roemer and economists like Bowles, Reich, and Schor, who take either a liberalist or neo-Marxist view. Their opinions, however, do not represent the general outlook of the people in the United States. More important, a great many Americans do not care much about any concept of equity that encourages an equal distribution of incomes and wages. They place importance on liberty and freedom by which unequal income distribution is inevitable. Economic freedom, or essentially the free market mechanism, pro-

motes open competition and thus an unequal income and wages. The more famous writings that expound on this theme are by Freedman (1962), Hayek (1960), Lipset (1996), Lipset and Marks (2000), among others.

When we argue the concept of equity or equality, it is important to distinguish between equality of opportunity and equality of outcome (consequence). The liberty and freedom cherished by the American people are inherent in equality of opportunity, which is preferred to equality of outcome. Thus it may be too simplistic to say that the majority of Americans do not care much about equity or equality. It should be said, more correctly, that they do not care much about equality of outcome. The Americans, in general, thus do not deny a wider disparity of income because this is a symbol of equality of outcome provided that equality of opportunity is assured in their society.

Why do people prefer equality of opportunity to equality of outcome? There are many reasons and answers. First, most Americans are descendants of immigrants. The tradition of autonomy, self-reliance, and fair competition has been passed on from generation to generation. The so-called American dream is representative of this tradition. Embedded in it is the Puritan ethic that people who work hard will be highly rewarded, so there is a strong connection implied between effort and income. These were the very points emphasized by de Tocqueville (1835) more than a century ago.

Second, clearly, along with the work ethic accepted by the American people that those who make great effort, and/or who perform well, deserve high rewards, or wages, is the opposite turn of affairs: those who do not make a great effort, and/or who perform badly, deserve no rewards, or low wages. It is thus important to note that the majority of Americans with low wages honestly attribute their wages to their own failure, be it lack of effort and/or of luck. Some may look for the opportunity to improve their work habits or change employers. Others may surmount a challenge and obtain a higher wage. Equality of opportunity is the crucial factor for workers who are unsuccessful but are motivated to keep on trying. Equality of opportunity is evidenced by the frequent job changes across US firms.

Third, a big factor that weighs in the issue of equity or income equality in the United States is the racial heterogeneity of its society. If equality of outcome were desirable, it would mean a strong redistribution income policy from the rich to the poor. Because the majority of the poor are other than white Americans, and mostly African

Americans or other racial minority groups, a strong income redistribution policy is not likely to be supported by the majority of white
Americans (e.g., see Lipset 1996).

My understanding about the racial heterogeneity in the United
States is that it is another reason why American people do not see
equality of outcome as appropriate. However, it should be appreciated
that the United States, more than most other advanced countries, has
made great effort to reduce racial discrimination at least in terms of
providing equal opportunities for all Americans socially and economically. Good evidence is in the quota policy that forces firms and organizations to hire a required percentage of minorities. Society as a
whole in the United States has made a better effort than in other countries to reduce racial discrimination and promote equal treatment not
only of nonwhites but also of women. Japan is very weak on this
gender issue, as will be shown later.

Fourth, because of changes in social norms, workers have started to
support socially acceptable wage differentials. Larger wage differentials can result within a workplace where the majority of concerned
workers agree on a fair allocation of human capital and observed level
of performance. (Atkinson 1997 discusses this phenomenon. For example, the "fair wage" hypothesis and the "social-norm" theory of wage
determination have been proposed to explain such wage differentials;
see, for example, Akerlof 1981 and Carruth and Oswald 1989.) The socially acceptable wage hypothesis seems to pertain, in particular, to the
Anglo-American culture of the United Kingdom and the United States.
The effect of the changing social norm on wage inequality seems to be
supported by the disinterest the American people show in equality of
outcome.

In the American society we therefore have a unique representation
of equality with the following characteristics: First, the inequality of
outcome in terms of wages and income distribution is the highest
among advanced and industrialized countries. Second, American people do not mind it much for various reasons, and find that equality of
opportunity is more important and crucial than equality of outcome.
Third, efficiency is regarded as an important principle, and thus equity
is sometimes sacrificed to guarantee efficiency. What forms does equality take in Japan and Europe? This will become apparent from place to
place in this book. The United States will serve as a useful reference
country for comparison.

1.6   Should Japan Become a Welfare State?

What Is a Welfare State?

Again, it is clear that since the 1980s Japan has been moving toward higher inequality in income distribution. Although Japan was counted at one time among the advanced countries that achieved the highest equality in income dispersion, this is definitely no longer the case. The same trend has been seen in the area of wealth inequality but to a lesser extent. The inequality of wealth declined slightly in the post-bubble economy (the 1990s), compared to the much higher inequality in wealth dispersion observed in the bubble economy period (the late 1980s). It appears that Japan currently has an equivalent level of income and wealth inequality to that in several major countries like the United Kingdom, France, and even Italy, very roughly speaking. Its inequality level is lower than that in the United States, while it is considerably higher than that in the Northern European countries.

I am more concerned with the latter fact, that Japanese inequality is considerably higher than that of the Northern European countries like Denmark, Sweden, the Netherlands, the so-called the welfare states. Because Japan and the United States are nonwelfare states, as will be shown statistically later, the market mechanism principle is highly valued, and the government does not intervene in the workings of the private sector. Japan currently faces the dilemma of moving away from the US market principle toward that of the welfare state. I see the move toward a welfare state as inevitable, regardless of the desire of the majority of Japanese people, specialists, and politicians of the ruling political parties who want to maintain the US market mechanism model (see Tachibanaki 2000, 2002). As I will discuss more fully later, Japan is at the turning point of becoming a welfare state, but we have to know more about what such change entails.

First it is necessary to define the welfare state. The term refers to a country where government often intervenes in order to increase the welfare of its people. The better-known examples of welfare states are the Scandinavian countries after the Second World War, but the United Kingdom figures prominently in the history of the welfare state. The starting point and the philosophical basis of the welfare state are due to the Beveridge Report, which was published in Great Britain during the war. The United Kingdom soon after adopted the "From the cradle to the grave" notion of the welfare state. The United Kingdom ceased to be a welfare state only in the age of Mrs Thatcher, the early 1980s. Today the government of Mr. Blair, although a Labor government, is close to that of the nonwelfare states like the United States and Japan.

In the 1990s when the Scandinavian countries were not doing well economically, their provisions of welfare were blamed for the poor performance. The Scandinavians thus attempted to make reductions in welfare to revitalize their economies. This strategy was related to the trade-off between efficiency and equity, which was mentioned earlier.

In general, the activities of welfare states have three purposes. First, the government provides public services that cannot be handled by the private sector. Among the usual public services are those we call public goods: military, foreign offices, education, police and fire protection, hospitals, roads, bridges, and other infrastructures. Second, the government manages social insurance services, among these old-age pensions, medical care, unemployment insurance, physical disability assistance, and poverty relief. Funding is collected through taxes and/or social insurance contributions. Third, the government commits to redistributing income from wealthy households to less fortunate households. Both taxation and social security systems work toward achieving the goal of redistribution.

Clearly, the welfare state's government must be large in size because the role of the public sector is large. The government, both nationally and locally, collects a large tax revenues and social insurance contributions in order to provide citizens with the large number of services described above. Since most of public services such as unemployment insurance benefits, medical care payments, public pensions, and social assistances to the poor depend on the collected taxes, the government behaves as an institution that redistributes incomes from rich to poor households. Similarly, because of the public expenditure on education, students at national universities pay less tuition and receive more subsidies than those attending private universities. In other words, the power of redistribution works even at the high levels of the educational system. More important, both the personal income tax system and the social insurance contribution system have progressive rates by which bigger contributions to the redistributed income come from the bigger earnings.

Therefore government in the welfare state prepares safety nets for people who fall victim to disasters or suffer other kinds of misfortune in the form of unemployment, disease, disability, bankruptcy, fire, traffic accident, and so forth. Safety nets can soften the impact of uncontrollable events by compensation payments for incurred damages. The provision of safety nets is essentially the rationale behind the welfare state.

Government, Family, and Enterprise
Not only government but also private sector entities like the family and the business firm can prepare safety nets. Tachibanaki (2000) found that families and business firms, and corporations in particular, provide more of a safety net in Japan than does the government.

The business firm has a special role in Japan. Among many services, large firms provide their employees with housing facilities, recreation centers, hospital care, retirement pensions, and medical insurance. How have Japanese large firms come to make such welfare provisions? Primarily this is due to the need to attract and keep qualified employees by generous financial packages, and it is these employees' higher productivity that enables the firms to make such policies. Second, as will be discussed later, the Japanese government's welfare programs are very limited. The government has for a long time ceded its welfare role to the firms eager to promote their "welfare capitalism," as it has been termed in the Japanese context by Jacobi (1997) based on the concept of "manor capitalism" of early twentieth-century America. See Tachibanaki (2003) for more on Japanese welfare capitalism.

The sign, however, is that the tradition of welfare capitalism will not survive in Japan. In recent years Japanese firms have been backing away from offering extensive welfare programs, as shown by Tachibanaki (2003). Besides the declining role of firms in welfare provisions, the role of families in the economic support structure is changing drastically. As I showed in Tachibanaki (2002), changes are occurring in the relationships between the elderly and their adult children, between husbands and wives, and to a lesser extent between parents and young children. In the past the elderly either lived with their adult children or were supported by them economically. This tradition is disappearing, mostly due to a rising divorce rate but also to an increasing number of adults choosing not to marry. In effect, family ties have already deteriorated.

The changes in both the firm and family in Japan cannot be ignored. Only the government is left to intervene and help the economically troubled among the population. Insufficient provision of the traditional safety nets is the main reason why Japan has to shift willingly or unwillingly to a welfare state from a society where families and firms have been the major insurers of welfare services.

In line with the notion of a safety net, or the welfare state more broadly, is the important issue of moral hazard, as is often raised where generous safety nets or welfare states are debated. Moral hazard is the definition given the case where individuals have the capacity to abuse the generosity of a service provider such as the welfare state. The following three examples are illustrative of the types of moral hazard that can occur. (1) If the unemployment insurance system compensates sufficiently well, the unemployed will not make a serious effort to find jobs. (2) If the poverty relief program is too generous, there will also be low incentive among the poor to look for work opportunities. (3) If the health insurance system is too comprehensive, people will arrange for more hospitalizations and/or doctors will insist on unnecessary health examinations, medical treatments, and medicines.

The Thatcher government in Britain and the Reagan administration in the United States were well known to be critical of the kind of welfare state abuses mentioned here. They expunged their social and welfare programs of many safety nets and generous welfare payments, and further deregulated and lowered the tax burdens on industries. Their reforms were successful to the extent that they led to economic growth in the 1990s. However, both countries have experienced widening income disparities, as was mentioned earlier. This is an excellent example of the trade-off in policy between equity and efficiency.

Welfare States versus Nonwelfare States

There are several criteria that can be used to classify advanced countries into welfare states and nonwelfare states. The most popular is the rate of government welfare in relation to national income, which is roughly equivalent to the rate of tax revenue and social insurance contributions in relation to national income. These variables can indicate to what degree the government commits to providing welfare services for its people.

Table 1.12 shows these rates for representative countries. The signs that the both Japan and the United States are the nonwelfare states are clear, since taxes as well as contributions to social security and social insurance are the lowest. In contrast, Sweden, which is a typical welfare state, has the highest rates, over 50 percent of each person's income. The United Kingdom, Germany, and France stay close to the

Table 1.12
Social security reimbursement versus proceeds from income and social security contributions (in percent)

		Social security benefits over national income[a]		Tax and social security contribution[b]		
				Total	Tax revenue	Social security contribution
Japan	(1993)	15.2	(2002)	38.3	22.9	15.5
	(1997)	17.8				
United States	(1992)	18.7	(1997)	37.0	26.2	9.8
United Kingdom	(1993)	27.2	(1999)	50.0	40.0	10.0
Germany	(1993)	33.3	(1999)	56.7	25.7	31.0
France	(1993)	37.2	(1999)	66.1	40.6	25.5
Sweden	(1993)	53.4	(1999)	75.4	55.8	19.7

a. Data from National Institute of Social Security and Population, *Social Security Benefits*, 2000.
b. Data from Ministy of Welfare and Labor, *White Paper*, 2002.

middle. The United Kingdom inclines toward the US position, and both Germany and France toward that of Sweden.

The size of government welfare payments and/or the size of social security and social insurance revenues cannot alone account for a country's classification as a welfare state. The qualitative aspects of these payments have to be factored in along with the quantitative evidence. For example, it is interesting to consider who receives the benefits. Then come the questions of whether there is a qualification limit and whether the source of financing is general taxes or social insurance. Last are the questions of whether the revenue side is progressive, proportional, or regressive and whether the social security benefits are proportional to the contributions or a flat rate.

Another important factor is the political or economic principles that determine the nature and the course of welfare services by the government. Esping-Andersen (1990) developed a classification of advanced countries based on the political and economic doctrines. Table 1.13 shows the three classification groups suggested by Esping-Andersen. The first column shows their political and economic orientations, and the second column some special features of their welfare programs.

The first group makes limited provision for welfare assistance, as is characteristic of nonwelfare states. The second group consists of countries where social insurance has a principle role, but the benefits are

Table 1.13
Welfare provisions classified by countries

Economic principle	Welfare services and payments	Countries
1 { Liberalism	Limited services	United States, Canada
Libertarianism (more correctly free market)	Means-test based	Australia
2 { Conservatism	Selective services	Austria, France
Corporatism	Social Security provisions	Germany, Italy
3 { Social democracy	Universal services	Sweden
Fraternalism	Liability premiums	Norway

Source: Esping-Anderson (1990).

selective in the sense that they are tailored to different needs of the people who receive them. The third group represents the typical welfare state where the services are available to all citizens and tax revenue is the main source of financing.

The political and economic distinctions among these groups are as follows: The system of the first group conforms to the classical laissez-faire market principle. The system of the second group conforms to a conservative, corporate principle, as the economy is run by a collaboration of government and organized worker and industry associations that can intervene where needed. The third conforms to the social-democratic principle of government as an instrument of a cooperative society that provides services to all citizens according to their needs. In this instance Japan was not among the countries classified by Esping-Andersen. Later, however, he did include Japan somewhere between the first and the second groups, and that classification is appropriate, in my judgment, based on its political and economic principles.

Therborn (1987) had a few years earlier made a similar study, in which he included among the variables the issue of unemployment. The criterion he used to class a country as a welfare state was its eagerness to reduce unemployment by adopting certain policies. The attention to unemployment is consistent with Keynesian economic theory, which considers economic policies that aim to reduce unemployment. More precisely, Therborn employed two criteria in defining a welfare state, the extent of welfare services and the extent of government intervention to reduce the unemployment rate through policy.

Table 1.14
Classifications of countries by welfare services

Income redistribution	Welfare services			
	High welfare provisions		Low welfare provisions	
	Universal	Selective	Universal	Selective
Strong	Sweden Norway Denmark	Netherlands Germany		
Weak		Italy France	Canada United Kingdom Australia	Japan Switzerland United States

Japan's Speciality

In my classification of advanced countries by their various welfare and nonwelfare state orientations, I have chosen mainly the criterion of a government's commitment to redistribution policies through taxation and social security. I regard any country that has a strong redistribution policy as a welfare state and any country with a weak redistribution policy as a nonwelfare state. Obviously the country with a stronger redistribution policy aims at higher equality in the disposable incomes of its people, and the aggressive transfers of incomes from the rich to the poor by taxation and social securities are with the consent of the people.

I add another important criterion, which I noted previously, that the available public services fall within a reasonable range. In all, I consider three criteria as characteristic of the welfare state: (1) the extent of welfare provided by the government, (2) requirements for welfare services, and (3) the extent of redistribution through taxation and social security policies. Table 1.14 shows my classification based on these criteria. The highest form of welfare state is that observed by Scandinavian countries Denmark, Norway, and Sweden, and at the other extreme are Japan, Switzerland, and the United States. The remaining countries are somewhere in between these two extreme cases, that is, in between the typical welfare and nonwelfare states.

In summary, in regard to the arguments on what is a welfare state, it is clear that Japan has never been a state where the government provides its people with a great many welfare services, and especially not any related policies such as to redistribute income or to reverse an unemployment rate.

The case made for Japan cannot be without some reservations, however. First, the level of welfare for the Japanese people is not that very low, despite Japan's classification as a nonwelfare state. This is because the family and the firm, particularly the large firm, have traditionally provided the needed welfare services, as was mentioned previously. So, although Japan is not a welfare state, it has a private sector that tends to the welfare of the people in its stead. As a result at the national level the concern for welfare has not had to be especially high.

Second, the people employed by medium and small size firms are not able to receive the same level of welfare services as those employed by large firms because these firms do not have the funds to provide their employees with welfare services. The differences between large and smaller firms in capital intensity, productivity, and wages, for example, are known feature of the labor market, and thus must be factored into the industrial relations in Japan (see Tachibanaki 1996a). The high level of welfare for workers in large firms and the low or nonexistent welfare for workers in smaller firms is what I call the dual structure of welfare in Japan.

Third, because the Japanese economy has not experienced high unemployment, it has not been necessary for the government to make policy to reduce the number of unemployed. For this reason the criterion on government reducing unemployment used by Therborn cannot be applied to Japan, where no such action is called for at all.

Fourth, my criterion on the extent of income redistribution needs careful qualification for Japan. While today Japan does not have a strong income redistribution policy, this has not always been true. In the past, in the 1970s and early 1980s, Japan had very strong income redistribution policies. In effect, there was a very steep progressive income tax in those years, amounting to about 80 percent (national plus local income taxes) of the marginal tax rate for the highest income class, which additionally faced a relatively high level of the minimum taxable income. The steep progressive income tax was significantly weakened over time, leading to the complete demise of income redistribution policy in the present day. This change in income redistribution policy is crucial to understanding the Japanese society's shift toward higher economic inequality. I will return to this subject and discuss it at length later in this book. However, although Japan was never a welfare state, the time has come for Japan to move to a welfare state willingly or unwillingly.

2

History of Income Distribution in Postwar Japan

2.1 Social Inequality in the Prewar Period and the Drastic Postwar Reforms

Japan a Very Unequal Country

The post–Second World War years were more than a time of reckoning for Japan. Japanese society and economy had been destroyed almost entirely by the war. The destruction appeared in all areas, not just in the extremely large number of human losses and casualties but in destroyed factories, offices, buildings, houses, bridges, and roads in most urban areas. People were injured, poor, hungry, unemployed, and desperate.

Complete devastation seemed ineludible, but not for long. Japan started to recover and moved to postwar redevelopment owing to rescue programs provided by the US occupation and the dedication of the Japanese people to help the programs succeed. The happy result, which could not have been possible without the defeat by war, was economic, political, and social reform. In particular, the prewar traditions that had characterized Japan as a very unequal country were largely removed by the democratic and liberal principles of the postwar reforms. These changes were initiated by the United States.

Japan has had two revolutions in modern history. The first, more than one hundred years ago, was the Meiji Restoration, which abolished the Tokugawa feudal shogunate. The second was the post–World War II reforms. Although the term revolution may not be appropriate for the second situation, its effect was enormous enough to justify this term. It was a revolutionary time in that there were abandoned the traditional and unequal features that had dominated all areas of Japanese life: in the family, in male–female and parent–children relationships, in schooling, in industrial production and industrial relations, in landowner–tenant farmer systems, and in the income tax and wealth distribution system.

In what sense was Japanese society traditional or unequal before the war? Japan was effectively an ancient regime in a modern age. Its economy was expected to work on a modern capitalist, that is, market-oriented principle, but its closed society was not at all modern. Many feudal features persisted in Japanese society, among them the traditional distinctions between social classes: between aristocrats and commoners, between landowners and tenants, between *zaibatsu* (very wealthy capitalists who controlled the capital market and the economy) and small workshop owners, and between white-collar and blue-collar places of employment. Further government policy was implemented by military power, and in accord with the patriarchal organization of Japanese society, women had no rights.

However, it is important to see that the submergence of modern capitalism within a feudal Japan was in a world where there had already emerged the totalitarianism, imperialism, and militarism that would be destroyed by the Second World War. The appeal of these powerful systems of social control extended to Japan, and the Japanese people suffered as a result.

As was noted earlier, ultimately with the defeat in war came a number of positive changes in the social and economic systems of Japan. The changes that would transform the economic life of Japan were (1) adoption of indirect financing in the capital and financial market, including the main bank system, by which bank lending achieved prominence over equity financing, (2) the introduction of long-term employment and seniority in the determination of wages and promotions, (3) the introduction of an old-age pension system and medical insurance for employees, and (4) stronger oversight of public authority over private industries. The changes initiated in the postwar era became the source of Japan's strong industrialization and rapid economic growth in subsequent years, as Okazaki and Okuno (1993) have suggested. The postwar imposition of institutional changes thus became the driving force of the Japanese success story.

Income Distribution
What was the equality–inequality argument on income distribution before the Second World War? Before proceeding further, it should be noted that the documentation on this issue in the prewar period is

Table 2.1
Pre-war and postwar inequalities of income distribution (Gini coefficients)

Year	Ohtsuki Takamatsu	Ono Watanabe	Minami Ono Year	Town	Village	Wada	Mizoguchi Takayama Terasaki
1890	0.311						
1900	0.417						
1910	0.420	0.357					
1920	0.463	0.417	1923	0.536	0.523		
1930	0.452	0.431	1930	0.525	0.477		
1940	0.641	0.467	1937	0.563	0.476		
1956						0.313	
1962						0.382	0.376
1968							0.349
1974							0.344
1980							0.334

Source: Mizoguchi (1986) and Minami and Ono (1987).
Note: The Gini coefficients are for the regions listed at the top of the rows.

limited. In fact the accuracy of the available information is so questionable that unless more reliable documentation on income is found, it is not possible to investigate adequately the income inequality issue in the prewar period. Therefore my discussion of the prewar period is based on only the work of other authors.

Table 2.1 lists some Gini coefficients resulting from income inequality estimates due to different studies using different samples. For the purpose of comparison both the prewar and postwar periods are represented. The problem is, however, that the sampling is limited. The figures for the prewar period are based only on the available taxpayer incomes. Incomes of nontaxpayers are thus not represented. Since only few households paid income taxes, the income data for households is incomplete.

What are the implications of such limited sampling of only income taxpayers? First, since only a small number of high-income households paid taxes in the prewar period, the incomes of the great majority of households cannot be accounted for. By the exclusion of a large number of both middle- and low-income class households, and instead concentrating on income in a small number of high-income households, there appears to be more equal income distribution. Second, there were besides the nearly all high-income households in the sample, a smaller number of extremely high-income households excluded from the samples; therefore including these income data would have showed more unequal distribution of income. The twist to the sampling is that while in the first instance the representation of only high-income households serves to lower the estimated income inequality, the exclusion of the extremely high-income households serves to raise it. Because the first effect appears to be the norm in studies reporting income distributions, the income inequality based on taxpayer households is lower than it should be for all households.

The estimates of Ono and Watanabe (1976) are based on only income data of taxpayers. The Gini coefficients for data between 1910 and 1940 hover around 0.36 to 0.47, which implies that the income distribution in the prewar period was fairly unequal. The inequality would, of course, increase if the incomes of no taxpayers could be included. Such an attempt to correct the sampling bias was made by Ohtsuki and Takamatsu (1982). They factored non-income taxpayers into the estimates and computed higher Gini coefficients than those of Ono and Watanabe for comparable years.

Minami and Ono (1987) estimated the income inequality for the Yamaguchi prefecture, a small region in western Japan, for which they found nearly complete household data. Since the samples from the prewar period come most often from taxpayers, the Minami and Ono estimation provides the most reliable result, at least in terms of the sampling bias. While their estimation may appear to be deficient in that the data are based on a single region and may not pertain to the national level of income distribution, Minami and Ono point out that Yamaguchi prefecture's general economic condition was similar to that of the rest of Japan. Consequently the estimates for Yamaguchi should represent the nationwide level of income inequality. As table 2.1 shows, in the Yamaguchi prefecture the income inequality was somewhat higher than what other studies reported for all of Japan, and this supports my conjecture that the sample income data should include both taxpayers and nontaxpayers in order to obtain the true extent of income inequality.

Overall, as can be concluded from table 2.1, before the Second World War Japan was a country where the income distribution was highly unequal. The evidence is, in terms of the estimates given by Wada (1975) and Mizoguchi, Takayama, and Terasaki (1978), that the prewar differences between the rich and the poor declined in the postwar period.

Table 2.2
Example of wage differentials within a firm

	Yearly wages (yen)	Index (male regular blue-collar = 1.0)
Factory head	10,808	17.27
Deputy factory head	6,419	10.25
Section head	5,008	8.00
Regular white-collar	2,463	3.93
Semi-regular white-collar	1,626	2.60
Contract white-collar employee	1,480	2.36
Semi-contract white-collar employee	1,338	2.16
Male foreman	980	1.57
Male regular blue-collar	626	1.00
Female forewoman	464	0.74
Female blue-collar	281	0.45

Source: Data from a paper-producing company's internal report in 1930.

Wage Distribution

Contributing largely to the income inequality in the prewar period was the unequal distribution of wages. Data on wages and earnings are in fact more reliable than data on income in this period. Table 2.2 shows wages in terms of the hierarchy of white- and blue-collar jobs in a single papermaking firm of the 1930s.

From the table it is clear that the distribution of wages in the prewar period was remarkably uneven. The factory foreman took home a wage 17.27 times higher than that of the assembly-line workers, and his deputy earned 10.25 times their wage. From these enormous differences we can infer the strong hierarchical distinctions observed in the firm. Today the differences in factory manager wages is at most around 4.0 to 6.0 that of the assembly workers.

Also today white-collar workers who have experienced promotions to managerial positions receive almost 4.0 times the wages of blue-collar workers (or assembly-line workers). The differences in wages between white- and blue-collar workers remain an indicator of class. The differences between white- and blue-collar factory wages today are at most 1.5 to 2.0. These smaller differences between white- and blue-collar wages are due to the more equal treatment of factory employees in Japan after the Second World War.

Last, the difference between men and women factory workers has not improved much. In 1930 female workers received half the wages of male workers. Today the wages of women are still around 30 to 40 percent lower than those of men. Although the difference between the prewar and the postwar periods is not so large as the difference by hierarchy or profession, the wage difference between men and women is still large by postwar standards.

In summary, the wage differentials in table 2.2 show that in Japan, before the war the disparities in wages were very large and based on a hierarchy of labor and on gender. The category of worker, in particular, was a strong indication of social class. The upper classes were rich because their workers could earn much more than the workers of the lower classes. Japan was socially stratified, and this stratification was secured through education and family wealth from generation to generation.

Extremely Wealthy Households
In the prewar period the inequality in wages led to only a very limited number of the extremely rich and wealthy families and households. Japanese society was entirely class-conscious and centered on an aristocratic group of families. As in the West where the upper classes were comprised of dukes, marquesses, earls, viscounts, and barons, the nobility were large landowners who controlled large numbers of tenants. Added to their ranks were the capitalists with equities in huge enterprises that dominated the economy. Although it is risky to claim that all the nobility were wealthy, it is certainly true that all among them who were landowners and capitalists were rich enough to exert economic power. The landowners were privy to huge rents from their lands and houses, and capitalists obviously to huge dividends.

A valuable study of extremely wealthy families before the Second World War is that by Yazawa (1992). His findings may be summarized as follows. First, the extremely wealthy families lived mainly in urban areas like Tokyo and Osaka because they were industrialists and capitalists who had invested heavily in their industries. Second, the number of huge landowners was small, and they lived outside urban areas. Their enormous wealthy was created at the expense of the 43 percent of the population of Japan that was too poor to own houses and had to rent instead. Thus these wealthy landowners who enjoyed huge incomes from their rental properties exacerbated the problem of high inequality. Third, the zaibatsu households were at the peak of this pyramid of wealth in the prewar period. They were even then what might be called "conglomerateurs," since they owned and managed many kinds of industries and businesses. Today the most well-known descendants of these zaibatsu families are the Mitsui, Iwasaki (i.e., Mitsubishi), Hattori, Furukawa, and Sumitomo families. These families were among the top-ten wealthy families in Japan.

How wealthy were they? Mr. Mitsui, who was the richest and had the highest income in 1936, was paid 2.54 million yen. As reported in table 2.2, the annual income of a white-collar employee was about 2.0 thousand yen. The difference in incomes is unbelievably large: 2.54 million yen is 127,000 times higher than 2.0 thousand yen. The major source that Mr. Mitsui and others had for their extraordinary wealth was the dividends from their industries.

It would be interesting to compare the 2.54 million yen with the income of a contemporary wealthy family. Mr. K. Matsushita, who owns the Matsushita electric company and enjoys the most wealth in Japan, took in an income of about 1 billion in 1982. The average income of white-collar employees in 1982 was about 3 million yen. Mr. Matsushita therefore received about 330 times more income than the ordinary white-collar employee. The difference between 127,000 and 330 is enormous, and from these figures there can easily be inferred a situation of very high inequality of income distribution in the prewar period that is incomparable to any such inequality of income today.

Postwar Economic and Social Reforms

Defeat in the Second World War brought an end to the extreme economic disparity as Japan adopted an alternate course that favored social equality due to reforms mostly initiated by the US occupation. The important reforms that facilitated the economic and social change were (1) the interdiction of zaibatsu activities through the anti-monopoly law, (2) land reform, (3) democratization of labor, (4) tax reform, and (5) equal opportunity in education.

Dissolution of Zaibatsu through the Anti-monopoly Law   The zaibatsu families such as Mitsubishi, Mitsui, Sumitomo, and Yasuda were judged by the US occupation to have led Japan into the war because they had close associations with members of the military. Thus they were ordered to disband their enterprises. The excessive concentration and monopoly powers within industries and the banking sectors were also viewed as being contrary to the US market principle of free competition and representative of unfair competition. Several institutional

reforms were made in order to break up the monopolistic industries. For example, the 1947 anti-monopoly law and abatement of excessive economic concentrations led to the divestment of holding companies and opened these companies to public shareholders. (See, for example, Hadley 1970 on the development of the anti-monopoly policy in Japan.) These postwar reforms were effective in bringing about the industrialization of Japan. It should be emphasized, however, that soon after the introduction of the anti-monopoly law, industrialists demanded to ease the strong anti-monopolistic conditions in order to be more competitive with foreign direct investors and industrial giants. Therefore the postwar history of Japanese industries took a gradual shift from anti-monopoly to mergers and acquisitions, and then entered an era of huge conglomerates in the 1960s and 1970s. Shifts in the industries are continuing to this day.

It should be emphasized that the zaibatsu dissolution and related economic reforms that were achieved after the war were effective in changing the social structure because extreme wealth of these families was reduced. In particular, those industrial leaders, who had huge dividend incomes, had to relinquish their equity holdings. Naturally the income and wealth inequalities declined dramatically because of the postwar industrial and economic reforms.

Land Reforms The land reform policy was radical. All land of deceased landowners was confiscated and sold, and the living landowners were ordered to sell excess land over the assigned limit of 10 *chos* (about 24.51 acres). Because the selling price of land was kept very low, a large number of tenants could obtain small areas of land at negligible cost, and even no cost. The number of large landowners decreased immensely, and equivalently the number of landowners with small or tiny areas increased immensely. The landowners who formerly enjoyed enormous rents had to accept huge losses of income, while the new landowners were able to increase their incomes because they no longer had to pay rent. (See, for example, Nakamura 1978 on the land reform.)

The thorough change in the structure of landholding through the postwar land reform moved the income and wealth inequalities toward equality. The share of assets income due to landholding—as rent over individual total income—decreased by about 20 percentage points, from 21.4 percent in 1940 to 3.4 percent in 1950. The land reform policy succeeded in dampening the impact of landholding on income inequality. The land reform was larger in eastern than in western Japan. This is significant because the redistribution of land in the east included the Tokyo metropolitan area.

Paradoxically, in the late 1980s when the Japanese economy entered into a bubble economy, as was noted previously, land prices increased immensely. Who gained from the bubble? The people who had at one time been tenants and had purchased land from landowners forced to sell during the land reforms of postwar Japan. Although the land areas were small in size, the inflationary price spiral of the bubble economy raised the real asset value of landholding enormously. As a result the former tenants who had remained farmers became in the late 1980s wealthy landowners. Some cashed in and sold their land at very high prices, becoming very rich.

Democratization in Labor   Labor movements in the prewar or during the war period were very weak for the following reasons. First, management control was so strong that employees had no power to organize trade unions or join in labor disputes. Second, despite socialist proclamations and agitations during the prewar period, only a small number of intellectuals and social leaders made demands for improvements; the majority of employees were not aware that they had the right to complain to management about their working conditions. Third, the right-wing government had during the war prohibited workers from joining labor movements to voice their disputes. Fourth, nearly all thoughts during the war were of dealing with the deprivations of war and not labor issues.

The US occupation introduced three fundamental labor laws, namely the labor unions law, the labor standard law, and the industrial relations law. These laws were regarded as representative of a democratic society. As a result many trade unions were organized after the war, and the union density rate (i.e., the ratio of union members to total workers) was well over 50 percent, close to 60 percent. The 50+ percent union density rate is an indication that the majority of workers chose to join labor unions after the war. (Today the union density rate is about 20 percent due to a substantial gradual decrease over the past 50 years.)

The strong voice of the postwar labor unions brought large improvements to factory conditions, especially in working hours and wages. A lot of labor disputes were settled by worker strikes and lockouts in the late 1940s and 1950s. Industrial settlements were prevalent, and a good many firms and industries were continually on the verge of upheaval. The most prominent labor disputes were in the coal-mining industries. The production losses throughout Japan due to these disturbances were considerable.

It must be, however, added that besides raising the rights of workers, the power to unionize contributed to the democratization of the Japanese people. The differences between management and workers narrowed. The earnings gap, which was so large in the pre-war period, narrowed too. Also the wages of workers began to be standardized. The trade unions were able to spread equality to many areas of Japan.

Until the late 1950s and 1960s labor grievances were aired through fairly violent labor strikes. Then the relations between management and labor took a cooperative turn. (See, for example, Taira 1970 for this historical development.) It is the cooperative, collegial industrial environment that is thought to be behind Japan's rapid economic growth. The productivity of industries increased, the employees worked hard, and the trade unions eased demands on management. (See, for example, Tachibanaki and Noda 2002 on the effect of trade unions on economic variables such as productivity, labor turnover, working conditions, wages, etc.)

As was mentioned above, over the years the improvements due to industrial settlements led to a steady decline of the union density rate in Japan. Today, some sixty years after the war, Japan's union rate is the lowest of the industrialized countries, including the United States. While there are a number of reasons that can be put forward to explain the decline in workers joining unions, the main explanation is both the increase in the number of non-regular workers (the part-time and contract workers) and in the number of white-collar workers. Part-time and contract workers are excluded from trade unions, and white-collar workers are not interested in joining trade unions. White-collar workers prefer to act independently and not through collectives like trade unions.

Second, although trade unions have declined in size, the egalitarian ideas they have introduced in the workplace have remained. Consequently, except for the wage differentials between men and women, the wages are much the same for each employee rank. One explanation is that the Japanese consider the trade union to be a business operation, and the different unions being separate business operations, and this is clearly different from American or European conception of a trade union. (See Tachibanaki and Noda 2000 about the above two notes for more detailed discussions.)

Tax Reform   Carl Shoup, an American public finance professor at Columbia University, was asked by the US occupation to reform the tax system in Japan. Shoup recommended a drastic change in the tax system, and the Japanese implemented it. It came to be known as the "Shoup tax reform." By this tax reform the distribution of income and wealth, and thus the social and economic structure of Japan, was entirely altered.

The reform was implemented in three important ways. The first the number of income taxpayers was enlarged significantly. As described previously, in the prewar period income taxes were levied only on rich households, so the majority of the people did not pay income taxes. The Shoup reform extended the income tax system to include all households. The second tax reform introduced the so-called comprehensive tax system whereby a single tax rate was levied on the sum of various sources of income such as wages, interests, and dividends. The third introduced a very steep income tax curve, amounting to a progressive income tax rate. Richer households had to pay a considerably higher income tax rate than poorer households. Extremely poor households paid no income taxes because the minimum taxable income level was set up at a high level. (Interested readers can refer to Ishi 1993 for more information.)

Through these three reforms a fairly strong income redistribution policy was set in place. This tax system continued until the 1970s, and it became a driving force for equalizing the after-tax income distribution. Shoup should therefore be remembered for promoting equality in Japan. His tax reforms, however, have not survived to this day. The progressive income tax rate has been eased many times since the early 1980s. The changes affecting income redistribution will be considered again later when we come to discuss the income distribution policy in use today.

Equal Opportunity Policy in Education   Reforms in education were made on the principle that Japan, in becoming a democratic society, should have schooling available to all individuals who desire it. This was an important component also of the economic reform because it is through education that equality of opportunity becomes open to the majority of the people.

There were three basic changes. First, obligatory schooling for children was extended to nine years—namely six years in elementary (or primary) school and three years in junior high school. Before the war not even the six years were obligatory. The noteworthy feature that made this initiative succeed was that parents no longer had to pay any educational costs except if they chose to send their children to private schools. Public funds were therefore allocated to cover nearly all the costs of the obligatory nine years of education.

Second, for a very low fee students who wanted to continue their education beyond the nine years could attend the three-year senior high schools. The senior high schools were public schools that charged tuition. Although the tuition fees were kept low, those sons and daughters of poor households who wanted to attend senior high schools could not do so because this meant foregone incomes as well. In other words, the majority of children after the war had to work to help their poor parents financially, and everyone was poor after the war. This became apparent to high school students who wished to continue on to college. For simple economic reasons a large number of senior high school graduates could not go to colleges.

In the prewar period only sons of rich families could go to college. It was therefore a small number of young people, about 10 percent of the youth population, that had college degrees, and these college graduates were at the very top of Japanese society, since only the upper-class families could afford to pay for their sons' higher education. A small number of college-educated elites who went into government and made decisions that shaped the economy were all scions of a single clan of the top ten wealthy families.

This imbalance, however, was not corrected in the postwar years until the 1960s. The rapid economic growth of the 1950s had by then considerably raised the average incomes of households and enabled a great many young people to attend college. In other words, the majority of parents were now able to finance their children's education. The sons were the first beneficiaries of higher education in the decade of the 1960s. Later, owing to the economic prosperity of the 1980s and 1990s, daughters of the middle classes were able to attend college as well.

Third, educational opportunity was afforded to young women. Before the war very few daughters of wealthy families went to colleges, since society was entirely patriarchal in those days. Men made the decisions in the family and held the dominant positions in educational institutions, community affairs, enterprises, and government. The position of a woman was to be a good wife and mother, and consequently women were not encouraged to seek higher education. At the time a great majority of women accepted this condition, fortunately or unfortunately and willingly or unwillingly.

The postwar educational reforms opened to young women equal opportunity also to attend college. However, as I noted previously, in the 1950s and 1960s not all young women desiring to continue their studies beyond high school had parents able to finance a college education. Junior college education (two years' education after senior high schools) was the usual compromise. A large number of young women ended up with a junior college education in the 1950s and 1960s, even if they preferred a four-year college program. Nevertheless, with the education of women there came a considerable increase in household incomes, and by the 1970s and 1980s the daughters of these women were able to attend four-years colleges.

A final important reform in education was the introduction of co-education. Before the war, at the middle school level, boys and girls went to separate all boy and all girl schools. That custom was changed, and boys and girls not only started to attend the same schools but also to be instructed together in the same classrooms. Nevertheless, by law, separate education for boys and girls was allowed in some senior high schools, and most parents and students preferred these schools.

In time, with the removal of barriers to higher education, some women were able to rise to high positions in business and government, and earn high salaries. But for most women such favorable turns did not come rapidly. Many yielded to tradition, married and stayed home; others joined the labor force and faced discrimination. The supply and unequal treatment of women workers will be discussed later in chapter 6.

2.2   Rapid Economic Growth, Bubbles and Serious Recession

Toward Rapid Economic Growth

By the mid-1950s the Japanese economy entered a period of rapid economic growth. This was owing not only to the democratic reforms after the war, as explained above, but also to the outbreak of the Korean War, during which the US government solicited the industry of the Japanese people in special military procurements. The result was a highly industrialized economy. Japan's economic growth continued its rapid rise until the first oil crisis of 1973. On average, the annual growth rate of the national economy was close to 10 percent, and Japan was the first non–Euro-American country in which such high growth rate was observed. However, the purpose of this book is not to discuss economic history of Japan, or its period of rapid economic growth. For the relevant facts on Japan's economic history, the interested reader is encouraged to consult Nakamura (1978), Kosai (1983), Tachibanaki (1996b, 2003), and Yoshikawa (1997).

It is useful nevertheless in this book to consider very briefly the developments behind Japan's rapid economic growth. All the Japanese people were impoverished after the war and needed to make a living. This translated into a high work incentive and hence diligence. As the Japanese worked very hard and saved, their household savings became very high. The banking sector, and bank financing, depended heavily on the savings of the Japanese households. Industries motivated to rebuild sought funds from banks, and the indirect financing system, consisting of principally commercial banks, worked fairly well in transferring savings from households to the nonfinancial firms. Industries were thus able to introduce new technologies from abroad and to gain in their own technical expertise. The relatively cheap yen, 1 US dollar = 360 yen until the 1970s, helped Japanese exports to a great extent.

Contributing importantly to the high economic growth after the war was the abundant stock of human capital. Japan had not only a large number of skilled and diligent workers, but they were nearly all literate and able to compute simple algebra. The Japanese illiteracy rate was the lowest it had ever been in one hundred years. This does not necessarily imply that all the people were educated at the higher education level, but that everyone had the minimum education and the skills to help in the drive toward high industrialization. While at this early stage of economic development everyone satisfied the condition of having the minimum standard level of education and skill, at the later stage of economic development, in the 1980s and 1990s, a considerably large number of more educated persons became engaged in R&D and new technology fields in industry. This was because the steady rise in the number of young people who attended colleges over the years.

Changes due to Rapid Economic Growth

The most interesting effects of the rapid economic growth were the shifts in the lives of ordinary people. For the almost twenty years that economic growth continued the lives of the majority of Japanese people were altered dramatically.

First, the enlargement of the industry sector brought down substantially the share of workers engaged in farming and small retail trades. There were employment opportunities in the manufacturing sector for both white-collar and blue-collar workers. The share of blue-collar workers was larger than that of the white-collar workers because of their need on the factory floors. Typically these factories produced textile products, iron and steel, electric machines, and motor vehicles (i.e., cars and trains), and the shares of these products within total manufacturing changed from initially mostly textiles to later mostly motor vehicles (i.e., mostly cars). At the different stages of the rapid economic growth period the names of the most prosperous industries changed accordingly. Simultaneously each considerable increase in number of employees brought a drastic decrease in the self-employed, chief among them the farmer, the small retailer, and the small family-run firm.

Second, the change in the industry and employment structure was accompanied by high regional labor mobility. People moved from rural to urban areas where there were lots of employment opportunities. The large metropolitan areas like Tokyo, Osaka, and Nagoya consequently increased substantially in population size. This led to the so-called, later observed urban problems of overcrowded dwellings, traffic congestion, air pollution, and petty crime.

Along with high regional labor mobility came also the beginning in Japan of what we call a "nuclear family." This family consists of a husband and a wife with a small number of children, if any. In the past adult children lived together with their parents. Three generations, namely older parents, their adult children, and any grand children, lived together mainly in rural areas in so-called "extended families." As the adult children moved to urban areas to take jobs there during the period of rapid economic growth, their parents stayed behind in the rural areas. This phenomenon of nuclear families settling in urban areas and older parents remaining in rural areas meant that the number of family members (i.e., family size) was smaller in both urban and rural areas than that in past.

The decrease in family size had an impact on the measurement of equity based on household incomes, and more precisely welfare measurement. The following example should suffice to illustrate the issue. It involves a comparison between a four-family-members household that earns 10 million yen and a two-family-members household that earns 5 million yen to see which household is the richer of the two or has a higher welfare. For simplicity, we will suppose that in the

four-member household both husband and wife work and that in
the two-member household only the husband works. This way both
the number of family members and the number of income earners are
essentially even in equity and measurement of welfare. During the
period of rapid economic growth, however, the number of family members greatly decreased while the number of income earners increased,
mainly because of the increase in married women joining the labor
force. It is for this reason that income inequality has become such a
large issue today.

Fourth, the manufacturing industries and their allied service industries benefited most from the rapid economic growth because of
improved productivity. These industries could pay higher wages com-
mensurate with the growth of their technologies, and thus the incomes
of households with members employed in these industries were higher
in growth than those of farmers and small retailers. So the income differentials between employees in urban areas, and farmers and small retail traders in rural areas increased. However, because the number of
farmers and small retailers declined in the period of rapid economic
growth, the income inequality among all households was not so apparent where wages were fairly equal. We will examine more closely this
issue below.

Effects of Postwar Reforms and Subsequent Rapid Economic Growth on Income Distribution

Tables 2.1 and 2.2 give measures of income distribution in Japan over
the past hundred years. Note in table 2.1 the drastic decline in the Gini
coefficients, which in the 1930s and 1940s were around 0.4 and 0.6 and
in the 1960s and 1970s around 0.3. The nearly 0.1 and 0.3 decline in
Gini coefficients is substantial in the estimation of income inequality.
As was discussed earlier, the postwar democratic reforms had equal-
ized the income distribution so much as to transform Japan into an
equality-oriented society.

Although the small rises in the Gini coefficient in the 1950s and 1960s
were signs of rising inequality, they were not large enough to halt the
general shift from inequality of the prewar period to equality. These
small rises in inequality are explained by Mizoguchi (1986) as due to a
surge of employment in the manufacturing industries, which paid the
different wages shown in table 2.2. As both tables 2.1 and 2.2 show,
some further income inequalities occurred in the 1960s and 1970s, but
overall, it is possible to conclude that incomes and wages were distrib-

Table 2.3
Changes in household incomes (Gini coefficients)

	All households	Non-farm households
1924	0.190	0.170
1938	0.297	0.273
1953	0.041	0.041
1960	0.054	0.054
1979	0.043	0.043

Source: Mizoguchi (1986).

uted fairly equally in the postwar period of rapid economic growth. Later, to obtain a better sense of how the high equality was achieved in the postwar period, we will apply the famous Kuznets inverted-U hypothesis to the income data. Here we consider several features of manufacturing suitable only to Japan.

First, in the early years of the postwar period, a few manufacturing industries began to experience increases in productivity, and they raised wages accordingly, as was mentioned previously. As the economy grew, other manufacturing industries began to increase their productivity as well, and the wages in these industries were raised. Consequently the wage gaps among different manufacturing industries narrowed, and the wages of employees in manufacturing industries could be standardized, as shown in table 2.3. (See Tachibanaki 1975 for a time-series distribution of the incomes in Japan.)

Second, in the early years of the postwar period, the wage differentials between employees at large firms and employees at small firms appear not to have been substantial. Eventually the gap widened, and Japan became characterized as a country with a "dual economy." Implied by this term is that the differences between large firms and small firms in the Japanese industries are not only in wages but also in productivities, capital intensities, and benefits packages. During the first decade of the postwar reforms the wide wage differentials were slight because small firms could increase their productivity to a certain extent as well. Owing to the increasing productivity and lower production costs, small firms were in the position to raise the wages of their employees.

One important additional effect on the small firm in the postwar period must be considered. That is the effect of the 1940s postwar baby boom that came of age in the 1960s. The high birth rate of the 1940s raised the labor supply of the 1960s, transforming the economy by an excess of labor supply where earlier there had been a shortage of labor in the entire economy. This was a fortunate social phenomenon, and along with the large numbers of workers who moved from rural to urban areas, it produced the necessary human capital to steer the economy forward and upward. However, by the late 1960s and early 1970s, an endless labor supply could no longer be assumed. Japan was thrust into an era of labor shortage from an era of excess labor supply. Particularly in the small firms, employers had to raise wages in order to attract workers, even if the wages offered were higher than what they were able to pay. This contributed to narrowing the wage differentials between employees at large firms and those at small firms.

Third, the income structure for farmers and agricultural workers was transformed. In the past farmers engaged exclusively in farming activities. So their average incomes was much lower than those of other occupations, and their incomes varied in accord with the uncertainties associated with agricultural production. The very high need for labor in manufacturing industries during the growth economy encouraged farmers to seek side jobs in these industries. This way, by factory work, farmers could add to their farming incomes, and this raised the average incomes of farmers substantially. It is mainly this reason why the income differentials between farmers and nonfarmers decreased. Of course, there was often also an increase in agricultural productivity that should be added in explaining the increase in incomes of farmers, but manufacturing jobs contributed more to equalizing the income gap between farmer and nonfarmer during the period of the rapid economic growth.

Fourth, the introduction of employment principles made important contributions to industrial relations in Japan. Wage increases and promotions based on long-term employment and seniority became the norm across industries. As the seniority system implies, increases in wages became determined mainly by an employee's age and job tenure, and at the same time this principle opened the possibility for promotion along a hierarchical ladder. The long-term service was a provision by which an employee became protected from being discharged, but this principle also indirectly supported the seniority principle, since long-term employees seldom leave their employers. These two systems are regarded as complementarities.

The seniority system is further egalitarian in principle because all employees are treated equally early in their careers. The only crite-

rion for wage determinations is an employee' age and job tenure regardless of other qualifications like ability, education, performance,
and productivity. Those employees who work year round are treated
equally, and thus the wages of these employees are raised at the
same rate in accord with their age and job tenure. This means that
employee wages are fairly close during their early years of employment, and that some wage differentials appear in their later years
if they are promoted to higher positions. Since the wage differences
appear around the time the promoted employees have reached middle
age and have accumulated their work experiences in the firm, the
equal treatments ensured by the long-term employment and seniority
systems, and thus wage equality, apply mostly to early stages of their
careers.

Why Egalitarianism?
There are several reasons why an egalitarian approach to wage payments was adopted in postwar Japan. The nature of production systems adopted in the period of rapid economic growth suggests the
motivation for a system of equal treatment of employees.

First, in the postwar period new factory systems were designed to
produce a small number of standardized goods but in large quantities
in order to lower the unit cost of production. The products affected
were textiles, iron and steel, electrical appliances (refrigerators, TV
sets, and washing machines, etc.), and motor vehicles. These products
became fairly standardized because they were produced on assembly
lines by a large number of factory workers engaged in relatively simple
job tasks. In other words, most factory work became routine, and
many workers were compelled to do repetitive tasks. In such circumstances it is hard to observe any qualitative differences among workers
doing the same type of job. Naturally equal wage payments were the
best choice for the assembly line jobs. This is the philosophical, though
practical, response to the question of why the egalitarian principle (i.e.,
seniority rule) was adopted. The same wage principle was also applied
to white-collar jobs, even though these involved more heterogeneous
job assignments.

The egalitarian principle accepted for both blue-collar and white-
collar workers seems to have worked to infuse the factory floor with
team spirit, which increased productivity of all workers. In sum, it was
the method of production at that time that was most responsive to
egalitarianism.

Second, the incentive to work hard was an inevitable by-product of
the egalitarian principle. Because of the equal treatment of workers,
less productive workers were motivated to raise their production
levels in response to their more motivated colleagues. Because of the
egalitarian principle employers did not fear the possibility of less productive workers shirking such as might happen if their wages were set
at a lower level. Shirking by any worker is harmful at any factory assembly line operation.

Were ambitious productive workers satisfied with their equal wage
payments despite their higher contributions to the firm? There was in
fact a reward system that provided such workers with relatively early
promotion to management levels, although the promotions did not
come with the same regularity as seniority-based promotions. Alternatively, a large number of ambitious productive workers applied themselves with diligence because they expected to be recognized for their
high productivity by promotions within the hierarchy later in their
careers.

Third, ten years after the war, in the late 1950s the per capita national income was still low. Thus the average wage was also low. Most
people in Japan were at a poverty line. Economically the country was
poor, although it was on the threshold of rapid economic growth. So
industrial managers chose to adopt a fairly uniform wage level to
bring their workers over the poverty line, and by their compassion
achieved a productive workforce.

After the Rapid Economic Growth and the Stable Economy

The first oil crisis in 1973 brought an end to Japan's period of rapid
economic growth. This was at the time when also the economies of
nearly all industrialized countries experienced stagflation. The stagflation continued through the 1970s, in the form of high unemployment
and high inflation in these industrialized countries. However, the Japanese situation was different; Japan's economy was already at a turning
point in the late 1960s due to several developments: chief among these
were a downturn in consumer spending, a shortage of labor, and no
new technologies. Yoshikawa (1997) contends that the symptoms of
the end of the growth economy had already appeared before the oil
crisis, and the oil crisis was only the point where the growth economy
came to a decisive end.

He makes some important observations on the developments that
led to the end of rapid economic growth and the events of subsequent

years. First, the per-capita national income, by which the household living standard is measured, was high in the early 1970s when the rapid economic growth period was nearing its end. Nevertheless, the per-capita income of Japan did not surpass that of other industrial countries until the late 1970s and 1980s, when in nominal terms it rose well beyond the incomes of these same countries. For the Japanese economy this was a moment of triumph.

Here Tachibanaki (2003) takes a more cautionary view and hesitates to view the revitalized economy of the 1980s in such positive terms. On the one hand, he points out that the real living standard in terms of purchasing power, quality of life, and working hours remained inferior to that in Euro-American countries. On the other hand, the Japanese yen was overvalued and thus the comparisons of Japan's per-capita income with other national incomes were misleading. In fact, if these comparisons were made accurately, the living standard in Japan could be shown to be inferior to that in other advanced countries.

Second, the two oil crises in the 1970s brought difficulties to many industrialized countries, namely the high unemployment rates and high inflation rates mentioned earlier. There was also a problem of foreign trade deficits suffered by some countries. Despite its economic recovery in the late 1970s and 1980s, Japan could not escape this problem. Fortunately, it did not last long. The Japanese economy succeeded in achieving a fairly quick turnaround, with an annual growth rate of around 3 to 4 percent.

More important, the rate of unemployment fell to 2 percent, which was the lowest of the industrialized countries where the average rate was 7 to 10 percent. So only Japan enjoyed a stable economy in the 1970s and 1980s. Because other countries still had serious economic problems, there was even a widespread movement in the West to find out how it was that the Japanese industries, and thus Japan's macroeconomy, were so healthy. The Japanese success story in these years appears to have been due to the workings of the labor market and industrial relations. Interested readers can refer to Tachibanaki (1987).

Third, the year 1973 has a special meaning for the Japanese. Besides signaling the first oil crisis, 1973 was the year a social welfare program was introduced in Japan. Previously, as was mentioned in chapter 1, the responsibility for an individual's welfare had been with the family and/or the large firm. But the opinion of social policy makers, government officials, and politicians, who admired the European welfare state model, persuaded the people to concede to making the change in the direction of a social welfare state. A public pension system and a medical insurance system became fully enacted in 1973 for all citizens. The old-age pension and health insurance had actually been gradually developed before 1973 but became open to all citizens as if that year.

Further the prosperous economy enabled local governments to provide the elderly with free medical services. Many people even thought that in ten to twenty years Japan would become a fully European type of welfare state. This, unfortunately, never happened for two reasons. First, there was the slowdown in the growth rate of the economy from the high of the period rapid economic growth, although the Japanese economy was doing better than the economies of other industrialized countries. Consequently tax revenues and social insurance contributions slowed as well. Second, there was the aging of the population age structure that had started to become apparent, and is currently rearing upon us. It should not be difficult to see that these two phenomena alarmed the government, which took a good look at its old-age pension and health insurance and modified the direction of its welfare state. Interested readers can refer to Tachibanaki (2000) about the history behind the development of welfare programs in Japan.

What was the impact of the economic slowdown and the subsequent recovery on the size of income distribution? As table 1.1 showed clearly, the distribution of income was fairly stable from the 1970s to the early 1980s; there was not much change in equality or inequality. As is usual in a stable macroeconomy, no significant change in income distribution occurred. Therefore no serious discussion of Japan's years of economic stability is required.

Effect of the Bubble: Income from Assets and Imputed Rents
The Japanese economy entered into the so-called bubble economy in the mid-1980s, and the bubble continued until the end of the 1980s. Over these four years the relentless rise in the values of both land and equities widened the disparities in income and wealth. Wealth from assets holding became a serious indicator of income inequality. We concentrate here on the income inequalities that ensued from the land and equity bubble; we explore more fully the issue of wealth inequality in chapter 4.

In assets holding, land yields rents and monetary assets yield interest income and dividends, and so forth. Capital gains are possible from both real assets and monetary assets. A factor that is as important but ignored in the literature is the contribution of imputed rents that

Table 2.4
Breakdown of income inequality by income sources

	Average income (million yen)	Concentration coefficient	Contribution rate (%)
Total income	9.574	0.371	100.0
Wages	7.012	0.275	54.3
Real assets	1.776	0.656	32.8
Financial assets	0.786	0.582	12.9

Source: Tachibanaki and Yagi (1994).
Notes: Real assets include imputed rents receipts, and rents, and financial assets incomes include interests, dividends, and capital gains. Financial assets based on a survey of financial assets by *Japan Economic Journal*, 1990.

arises from land and home ownership. Table 2.4 takes into account these imputed rents in the estimations of the contribution of real asset holding to income inequality.

The analysis of national income inequality in the table is based on the following three components: wage income, income from real assets including imputed rents, and income from monetary and financial assets. There are three measures used: the average income from each component, the concentration coefficient showing a small number of households forming the larger part, and the portion of each component's contribution to national income inequality. Several of the computations in the table give noteworthy results.

The average income from real assets is 1.78 million yen. The major source of this income is imputed rents. This amount is fairly larger than that from monetary and financial assets, averaging 0.786 million yen. More important, the concentration rate of rents, 0.656, is very large, and its contribution to national income inequality is very high, 32.8 percent. It is higher than the contribution of incomes from monetary and financial assets. Nevertheless, that the concentration coefficient of incomes from monetary and financial assets is not low, 0.582, although it is slightly lower than that of incomes from real assets. Its contribution to national income inequality, however, is a surprisingly low 12.9 percent.

A comparison of wage and property incomes, meaning income both from real assets and from monetary and financial assets, suggests that the average income of the former (i.e., 7.012 million yen) is much larger than that of the latter (combined as 2.562 million yen). But the concentration coefficients and contribution to national income inequality give a different story. In particular, the income effect of real assets is very large in both the concentration rate and the contribution rate. Households that own both land and houses benefited in increased income flow from real asset holdings.

The general argument is that wealth inequality rose during the years of the bubble economy. That is to say, in the bubble economy the very large difference in wealth figures between those who held real and monetary assets and those who held no assets widened further. The discussion of this section thus will focus on the story behind the numbers in table 2.4, on the difference in income flows due to wealth holdings and no wealth holdings.

The results in table 2.4 have a policy implication because it takes into account the role of imputed rents in national income inequality. As the table shows, real assets holders can enjoy high rents in the form of tax-free incomes. Households that rent their homes normally pay taxes on the income they use to pay their rent. It is evident that this treatment is unfair, and thus that some tax should be levied on imputed rents. There are several countries where imputed rents are regarded as taxable incomes, for example, the Netherlands. Although it is not an immediate issue, it is bound to become a future issue in Japan.

Serious Recession
The bubble economy ended around the late 1980s or the early 1990s. History teaches us that bubbles do not continue in perpetuity. Japan was not an exception to this idea. Within just two to three years land and equity prices fell drastically, and Japan entered a serious recession that has continued for nearly fifteen years. A great many bankruptcies, devaluations, negative GDPs and GNPs, high unemployment rates, and government deficit spirals have followed. Their impacts are still being felt in the Japanese economy.

It may be fascinating to learn why the bubble occurred, and why its duration was only four to five years. Because the macroeconomy or monetary economics is beyond the scope of this book, the reader is referred to an important book on the bubble economy edited by Muramatsu and Okuno (2002). As fascinating a subject that will, however, be examined here is the effects of the bubble economy on Japan's income and wealth distributions. The first part of this subject has been just discussed regarding the implication of property incomes, including the role of imputed rents, that arise from real assets holding; the second part will be covered in chapter 4. There remains to be discussed in this chapter the effect of the current serious recession on income distribution.

The persistent recession has completely changed the lives of the Japanese people. In Japan today the unemployed number close to 4 million and the homeless people over 30 thousand. The official rate of unemployment is about 5 percent, and the rate of potential unemployment, which includes discouraged workers drop out of job seeking, is over 10 percent. Wage cuts are seen everywhere, and welfare provisions are cut too. The number of low-income earners has increased greatly. Everyone has suffered enormously. It is natural to think that income inequality has increased, but it is necessary to see if this supposition can be supported empirically. This is the task we turn to next.

Change in Income Inequality over Time
Since the 1970s the two basic sources used to evaluate a time-series change in income inequality are the *Income Re-distribution Survey* by the Ministry of Welfare and Labor and the *Family Expenditure Survey* by the Ministry of Management and Coordination. Both have strengths and weaknesses as statistical sources in providing a description of Japan's income distribution over this long period. First, the *Income Re-distribution Survey* includes all people, by age group, occupation, and household characteristics (celibate, widowed, young unmarried, etc., or extended family households), while the *Family Expenditure Survey* excludes farmers and single unmarried taxpayers. Therefore the *Income Re-distribution Survey* is the preferred source for more complete sampling.

Second, the *Family Expenditure Survey* is published every year, while the *Income Re-distribution Survey* is published every three years. For this reason it is useful for gauging yearly changes.

Third, information on taxes and social security contributions are reported fairly accurately in the *Income Re-distribution Survey*. While these figures are not available for all samples in the *Family Expenditure Survey*, they are marginally available for all that are employed. Because we are interested in all kinds of Japanese people, and not in selected samples of employees, or of households receiving earnings (i.e., excluding retired people), the former source is better for our purpose than the latter source.

In summarizing the three points above, it is possible to conclude that the *Income Re-distribution Survey* is a better source than the *Family*

Table 2.5
Income redistribution through tax policies and social security programs

	Inequality before redis-tribution	Inequality after redis-tribution	Redistri-bution coefficient	Redistri-bution coefficient due to taxes	Redistri-bution coefficient due to social security
1961	0.390	0.344	11.8	—	—
1967	0.375	0.328	12.6	3.7	8.7
1972	0.354	0.314	11.4	4.4	5.7
1975	0.375	0.346	7.8	2.9	4.5
1978	0.365	0.338	7.4	3.7	1.2
1981	0.349	0.314	10.0	5.4	5.0
1984	0.398	0.343	13.8	3.8	9.8
1987	0.405	0.338	16.5	4.2	12.0
1990	0.433	0.364	15.9	2.9	12.5
1993	0.439	0.365	17.0	3.2	13.2
1996	0.441	0.361	18.3	1.7	15.7
1999	0.472	0.381	19.2	1.3	17.1
2002	0.498	0.381	23.5	0.8	21.4

Source: Ministry of Welfare and Labor, *Income Re-distribution Survey*, various years.

Expenditure Survey as long as we are interested in changes in income distribution for all people or samples, and in income redistribution policy through taxation and social security. Thus the subsequent discussion, including the next chapter, is based mainly on the *Income Re-distribution Survey*. The other statistical source is used to supplement survey areas not reported in the *Income Re-distribution Survey*.

Income Re-distribution Survey

Table 2.5 and figure 2.1 give the Gini coefficients on income inequality for primary incomes and before-tax incomes respectively. The primary incomes listed in the table from the *Income Re-distribution Survey* do not include social security benefits such as old-age pension benefits, whereas the plot of before-tax incomes in the figure based on data from the *Family Expenditure Survey* includes social security benefits. Clearly, the incomes represented in these two measures of income are not comparable, strictly speaking. However, because in each survey the spread of income is over a common long-term period, together they give at least a reliable indication of time-series changes in income inequality.

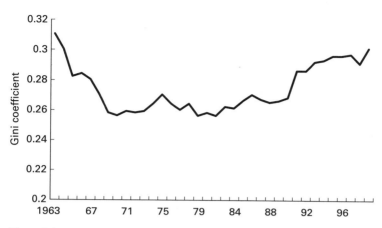

Figure 2.1
Changes in income inequalities in the postwar Japan for two or more member house-holds. Gini coefficients are used to indicate the income inequalities. Source: Ministry of General Affairs, *Family Expenditure Survey*

The following observations can be made from the *Family Expenditure Survey* results shown in figure 2.1. The distribution of income in the 1960s, when the most rapid economic growth occurred, was also a period of high inequality, as was explained earlier. Around the time of the two oil crises in 1973 and 1975 the growth of income inequality slowed. Within a short time there was, once more, high income equality, and this level of equality continued for nearly ten years. In the mid-1980s the trend changes. Income inequality starts to edge up, and continues its rise—and ultimately to the high level of inequality at which it is today.

The numerical values from the *Income Re-distribution Survey* support the last point. The Gini coefficient in 2002 for primary incomes was 0.498, while the lowest figure in the 1980s was 0.349 in 1981. The increase in the Gini coefficient over the 21 years is 0.149, which is a huge increase. The increase in the coefficient for redistributed incomes, which take into account the contribution of tax payments, and social security contributions and benefits, is 0.067, that is, from 0.314 in 1981 to 0.381 in 2002. This is again a very big increase. The last figure, 0.381, indicates considerably high inequality by international standards. From these two increases in inequality it is not difficult to see that Japan is no longer an equal society. While income inequality is not the only criterion to use in judging whether or not the country is equality or inequality oriented, it is one of the more obvious criteria, so much attention is given to income distribution. Other factors such as wealth, inheritance, education, and occupation will be examined later in relation to income distribution.

As was mentioned earlier, the plot in figure 2.1 is based on the *Family Expenditure Survey*, which excludes farmers and single households from the samples. Thus it has no purpose as an indicator of income inequality but as an indicator of change in income equality over time. It is important that from the 1960s to the late 1990s (for about 30 years) the time-series trend in income inequality from the *Family Expenditure Survey* is almost parallel with that from the *Income Re-distribution Survey*. These statistical sources thus support a pattern in the time-series change in income inequality over the same period of time.

The Hundred Years' Story
It may be useful to put the more recent thirty-year trend into the hundred-year perspective with which we began this chapter. Figure 2.2 summarizes the change in income inequality from 1900 to 2000. The plot in the upper panel is based on the Gini coefficients, and the plot in the lower panel is a very rough approximation that can be used to understand the general flow of inequality. The upper plot, however, is not strictly accurate, as it is based on an average of different statistical sources deriving Gini coefficients for the years in question.

For convenience, we will classify the hundred-year period into three subperiods. The first is from the prewar years; that is, from the middle of the Meiji period, *A*, to the immediate prewar years, *B*. This is a period of rising inequality. The second is from the immediate postwar age, *B*, to the first oil crisis, *C*, which is a period of rising equality. The third is from the post–oil crisis, *C*, to the end of the hundred years, *D*, which is the present period where we have, again, rising inequality. The three classifications covering the hundred years thus follow a pattern of inequality–equality–inequality. This alternating pattern is represented by the curve in the lower panel of figure 2.2. Recall that the first subperiod is when industrialization was introduced to Japan, bringing along an increasing trend in income inequality. The second subperiod is when industrialization matured, bringing along a decreasing trend. The third subperiod is the postindustrial economy of the present day, showing again an increasing trend. This is nothing but a sine curve. Income inequality thus can be seen to be refluent when viewed from a longer term perspective of economic development.

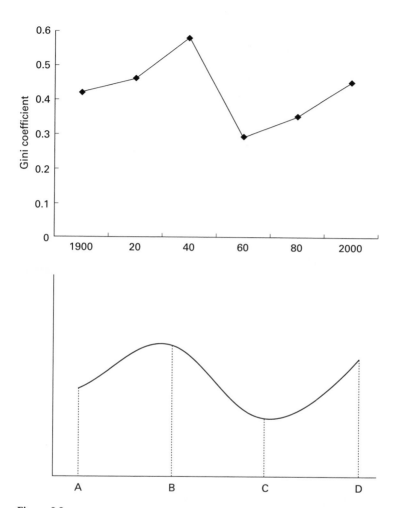

Figure 2.2
Shape of income inequality in Japan since the Meiji Restoration corresponding roughly to
the Gini coefficients (*upper curve*) and the cubic representation (*lower curve*).

2.3   The Cubic Hypothesis and Income Inequality

Kuznets's Inverted-U Hypothesis

Simon Kuznets (1955), a Nobel laureate, introduced the now famous inverted-U hypothesis, also called the Kuznets hypothesis. Kuznets proposed that income inequality increases at the early stage of economic development and industrialization; then after reaching a peak point of inequality (i.e., the late stage of economic development), it starts to decline. Kuznets supported this idea using fairly long time-series data for the United Kingdom, United States, and Germany. Although he did not have data for the immediate postwar period, his investigation found these countries' past income inequality and economic development to take the shape of an inverted U.

The Kuznets hypothesis opened the way to a large number of cross-country studies mostly comparing developing countries. In Japan some representative econometric studies applicable to developing countries are those by Agluwalia (1976), Ogwang (1994), and Anand and Kanbur (1993a, b). Both Agluwalia and Ogwang support the inverted-U hypothesis, whereas Anand and Kanbur see only a weak inverted U, and even an upright U in their evaluation. There are many different issues to address in regard to these results, including data problems, estimation methods, and sample periods. Also there is the question whether the data for developed countries should be included for comparison. Because these are complicated issues, I will not deal with them further.

For the present study, it would be more interesting and scientifically attractive to see whether the Kuznets hypothesis could be fitted to Japan. From Kuznets we know that at least in the United Kingdom, the United States, and Germany, income inequality and economic development processes followed the inverted U until the Second World War. How do the circumstances of Japan fit into this reasoning? In my judgment, it is possible to support the inverted U if we consider only the period between A and C (about 60 to 70 years) in the lower panel of figure 2.2, whereas it is impossible to support the hypothesis if we include the period between B and D (about 50 to 60 years). If we take the period between A and D (the entire 100 years), no such simple inverted-U hypothesis can be accepted. The result is neither an inverted U or a upright U but a sinusoidal time-dependent curve for the 100 years since the Meiji Restoration, which spans the beginning of the modern era to roughly the present day.

More precisely, we could recognize the starting period of Japanese industrialization to be the 1910s and 1920s when there was a sudden surge in Japan's economic development. If the Kuznets hypothesis is applied to the period starting in the 1910s and 1920s, slightly after point A, and ending in the 1960s and 1970s, the relationship between income inequality and economic development over this longer period does yield an inverted U. Tachibanaki and Yagi (1997) attempted a statistical test for the period of 1963 to 1991, and obtained an upright U pattern rather than an inverted U. This is because the first half of this period corresponds to a decreasing trend of income inequality, and is equivalent to the second half of the Kuznets effect. Thus Tachibanki and Yagi were able to support the second half of the Kuznets effect, but the second half of the Tachibanaki and Yagi sample, period C to D, cannot be explained by the traditional Kuznets hypothesis. In period between C and D income inequality is clearly on the rise again. So, how can we explain the increasing trend in income inequality in terms of the Kuznets effect? First of all, Kuznets did not predict any such turning point C, at which income inequality restarts. Kuznets focused on only the period between A and C, and was not interested in activity beyond C. Effectively this was beyond the scope of his concern.

The Postindustrialization Period: The Cubic Hypothesis
Here we elaborate on the period between C and D in figure 2.2, which represents postindustrial Japan during the period when its market economy matured. As we saw, the increasing income inequality Japan experienced was also a phenomenon experienced by both the United Kingdom and the United States. The United States had, however, remarkably higher increases in income inequality. Other industrialized countries showed mixed patterns of income inequality. Several industrialized countries showed no increase in inequality, and some other countries more or less followed with increases. In general, the income inequality appears to be higher in economies that have matured and entered into a postindustrialization era and in highly developed economies that have experienced a period of decreasing income inequality as is represented by the second half of the Kuznets inverted U. In other words, the cubic outcome in income inequality is natural for a mature postindustrial society. Only a few countries, among these Japan, the United Kingdom, and the United States, are at the advanced third stage between C and D.

It may be useful to delve briefly into the causes and outcomes of the events experienced at the three stages on the time curve. The first two stages, of course, accord well with the Kuznets inverted-U hypothesis. At the first stage of economic development the skillful managers of businesses, public policy makers, and other leaders are important initiators of economic growth. They are normally well-educated individuals who reside in urban areas, but they are the minority in any population. Since these are the prime movers in the industrialization process, their positions tend to be influential and their salaries high. The rest of the population, which is not as educated, is employed at the factories in urban areas or is engaged in farming in the rural hinterlands. Their incomes tend to be low. This demographic is one reason for the high income inequality present at the first stage of economic development.

Another reason is that the high-income earners have the capability to accumulate capital and manage their financial assets. By this means they can augment their earnings. Since the capital market at this stage is imperfect, the rate of interest is usually high, so up go the incomes of this group much more from their assets holdings. It is unlikely for factory workers and farmers to have the savings and know-how to invest in the capital market. So by a market mechanism, income inequality broadens because educated and skillful entrepreneurs can keep adding to their incomes.

What effect does the insatiability of the rich have at the second stage of economic development? As industrialization proceeds, many individuals at the poverty level are motivated to seek employment in the urban areas and move away from rural areas. At the same time the educational levels of some low-income earners is increased because they find opportunities to invest in education thanks to capital market perfections. Their skill levels increase then as well. The differences in education and skills between high-income earners and low-income earners shrink, and income gap narrows. Since the rate of interest at the second stage normally is lower, the advantages the high-income earners enjoyed in high returns on financial investments disappear. This is yet another reason why the differences in incomes between high-income earners and low-income earners are smaller at the second stage.

Interestingly before the Second World War, as we saw in table 2.2, the differences in earnings in Japan between educated white-collar workers high on the hierarchical ladder at a firm and the less-educated manual workers was very large. Also in accord with the Kuznets effect, the capital incomes for entrepreneurs and equity holders were very high. We can add to this the huge income difference between land-owners and tenants. These three phenomena are in fact typical of what is observed during the first stage of economic development.

At the second stage, an entirely different picture emerges. In Japanese history this was the time of postwar reform, which enabled large numbers of people to become more educated. As a result the earnings differentials between educated people and less educated people became lower. As economic development raised average household incomes, the differences in incomes between white-collar and blue-collar workers became smaller because of the small differences in education. Because interest rates were relatively low during this period of rapid economic growth, the difference in incomes declined between high-income earners and low-income earners. These results seem to be what led to the idea that income inequality in Japan was low during the rapid economic growth period. The vast majority, about 100 million people, felt that they belonged to the middle class. There were very few super rich people and very few extremely poor people, and this phenomenon gave rise to the so-called myth of equality in Japan.

The preceding very simple explanation of how the Kuznets inverted-U hypothesis might apply to Japan is nevertheless one of many interpretations of the Kuznets hypothesis in the economics literature. Because the main concern of this book is inequality in a society with a mature and highly developed economy, no further interpretation of the Kuznets effect in Japan is needed. The important point is that once the period when the inverted U was manifested was over, the period between C and D set in, when income inequality once more started to increase. The discussion in the next chapter will fully parse the causes behind this increase. Here we will look at them very briefly.

Why did income inequality start to increase again when the Japanese economy matured in the present era of postindustrialization? Since 1986 the service sector and high technology sector have been the major employers in Japan. Because the demand for highly educated and technologically skilled workers is very high, these workers receive very high earnings. Then there are the newly established entrepreneurs who engage in risk-taking to obtain even higher incomes. Finally added to this mix of very high-income earners are the very talented sports-players, artists, novelists, and financial managers, who are rewarded in kind, because they are outstanding in their fields.

Unfortunately, the average worker in the service sector is unable to earn a high income.

Nevertheless, it is important to point out that most people do not take a negative or hostile view about the widening income differentials. This is because the average income in the present economy is fairly high, so most people do not face much economic difficulty. Of course, there is the rising number of the elderly poor in this highly developed economy, and the issue of the aging population is important, as I have already discussed (and will return to later), in the debate about introducing the welfare state to Japan.

2.4   An International Comparison of Income Inequality; Past and Present

The previous section examined income inequality in Japan historically. This section proceeds to contextualize Japan's income inequality by an international comparison. Because an international comparison is not an easy task to undertake, it will not be as comprehensive as such an attempt would demand.

Difficulty in International Comparison

As was mentioned in chapter 1, there are some difficulties in making international comparisons of income inequalities. Here we discuss the extent of these difficulties.

First, internationally it is not easy to standardize the samples used for data collection and compare them because each country's government collects data differently, such as for employees only, farmers only, active labor forces only, or aged people only. Some countries distinguish between households with more than two members and households with only one member. In chapter 1 we saw that in Japan the size of family is a big problem. Also ideally samples that include all people regardless of age, profession, family status, and so forth, would be compared. In the real world this is far from an achievable task.

Second, there are different methods of measurement. Whether the data depend on questionnaires or reported income to a tax bureau is important. If the tax bureau's income data are used, it is natural to presume that incomes are underreported. Even errors in questionnaires are unavoidable because few respondents keep detailed household accounts. Also the definition and method of income measurement can differ from country to country. Two good examples are the treatment of imputed rents and the measurement of capital gains (or losses). So we have to take care not to accept the measurement of incomes as entirely accurate but as adjustments of incomes that are especially difficult to make internationally.

Third, it is necessary to adjust for the number of family members and/or number of income earners when household incomes are compared internationally. Useful for adjusting the family size is a technique called "equivalent scale," but there is no standard technique for adjusting for the number of income earners per household. If it were just the issue of both a husband and wife being employed, that would not be so difficult. However, Japan has extended families where elderly parents live together with their adult children. Also some families have young children who work and receive earnings. Such cases are not easy to adjust internationally, since the comparison requires the adjustment for number of income earners to be uniformly made.

Fourth, incomes are the most common and popular variable by which the welfare of a people is compared internationally. However, the usefulness of incomes is debatable when the interest is in well-being or affluence. On the one hand, household consumption level might be a better indicator than household income, and on the other, the disutility derived from working might be taken into account. Such questions are crucial when it comes to a people's welfare and an international comparison of that welfare.

Fifth, summary statistics are used to compare income inequalities or the size of any variable's inequality. I have used so far the Gini coefficient partly because it is the most accepted measure and is used widely. There are a large number of other measures such as the Atkinson index, the Theil measure, and the Dalton measure. Where an income inequality calls for rigorous study, in particular, where fine distinctions must be made, measures other than the Gini coefficient might be used instead. Because our concern in this book is with general economic inequality and its implications for a society, we can set aside many of the more academic measurement methods.

Equivalent Scale and Micro Data
Even with the equivalent scale technique the problem of obtaining accurate counts of income earners and household members using the equivalent scales is not particularly easy to surmount. There have been several attempts to minimize insufficient data. One method is to divide

total household incomes by the number of income earners in order to obtain per-earner household income. Another method is to compute the household income by taking a weighted average of the number of household members and their ages. By the latter method the welfare level of each household member is accounted for. Both methods, however, require data on the number of income earners, household members, and their ages. Also the computations used to adjust the income figures are fairly complicated. For this reason several simplifications have been made. For example, the OECD uses a SQRT method whereby total incomes are divided by a square root of the number of household members to obtain the adjusted incomes. Although this method may seem too simple, it is better than doing nothing because it is nearly impossible to adopt a method for international comparative studies that satisfies the requirements of all countries.

An equivalent scale adjustment technique is used in Yagi and Tachibanaki (1996) in an empirical study of income distribution. The technicalities involved in the adjustments made by Yagi and Tachibanaki to estimate the income inequality for Japan turned out to be fairly complicated, so the technique itself will not be presented here. Rather we will consider the interesting difference between income inequality with no adjustment and income inequality with the equivalent scale adjustment.

Table 2.6 shows the income figures and the Gini coefficients for the following three cases: (1) no adjustment, (2) adjustment in the number of household members (i.e., per-member incomes), (3) adjustment by equivalent scale. The adjustment in household members was obtained by dividing household income by the number of family members, and then the equivalent scale was obtained. Obviously the method used to

Table 2.6
Income inequality with no adjustment and with some adjustments, 1984

	Household income (thousand yen)	Per-member income (average) (thousand yen)	Equivalent scale income (average) (thousand yen)
Before-tax income	4128	1299	3240
Gini	0.408	0.441	0.419
After-tax income	3952	1245	3154
Gini	0.356	0.369	0.359

Source: Yagi and Tachibanaki (1996).

adjust the number of household member was simple, but the method to obtain the equivalent scale involved complicated computations.

Two observations can be made from the results in table 2.6. First, the Gini coefficients increase where per-member incomes and equivalent scaled incomes are used unlike where no adjustments are made. So income inequality measured without adjustments is downward biased. This is true for both before-tax income and after-tax income. Second, income inequality that is equivalent scaled falls between the adjusted per-member income and the nonadjusted income. This is again true for both before-tax income and after-tax income. The adjustments in income effectively yield Gini coefficients that are higher than those for nonadjusted income but lower than those for the per-member income.

The slightly higher Gini coefficient for the equivalent scaled income should not, however, imply that the nonadjusted income inequality data are useless. Nonadjusted income figures have value as a first approximation, before they are submitted to the demanding job of committing them to a proper equivalent scale adjustment.

The Luxembourg Project

Today the data on income inequality among individual households include not only income figures but also related variables such as tax, social security, age, profession, and family size. The equivalent income adjustment that was attempted for Japan, and explained above, is particularly useful if these other household survey data are available. Further the computers are more capable of using statistical techniques to produce more reliable income adjustments. So it is not an overstatement that today we can interpret more reliably survey data than was possible to imagine only ten years ago.

A good example of the progress made due to computer technology is the *Luxembourg Income Analysis Project*, which was briefly mentioned in chapter 1. Recall that this is an international attempt to collect survey data of participating countries and adjust the income figures based on a common principle and method. The goal is to obtain an internationally database on income distribution and related subjects. A large number of countries have supported this project, and we have now fairly reliable international comparative studies on income distribution that derive from the Luxembourg project.

Unfortunately, Japan is not a member country of the project. Therefore the international comparative studies of this project do not contain results for Japan. In other words, Japan is excluded from today's most reliable international comparative study on income distribution. This is unfortunate not only for Japan but also for the world. Although Japan was invited many times to join the Luxembourg Project, the government is reluctant to comply. The reasons are unclear, but it is said that there is fear of possibly private information on individuals' income being leaked. Since anonymity can be assured by various technicalities, it appears that there must be other reasons why the Japanese government is unwilling to participate. I would dare to speculate that the government is afraid of a possible finding that Japan will be exposed to be a very unequal country in income distribution. It is my hope that Japan will join this Project in the near future so that the valuable international analyses being made in Luxembourg will include Japan.

International Comparison: Past Evidence

The only other international comparative study on income distribution was that by the OECD (1976) on the state of income distribution in advanced and industrialized countries (refer to table 1.4). The OECD reported the conditions in the 1960s and 1970s, which is thirty- to forty-year-old history. The data, of course, are inferior to that of the Luxembourg Project because the estimation method for income inequality was primitive in comparison, especially since, unlike the recent method, it did not use individual survey data. It used only data aggregated by income class.

The OECD report nevertheless received a considerable attention at the time. A big concern was that it reported France to be the country with the highest income inequality because it had the highest Gini coefficient, 0.414. The French government, including President Giscard d' Estang at that time, protested vigorously against the OECD report, claiming the data treatment and estimation method used for France were inaccurate. As the French case suggests, people—and the government—can become very concerned about the state of income distribution if it is revealed to be highly unequal. In the worst case, a state of income inequality that is shown to be very bad (i.e., very unequally distributed) can be enough to incite people to a political revolution. Remember, there have been numerous instances of riots, political unrests, and even revolutions in the developing countries of Africa, Asia, and South America brought on by serious poverty issues.

Interestingly, in the Japanese case, the government used the OECD report as advertising. Japan was determined to be on equal footing in income distribution with Australia, Norway, and Sweden, as table 1.4 indicates. The problem, as was noted earlier, was that the Japanese statistics were based mainly on the *Family Expenditure Survey*, which does not represent all the possible samples in Japan. It excluded farmers and single-member households from the samples. This way a downward bias was achieved in income inequality since the excluded households are normally low-income earners.

The story of France, Japan, and perhaps other countries reminds us that the state of income distribution in a country is important both socially and politically. If a country is found to have an unequal distribution of income, the majority of people in the country, including the government, will be troubled by the result. Of course, most unhappy will be the very high income earners who will want to maintain the status quo.

An exception to the observations above may be the United States in which there is known to be the highest income inequality among advanced and industrialized countries. I gave earlier some reasons why American people do not pay much attention to their very high income inequality. Foremost is the American love of free competition, so if there seems to be a wide difference between higher earnings due to great effort and great contribution, and lower earning due to little effort and a small contribution, they don't seem to mind that at all. What they do care about is equality of opportunity.

In the case of Japan, however, the OECD study gave the impression to the world that the Japanese society was equality-oriented at least in the distribution of income. The myth of equality due to this OECD report made the Japanese people very proud of the achievement, since already in the 1950s and 1960s their economy had experienced remarkable growth. The success story of Japan spread the world over in the 1970s. The success story, however, began to change in the 1980s, as I described it in chapter 1. Income inequality was noticed to widen, although the economy enjoyed stable growth with very low unemployment at a time when after two oil crises almost all industrialized countries suffered from a so-called stagflation in the late 1970s and the 1980s. How was it that Japan's high inequality appeared in the 1980s, and has continued until now? The Japanese society and economy have changed greatly over the past twenty years in age-population structure, family relations, industrial structure, industrial relations, work ethic, tax and social security systems, and so forth. The next chapter discusses these subjects fully.

Table 2.7
International comparison of income distribution based on equivalent scale adjusted Gini coefficients

	Year	Gini coefficient
United States	1986	0.341
Ireland	1987	0.330
Switzerland	1982	0.323
Italy	1986	0.310
United Kingdom	1986	0.304
France	1984	0.296
Netherlands	1987	0.268
Germany	1984	0.250
Luxembourg	1985	0.238
Belgium	1988	0.235
Norway	1986	0.234
Sweden	1987	0.220
Finland	1987	0.207

Source: Atkinson (1995).

International Comparison: More Recent Evidence

In the 1980s and 1990s comparisons of income inequality were made with regard to past experience in the 1960s and 1970s. The first study of note attempting an international comparison of advanced countries was that by Atkinson et al. (1995). This study used Luxembourg Project data, so Japan was not included. The income distributions of these advanced countries were estimated based on a common means of data collection, definition, and analysis. Table 2.7 gives the Gini coefficients.

The levels of income equality of these countries can be grouped according to their high, medium, and low Gini coefficient values shown in the table. In the first group of high income equality are the Scandinavian countries of Finland, Sweden, and Norway plus the two Benelux countries, Belgium and Luxembourg. The evidence in the table supports common knowledge about the Scandinavia and the Benelux countries. In the second group are the two European countries, Germany and the Netherlands, whose income equalities range in the middle. In the third group are France and Italy, the United Kingdom, Ireland, the United States, and Switzerland whose Gini coefficients are much higher than those of other countries, and whose income distributions are thus much more unequal as well. It is possible to further break up the third group into the following two groups: the United

States and the rest. By this classification the United States and the Scandinavian countries represent the two extremes, namely the highest inequality and the highest equality in income distribution. (For an interesting study comparing these two polar cases, see Aaberge et al. 2002.)

Because Japan was not included in the Project, it is not possible to obtain a precise fit for Japan among the countries presented in table 2.7. My guess is that Japan in the late 1980s, the observation years in the table, was somewhere between the second group and the third group. In other words, its income was slightly higher in inequality than the average level but somewhat lower in inequality than the highest level.

A paper by Förster and Pearson (2002) investigating income distribution and poverty in the OECD area describes the state of income inequality among advanced countries from the mid-1980s to the mid-1990s. Japan is included in this study. Unfortunately, equal attention is not given Japan in the statistical comparisons of the countries. So it is a bit risky to use this study to position Japan in a country order of income inequality. However, it may be acceptable to disregard this infelicity and note an interesting result presented by Förster and Pearson.

Table 2.8 gives the estimated Gini coefficients of disposable incomes for 17 OECD countries. Reported also in the table are the decile ratios, SCV (squared coefficient of variation) and MLD (mean log deviation), used in the original study. The Gini coefficients are discussed here because they are useful in making observations about time-series changes. The years covered are the mid-1990s, which amounts to around five to eight years after the results in table 2.7 were obtained. Note that many countries show increases in their Gini coefficients, such as to imply that income inequalities in those countries, including Japan, increased from the mid-1980s to the mid-1990s. There are nevertheless some countries where income inequality decreased.

What is the relative position of Japan in table 2.8? It seems to be somewhere between the group of average inequalities and the group of highest inequalities, as is evident in table 2.7. It is not possible to say that Japan belonged to the group of countries that had high income inequality in the mid-1980s and mid-1990s, at least on the basis of these international comparisons.

Is this result still correct? The answer is, no. As discussed in chapter 1, income inequality increased from 1996 to 2002 dramatically. The

Table 2.8
International comparisons of income distributions based on Gini coefficients, Desile ratios, SCVs, and MLDs

| | Levels | | Absolute change* | | | | | | | | |
| | Gini coefficient mid-1990s | P90/P10 decile ratio mid-1990s | Gini coefficient | | Decile ratio | | SCV | | MLD | | |
			(A)	(B)	(A)	(B)	(A)	(B)	(A)	(B)
Australia	30.5	3.9	2.1	-0.7	0.2	-0.4	3.2	1.2	1.8	0.5
Austria	23.8	3.0	—	0.2	—	0.1	—	1.4	—	-0.2
Belgium	27.2	3.2	—	1.2	—	0.0	—	9.1	—	0.4
Canada	28.5	3.7	-0.8	-0.4	-0.6	-0.2	4.0	0.7	-2.5	-1.0
Denmark	21.7	2.7	—	-1.1	—	-0.2	—	0.4	—	-1.5
Finland	22.8	2.8	-2.8	2.1	-0.5	0.1	-3.7	7.8	-3.0	1.2
France	27.8	3.4	—	0.3	—	0.1	—	6.9	—	-0.8
Germany	28.2	3.7	—	1.7	—	0.4	—	-2.2	—	1.6
Ireland	32.4	4.2	—	-0.6	—	-0.1	—	32.0	—	-3.0
Italy	34.5	4.6	—	3.9	—	0.8	—	18.1	—	6.7
Japan	26.5	3.3	-1.4	1.2	-0.1	0.2	-5.8	5.3	-1.0	1.5
Netherlands	25.5	3.2	0.7	2.1	0.1	0.4	2.7	2.5	0.6	2.3
Norway	25.6	3.0	—	2.2	—	0.1	—	2.3	—	3.1
Sweden	23.0	2.7	-1.6	1.4	-0.2	0.1	-2.1	8.0	-1.8	2.0
Switzerland	26.9	3.1	—	—	—	—	—	—	—	—
United Kingdom	31.2	4.1	3.8	2.5	0.5	0.5	10.3	8.6	3.1	3.0
United States	34.4	5.5	2.7	0.4	0.8	-0.2	7.7	1.2	3.2	0.5

Sources: Foster and Pearson (2000) based on OECD questionnaire on distribution of household incomes.
Notes: (A) Mid-1970s to mid-1980s. (B) Mid-1980s to mid-1990s. Absolute change is the difference in the value of the index indicated by an asterisk (*).

increase in the Gini coefficient in this period for redistributed income is 0.02, that is, from 0.361 to 0.381. Also because, as shown in table 1.2 of chapter 1, nowadays Japan belongs to the group of OECD countries with the highest income inequalities, the answer is strictly, no. All that is certain is that Japan is no longer an equal country in income distribution, and that its inequality is approaching the highest among advanced countries.

3.1 Observations Based on Statistical Data and Actual Feeling of Living Standard

Limits of Statistical Data

In the preceding chapter we learned about changes in Japan over time and about how Japan's income and wealth inequalities compare internationally. In this chapter we delve into the statistical sources introduced earlier and examine the various components of income, such as wages, rents, tax payments, and social security contributions and benefits, as well as changes in family and age-population structures, to understand why income inequality has increased over the past twenty years. Each statistical survey has its own objectives, which gives it special features. So it is important to find the relevant statistical source that satisfies the particular needs of an analysis. Also it is necessary to recognize the limits of a data source before using it. As we saw in the last chapter, this is particularly true for the analysis of income and wealth data.

Some of the difficulties in sampling are worth observing. Often certain groups or individuals are excluded from a sample. Typically these are the homeless, the aged living in nursing homes, and individuals who change their addresses frequently. Since incomes of such people are very low or even nonexistent, data that exclude these samples give misleading findings on income inequality. A different problem arises when immigrants are included or excluded in the sampling. Finally there is the problem noted in chapter 2 of the tax bureau's data containing serious measurement errors because of individuals able to evade or avoid paying taxes on all their income.

Therefore, in being careful about sample data, we need to consider who is included or excluded in the data. So far in the statistical data for Japan, as explained in chapter 1 and illustrated in chapter 2, we saw that the *Income Re-distribution Survey*, the *Family Expenditure Survey*, and the *National Survey of Family Income and Expenditure* involve different sampling methods. Yet another sampling bias to consider is that of the *Wage Structure Survey*. This is an income data source frequently used by authors in Japan to examine "income" changes over time. Because this source contains over one million samples, it is regarded as a very reliable statistical source. In fact it is the very large number of samples that tempts researchers to use this source.

The *Wage Structure Survey*, nevertheless, has certain critical limitations. First of all, the data cover only "wages," not "incomes." "Wages" are only one component of income. If the subject of interest is the analysis of "wages," then this source is valuable. However, income cannot be appropriately considered in terms of wages alone, although it is possible to talk very roughly about income using wages as a major part of it. Moreover the samples are limited to employees who work in private firms that employ more than ten workers. Excluded from the samples are civil servants, self-employed entrepreneurs, part-time employees, employees in extremely small firms, and retired people living on pensions. As a result the *Survey* cannot be said to represent all employed individuals, much less to claim that it provides conclusive data on all forms of wages. This example of the *Wage Structure Survey* is provided to show that it is necessary to keep an open eye on the limitations in a statistical source, including the most touted source.

Do Statistics Tell about the Cost of Living Standard?

There is, no doubt, some skepticism that the numbers indicating high income and wealth adequately reflect the well-being or happiness of people. There is even skepticism that human happiness can be measured by economic prosperity. The last is a fundamental point of view that cannot be resolved easily because some people do prefer mental stimulation to material possessions.

The field of economics offers some controversial perspectives on these issues. Foremost is the consumption level, rather than income level, as a proper variable with which to measure the welfare or economic prosperity of a people. This is because people feel utility from consumption rather than income. In treating consumption as a measure of welfare, the neoclassical economics assumes that the utility function can be used to explain the condition of a household in terms of income and leisure time. Next in importance, in addition to consumption as a relevant measure of welfare, is the difference in the number of family members. Last is the disutility of working, where consumption is still an optimum. This is because, although working activity produces income, it is usually not without pain and fatigue.

These issues are pure economic abstractions. In the real world uncertainties prevail in measurements of household welfare in terms of consumption and/or income. In Japan there are first the regional differences in general price levels. Very large cities like Tokyo and Osaka show higher prices, and small cities and towns show generally lower prices. However, the purchasing power, or economic satisfaction, are very different, even were a household in Tokyo and a household in a small town outside the Tokyo area to receive the same nominal incomes. Because in the large urban areas land prices are high, most people cannot afford decent housing, but people in countryside can afford to live relatively large homes. Traffic congestion is an inconvenience for urban people, but they can enjoy a variety of cultural activities such as museums, concerts, theaters, and sports tournaments. Of course, it is a matter of individual choice whether one lives in the city or country. However, when a people's lifestyle preferences are considered, they can confound any measure of welfare.

Something similar can be raised about the differences in price levels internationally. When a country comparison is made using incomes and/or consumptions as the major consideration, it should be crucial to show how any nominal income figures and/or consumption figures reflect the living standard of people in the countries involved. The difference in price levels between urban areas and country areas within a single country, of course, adds to the complication.

An interesting difference in price levels to observe in this regard is that among major cities in the G-5 countries. Table 3.1 shows in two panels the general price levels for New York, London, Paris, Berlin, compared with Tokyo, and the expenditures adjusted in terms

Table 3.1
Comparison of Tokyo prices with those of some other major cities

	Tokyo	New York	London	Paris	Berlin
Reported price base, 1994	1.0	0.757	0.694	0.709	0.704
Purchasing power parity and real expenditure base, 1993	1.0	0.568	0.561	0.685	0.727

Source: Maki (1998).

of purchasing power parities. As should be clear from this comparison, people who live in Tokyo face the highest price levels compared with people in the large cities of the other G-5 countries—as do the Japanese people in general in comparison with people in the other G-5 countries. This is a critical problem, especially when the concern is an international comparison on poverty because there is no common measure of the poverty line that takes into account the differences in price levels.

In summary, consumption is probably a better measure than income in representing the welfare of a people. However, because of several technical difficulties encountered in using consumption data to determine economic inequality, income has become more useful generally. Another advantage of income is that it is measured in terms of a simple monetary unit, while consumptions are difficult to measure because there are innumerable consumption goods. Household total expenditure is a better indicator, but that requires household account books in order to obtain accurate expenditure figures. Thus, although incomes are really the second best choice, for practical reasons they are the first best choice for welfare evaluation because they provide the most reliable and comparable data.

Lifetime Incomes and Income Mobility

Measurements of income are made annually, and income inequality is based on comparisons of household annual incomes. Incomes can fluctuate from year to year for households. Consequently it is risky to discuss the size distribution of income based only on annual income. All households face uncertainty in income. A person may receive an income of 8 million yen this year, but next year it may be only 2 million yen because he becomes unemployed. The same person may receive 15 million yen two years from now as he sells off all his equities. The fluctuations of income in this case are 8, 2, and 15 million yen for three successive years. Statistics of annual incomes can thus vastly change depending on circumstances that occur within a particular year. It is possible to take the average income of these three years to minimize the fluctuation in incomes. The ideal statistics is, of course, to do the same for the lifetime incomes of all individuals and households. However, it is nearly impossible to obtain the lifetime incomes from the starting year of work to income at time of death for every household or individual.

The income statistics that meets the requirement of averaging income over a lifetime involves following each individual and/or household continuously over as many years as annual incomes are being reported. Statisticians call such data "panel data," because the statistical information is taken of the same individuals or households over a block of years. There are several countries that collect panel data. Consequently some improvement is being made in income statistics, although it is almost impossible to obtain such lifetime incomes for these countries. The desired developments in statistical techniques are to extrapolate the panel data of five to ten years to estimate the expected lifetime incomes.

Another important measurement that cannot be ignored in the analysis of income distribution is the difference in ages or life-stages of individuals or households. Because annual incomes are the principal objective of the analysis, the ages and life-stages of people earning incomes must be recognized at this point. In order for the differences in income to be interpreted adequately, the differences in ages— between aged people (or retired people) and people in active labor forces—is important. Remember, the major income source for the elderly is the pension benefit whereas it is wages for the active worker.

In Japan there is further the difference in measurement due to seniority, where the wage amount is determined by both the worker's age and seniority in the firm. In the Japanese system usually no wide wage differentials are observed among workers of a common age and seniority. Of course, there are some employees who later in their careers are promoted up the company hierarchy and other employees who are not promoted. So larger wage differentials are present among middle-aged or older employees than among young employees. Because wages are a large component of income among the working population, the differentials associated with seniority are important to factor into the wage and income distributions in Japan.

Income Fluctuations and Income Inequality

There are insufficient statistics on fluctuations in annual income that are due to income mobility. Income mobility can occur when individuals move up within a firm and/or when they relocate their households within a country. Such a change, which adds to income inequality, may be observed to accumulate over many years in international comparisons. So income inequalities due to income mobility may change over time the relative position of a sampled country in the comparisons of inequalities. On the mobility of workers within a country, the following simple example should prove the point. Two individuals, *A*

Table 3.2
Four combinations of income inequality and income mobility conditions over time

		Mobility	
		High	Low
Inequality	High	(1)	(3)
	Low	(2)	(4)

and B, in a country have annual incomes of 10 million yen in year 1, and 6 million yen in year 2 (individual A), and of 8 million yen in year 1, and 5 million yen in year 2 (individual B). In these two years their ranks remain unchanged because no mobility occurs. Say we introduce a small change. The annual income of individual B is 8 million yen in year 1 but increases to 15 million yen in year 2 (instead of 5 million yen). The income rank of individual B has moved up. The income mobility of this individual is up, and therefore high.

The intuition is that a person whose income is low in one year may experience a sharp increase in the following year. When the change is upward, we say that the individual's income mobility is high. It is possible to say that a country with higher income mobility is justified in having a higher degree of income inequality on average. The reason is that an individual can expect to have a better future in this country example.

Table 3.2 shows the different ways that conditions of income mobility and income inequality can combine. Note that there are four possible ways to relate income inequality and income mobility. In each case, these are assumed to combinations of high or low income inequality and income mobility. Finding the optimal combination, of course, depends on value judgments or a society's preferences. It is, at least, possible to say that high income mobility is better than low income mobility. However, whether in a country high income mobility or low income mobility is desirable in conditions of high income inequality or low income inequality cannot be determined generally because people have different preferences depending on how these condition affect their welfare. In democratic societies the optimal combination should technically be determined by the majority rules principle. In my opinion, this would be the combination high income mobility and low income inequality.

In any case, it is clear that income mobility is a factor that must be accounted for in policy making on income redistribution. An understanding of income mobility can give useful information on the mechanisms underlying an income distribution. No indexation is available on income mobility, however. Japan does not yet have an indexation method by which to analyze income mobility scientifically. We have to wait several years.

3.2   Types of Income Collected by Government

There are several ways to consider the causes of the increasing inequality of income observed in Japan. One way is to examine separately each of the components of the primary income data collected by the government and their contributions to income inequality. This is the task that is attempted here.

The Japanese statistical office pays attention to different types of earnings in the income data. Earnings are categorized as (1) wage income, (2) business income, (3) farm income, (4) home industry income (i.e., wages earned by family working at home), (5) assets income, or (6) other income. Items from 1 through 4 are based on the different conditions of employment: (1) as employee, (2) as self-employed, (3) as farmer, and (4) as family unit working at home. Items 5 and 6 produce earnings regardless occupation. Assets incomes consist of interests, dividends, rents, and capital gains (or losses) that arise from financial and real estate holdings.

Social security benefits such as pension payments, health insurance benefits, and unemployment compensations are not included in this definition of primary income. The government definition of primary income is adopted by the *Income Re-distribution Survey*, which is the source used most often in this book. An alternative definition would be to include social security benefits in primary incomes. There are benefits and costs to this alternate definition.

Another concept is after-tax income. In this case the income recorded is that obtained after deductions are made in the primary income for income taxes and social security contributions. The same issue about the treatment of social security benefits remains for after-tax incomes. In other words, the two ways to measure income are distinguished by whether or not social security benefits are included.

Yet a third concept is disposable incomes, or redistributed incomes. This is income that is obtained after social security benefits are added from the after-tax income. In this case the question of whether to include or exclude social security benefits does not arise. In other words,

Table 3.3
Breakdown of income inequalities by income sources

Income source	1978 Income shares	R_V	R_G	R_T	1981 Income shares	R_V	R_G	R_T
Wages	89.7	68.6	98.3	90.7	90.0	91.2	102.8	107.3
Business	10.3	24.2	10.0	18.0	12.0	23.8	10.5	16.7
Farm	3.3	−0.9	−1.4	−5.2	2.6	−1.0	−1.6	−4.9
Home industry	0.7	−0.0	0.1	−0.6	0.5	−0.0	−0.2	−0.7
Assets	4.6	12.7	7.9	14.3	3.9	15.0	7.5	15.0
Other	1.2	11.4	1.9	6.0	0.7	0.4	0.3	−0.2
Tax revenue	−8.6	−14.6	−13.5	−19.2	−10.7	−28.5	−17.9	−30.1
Social security	−1.2	−1.4	−3.1	−3.9	1.0	−0.8	−1.5	−3.2
Contributions	−6.4	−2.5	−4.4	−1.8	−6.8	−4.5	−5.2	−3.3
Benefits	5.1	1.0	1.3	−2.1	7.8	3.8	3.8	0.1

Source: Atoda and Tachibanaki (1985).
Note: R_V: relative contribution for relative variance; R_G: relative contribution for Gini coefficient; R_T: relative contribution for Theil measure.

disposable income, or redistributed income, provides the best concept for comparisons of primary incomes. Consequently disposable income is used in international comparisons.

The three statistical sources noted earlier—the *Income Re-distribution Survey*, the *National Survey of Family Income and Expenditure*, and the *Comprehensive Survey of Living Standards*—record the contributions of each component to national income, and in particular, to national income inequality (see table 1.1). Table 3.3 shows the breakdown of total income inequality by income source based on the statistical data provided in the *Income Re-distribution Survey*. The computations are from Atoda and Tachibanaki (1985). Although the reported results are not recent, the income sources of income inequality are still relevant.

From table 3.3 we can observe the following: First, the largest source of income inequality is wage income. The difference between high-wage earnings and low-wage earnings appears to account for much of Japan's income inequality. Second, the next important source is business income, and after that is assets income. The relative contributions of farm income, self-employed income, and other incomes to income inequality are small. Third, tax and social security are both negative, indicating that both the tax system and the social security system serve rather as means of income redistribution. Fourth, the tax system

Table 3.4
Breakdown of income inequalities by income sources weighted by income shares

Income source	1978			1981		
	R_V	R_G	R_T	R_V	R_G	R_T
Wages	0.76	1.10	1.01	1.01	1.14	1.19
Business	2.35	0.97	1.75	1.98	0.88	1.39
Farm	−0.27	−0.42	−1.58	−0.38	−0.62	−1.88
Home industry	−0.00	0.14	−0.86	−0.00	−0.40	−1.40
Assets	2.76	1.72	3.11	3.85	1.92	3.85
Other	9.50	1.58	5.00	0.57	0.43	0.29
Tax revenue	1.70	1.57	2.23	2.66	1.67	2.81
Social security	1.71	2.58	3.25	−0.80	−1.50	−3.20
Contributions	0.39	0.69	0.28	0.66	0.76	0.49
Benefits	0.20	0.25	−0.41	0.49	0.49	0.01

Source: Atoda and Tachibanaki (1985).

appears to be stronger than the social security system as an income redistributor in the early 1980s.

In table 3.4 the measures in table 3.3 are discounted to determine the relative share of each source in producing income inequality. Each income source is adjusted by its weight over total income. The weights over total income were 0.900 for wage income, 0.120 for business income, 0.039 for assets income, −0.107 for taxes, and 0.01 for social security contributions. The dramatic difference from the results of table 3.3 is the very large impact on total income inequality coming from assets income, if the social security contributions are disregarded. Also business income appears to increase enormously as a source of inequality in this table. In contrast, a very large decline of wage income is seen, which may be due principally to its high adjusted weight over total income. These relative weights are important to keep in mind as we proceed to investigate the contributions of these income sources to total income inequality.

The methods used to obtain the measures in tables 3.3 and 3.4 are both viable means of determining contributions to income inequality. So it is not easy to choose one over the other. My own preference is for the method of table 3.4 because of the consideration given the weight of each income source in its relative contribution to total income inequality. In sum, the order of importance of the four income sources in contributing to total income inequality is (1) assets income, (2) taxes, (3) social security contributions, and (4) wage income; the contributions

Table 3.5
Breakdown of total redistributed income by the Shorrocks decomposition method (in percent)

	1984	1994	Change
Income contribution			
Wages	94.1	94.8	0.7
Rental and business	41.2	41.8	0.6
Transfers	2.6	4.3	1.7
Taxes	−37.9	−40.9	−3.0
Total transfers and taxes	−35.3	−36.6	−1.3
Income share			
Wages	82.5	93.0	10.5
Rental and business	30.8	16.8	−14.0
Transfers	6.7	10.8	4.1
Taxes	−20.0	−20.6	−0.6

Source: Nishigaki, Yamada, and Ando (1998).

from business income, farm income, home industry income, and any other income are relatively minor. The few cases where the sign (whether positive or negative) changes in the two tables have no explanation and may be due to noise.

Table 3.5 shows more recent income sources of Japan's income inequality from the *National Survey of Family Income and Expenditure*. The computations are by Nishizaki, Yamada, and Ando (1998) who used the Shorrocks decomposition method. As in table 3.4, there is given the relative share of each income source in contributing to income inequality. Note that the largest share is that of wage income, and next in size come assets income and business income. Note further that the relative shares of assets income and business income are high despite their smaller share of national income than that of wage income. Something similar was observed in table 3.4, where a more rigorous statistical method was applied than table 3.5. Intuition tells us that this has to do with the small number of entrepreneurs and wealth holders who received extraordinarily high incomes from the mid-1980s through the mid-1990s.

So how is it that the tax system and social security system contribute to income redistribution? Because the statistical methods and the objectives of tables 2.5, 3.3, and 3.4 are different, it is risky to comment on this issue by way of a comparison of the three tables. The results in table 2.5 suggest that the income redistribution effect due to taxes to have declined while that due to social security contributions increased. The results in table 3.4 suggest that taxation can substantially reduce income inequality but not by transfers by the social security system, for which the results are negative and thus imply a contribution to wider inequality. Nothing more can be said about the results in these two tables because there are different statistical methods and purposes involved. A more extensive evaluation will be made later.

The final data source to consider is the *Comprehensive Survey of Living Standards*. This source provides us with the latest information (i.e., 1998) on rich households shown in table 3.6. The results are classified by source of income and individual's occupation. Note that for households with higher than 20 million yen per year—the so-called super-rich—the shares of business income (0.321) and of assets income (0.065) are much higher than for the others. A similar observation can be made about the highest share of the self-employed (0.377) compared with other occupations. People who are self-employed and earn very high incomes are mainly receiving their incomes from their businesses and secondarily from their assets. Self-employment is risky, and people who undertake this risk and succeeded in their business ventures are financially highly rewarded. See Tachibanaki and Mori (2005).

There is no reason to criticize successful self-employed entrepreneurs since they do take on high risk. Rather we should be most concerned about the low-income earners represented in the table. The great majority of low-income earners are employees. Unfortunately, because already in 1998 the Japanese economy was in trouble, many employees accepted cuts in wages, and some had to be laid off. This was a very sad turn for these Japanese workers. Their big source of income was wage income, and naturally they were not in the position to own significant property that can amount to assets income. Particularly affected by the economic downturn were those in low-level blue-collar jobs and in part-time jobs.

In sum, tables 3.4, 3.5, and 3.6 illustrate how two income sources, namely business income and assets income, combined to skew the growth of income toward inequality.

3.3   Change in Wages

This section investigates changes to wage income, which is the largest share of national income, but takes the third or fourth rank in the importance of the relative contribution to total income inequality after

Table 3.6
Share of total income for each income source and occupational class

	Total income	Wages	Business income	Farm income	Rental income	Social security benefits	Other income	Average age
Classification based on income source								
Higher than 20 million yen								
Share	1	0.5819	0.3212	0.0028	0.0649	0.0151	0.0141	56.5
Average (0.01 million yen)	3299.7	2386.1	3056.3	678.0	525.4	250.9	419.2	
10 to 20 million yen								
Share	1	0.7579	0.1563	0.0041	0.0499	0.0168	0.0149	53.3
Average (0.01 million yen)	1523.9	1275.2	1503.2	272.2	299.5	220.8	260.4	
Lower than 9.99 million yen								
Share	1	0.7985	0.0714	0.0128	0.0153	0.0882	0.0138	50.5
Average (0.01 million yen)	442.5	469.9	280.6	101.4	90.6	151.9	92.0	

	Total	Regular employees	Contract employees	Part-timers	Self-employed	Other
Classification based on occupation						
Higher than 20 million yen						
Number of samples	297	181	0	0	112	4
Share	1	0.6094	0.0000	0.0000	0.3771	0.0135
10 to 20 million yen						
Number of samples	2196	1761	13	3	399	20
Share	1	0.8019	0.0059	0.0014	0.1817	0.0091
Lower than 9.99 million yen						
Number of samples	22567	17537	478	173	4013	366
Share	1	0.7771	0.0212	0.0077	0.1778	0.0162

Sources: Ministry of Welfare and Labor, *Comprehensive Survey of Living Standards*, 1998.

some adjustments are made for the weight of the share over total income figures. There are four ways to measure wage income. The first is by the differences in wages among employees in the total workforce, to see the range of wages paid to employees. The second is by a time-series change in total wages, to see if national wages increase or decrease in equality over a period of time. The third is by the relative importance of various variables such as age, sex, education, size of firms, and seniority, to see if there are wage differentials involved in these cases. The final way is to follow these effects over time in a time-series analysis.

Interestingly, as was noted in chapter 1, the wage experiences in Japan compare with those of the United Kingdom and the United States over the past twenty to thirty years. Our next objective is to discuss the wage differentials in Japan in more depth.

Changes in the Labor Force
We can safely classify the labor force in Japan as consisting of three parts: employees, self-employed, and family members engaged in small trades or small factories. Most family workers are wives and children of small traders and small factory owners (largely self-employed men). In 1953 only eight years after the war, the share of self-employed and family workers was around 58 percent, and in contrast, the share of employees was around 40 percent. The share of employees continued to grow as time went on, and it is currently around 80 percent. About four-fifth of total workforce consists now of employees. So it is natural that wages now occupy the largest share (over 90 percent currently) of the national income.

Two other characteristics to add to the rising number of employees in the share of total workforce must be mentioned. The first is a steady increase in part-time and short-term employees. In particular, there has been a tremendous increase in part-time employees, amounting to a share of about 35 percent of total employees if we consider both males and females. The definition of part-time employees in Japan is somewhat problematic, however. Formally, it is a category defined by employees who work less than 35 hours a week. There are nevertheless a large number of employees who work over 35 hours and do work similar to that of full-time employees but are still called part-time employees because their working conditions such as hourly wages, bonus payments, fringe benefits, promotion possibilities, among other things, are inferior to those of full-time employees. They cannot rise to

the status of full-time or regular employees even if they accept jobs
nearly equivalent to full-time or regular employees. Women form over
85 percent of this part-time group, and the aged and youth the remaining 15 percent share.

The second is the rise in participation of women in the full-time
workforce. The rate of female workforce participation was already
high before the age of the rapid economic growth. In the 1950s it was
over 50 percent, but these were mostly women engaged in farming
jobs and in running small trades with their husbands. A small number
of women held full-time employee positions. The participation rate of
women in the workforce then started to decline in the 1970s for two
reasons. On the one hand, women bought into the marketing of the
perfect American housewife in that television era, and on the other
hand, the wage incomes of their husbands had become sufficiently
high to allow this change in lifestyle, thanks to the rapid economic
growth.

Only recently has the participation of women in the workforce
started rise again, in particular, for women aged between 20 and 59
years old, and currently it is over 60 percent. Why did it start again?
The reasons are the same as those in other advanced countries: mainly
the increase in women's wages, the increase in higher education, the
desire for financial autonomy and/or a desire to remain independent
of their husbands financially, and the availability of superior home
appliances to tend to domestic tasks.

In sum, the women joining the workforce as part-time employees,
and later as an increasing share of the full-time workforce, have
sharply influenced the state of wage distribution and thus income distribution. This is also the reason why the large majority of part-time
workers are female.

Wage Differentials by Sex
We are now ready to examine wage differentials not only by overall
dispersion (i.e., total inequality) but also in terms of various factors
such as sex (gender), occupation, size of firm, seniority, and age. The
main statistical source is the *Wage Structure Survey*. Before we turn to
this source, however, it is important to recall the limitations of its data.
First is that the samples are restricted to workers in the private sector
and employed by firms with more than ten employees. This implies
that employees in extremely small firms, who receive normally low
wages under the "dual" labor structure, are not covered in this survey.

Second is that only full-time employees are represented in the main data, although an appendix does cover part-time employees separately and marginally. This implies that low-wage earners as explained by the widening hourly wage differential between full-timers and part-timers are excluded from the samples. The combined effect of these two limitations is that a substantial number of low-wage employees (roughly 30 to 40 percent of total employees) are excluded. So it is hard to say that the *Wage Structure Survey* represents a wide sample of employees. Almost all studies of wages nevertheless use this source because information in it is extraordinarily rich.

An international comparison of the share of women's wages helps us see how these wages are lower in Japan. Table 3.7 shows female/male ratios for median weekly earnings of full-time workers given by Blau and Kahn (2000). Note that Japan is the lowest in women's wages. This remains the pattern from 1979 to 1998, the entire sample period. One optimistic indication is that the ratio in Japan has been recently observed to be on an increasing trend, such as might signify that the wage differentials between men and women have been narrowing, albeit slowly. In general, the countries that have low wage differentials by sex are Australia, Belgium, Italy, and Sweden, and the countries with the larger differentials are Austria and Canada. The United States has stayed somewhere in the middle.

There have been several country studies to explain wage differentials in Japan. Tachibanaki (1996a) and Genda (1998) found that overall the male-female difference in wages to be largest when the effects compared are education, age, seniority, occupation, and size of firm. The influence of gender is far more important than other variables. Why are females so disadvantaged? We can point to several reasons such as their fewer years of education and their shorter lengths of services in a company, and thus lack of seniority and low possibility of promotion to better paying positions. The biggest reason, however, is discrimination against women in certain employment areas, so they are denied promotion opportunities and better wages, as shown by Tachibanaki (1996a), Nakata (1997), Kawaguchi (1997), among others. Many advanced countries have adopted policies to enforce equal treatment of men and women, and these countries have been succeeding in reducing the discrimination against women. Japan has also in place legislation to prevent unequal treatment of women. This law has not been particularly successful because there are only weak monitoring activities and no sanctions against any violation of the law. More

Table 3.7
Female–male ratios, median weekly earnings of full-time workers

Country	1979–81	1989–90	1994–98	Change 1979–81 to 1994–98
Australia	0.800	0.814	0.868	0.068
Austria	0.649	0.674	0.692	0.043
Belgium	na	0.840	0.901	na
Canada	0.633	0.663	0.698	0.065
Finland	0.734	0.764	0.799	0.065
France (net earnings)	0.799	0.847	0.899	0.100
(West) Germany	0.717	0.737	0.755	0.038
Ireland	na	na	0.745	na
Italy	na	0.805	0.833	na
Japan	0.587	0.590	0.636	0.049
Netherlands	na	0.750	0.769	na
New Zealand	0.734	0.759	0.814	0.080
Spain	na	na	0.711	na
Sweden	0.838	0.788	0.835	−0.003
Switzerland	na	0.736	0.752	na
United Kingdom	0.626	0.677	0.749	0.123
United States	0.625	0.706	0.763	0.138
Non-US average				
1979–81 sample	0.712	0.731	0.774	0.063
Full sample	0.712	0.746	0.778	0.067

Source: Blau and Kahn (2000).
Notes: The years covers for each country are as follows: Australia: 1979, 1989, 1998; Austria: 1980, 1989, 1994; Belgium: 1989, 1995; Canada: 1981, average of 1988 and 1990, 1994; France: 1979, 1989, 1996; West Germany: 1984, 1989, 1995; Italy: 1989, 1996; Japan: 1979, 1989, 1997; Netherlands: 1990, 1995; New Zealand: average of 1988 and 1990, 1997; Sweden: average of 1978 and 1980, 1989, 1996; Switzerland: 1991, 1996; United Kingdom: 1979, 1989, 1998; United States: 1979, 1989, 1996.

important, there is no social pressure to promote equal treatment, and this is due partly to Asian culture and partly to the fact that the economy is so weak at the present time that businesses must reduce labor costs where possible and equal treatment of women naturally levies a cost on an enterprise.

A more serious difference appears in the widening gap in hourly wages between full-timers and part-timers. Because the majority of part-time workers are women, the widening differential in hourly wages has resulted in the overall male–female wage differential widening enormously. Note that this is contrary to the results in table 3.6 and

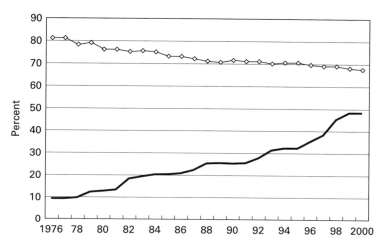

Figure 3.1
Wage differentials for part-time and full-time women employees (*boxed line*) and percentage of part-time women employees of total women employed (*solid line*). Source: Ministry of Welfare and Labor, *Wage Structure Statistics*

some other studies cited previously. The wage differential will appear to be undeniably shrinking, as in table 3.6, so long as the data examined are for full-time employees. Once the part-time women workers are included, whose share in the workforce has been increasing rapidly, the outcome for women becomes entirely different.

Figure 3.1 shows the hourly wage differences between part-time and full-time women workers, and the rising share of the part-timers in relation to the total number of women workers. Most dramatic is the increase in the share of part-timers from nearly 10 percent in the mid-1970s to nearly 50 percent in 2000, with nearly half of the female workforce becoming part-timers. Conversely, compared with full-timers, the hourly wages of the part-timers declined from about 80 percent to between 66 and 77 percent. To the reasons for the increase in part-time employees, and the decrease in part-time versus full-time hourly wages, discussed above there should be added another fact. Part-timers normally do not receive any of the bonuses paid twice a year to full-time employees, which amount to from three to five times their monthly wages. If bonus payments are taken into account, the widening differences in wage payments between part-timers and full-timers would widen and be more significant than shown in figure 3.1. So where the difference between men and women is concerned, it has narrowed only when full-time workers are surveyed. If part-timers are included, the difference increases because women part-timers, whose wages are low, constitute about 50 percent of all women workers. It is thus misleading to suppose that the wages differences between men and women have declined in Japan.

Changes in Occupation Structure and Wages

Structural changes of the workforce are reflected in time-series analyses in table 3.8. From the changes in the share of workers engaged in particular areas of employment we can make the following observations: First, the greatest change (a decrease) occurs in the number of workers engaged in agriculture and fishery related industries. Their share declined from 48 percent in 1950 to only 7.1 percent in 1990. The trend this implies is toward strong industrialization. Second, the share of blue-collar workers in manufacturing and construction industries has remained nearly constant. This group is still the largest, at about 30 percent of the workforce even today. Third, the share of skilled white-collar workers in professional and technical, and managerial areas has increased constantly. The current share is at about 15 percent, which is not particularly high. Fourth, the share of lower level white-collar workers, namely sales and service workers, has increased substantially. The reason for the importance of these last occupational areas, today, is the shift from manufacturing to service and tertiary industries.

In sum, we see in the table a decreasing importance of agricultural and fishery workers and an increasing importance of skilled white-collar and service workers. These changes, however, are not reflected in the structure of occupational wages because the differences in wages are small among blue-collar, sales, and even skilled white-collar workers. The wages of skilled white-collar workers in the professional and technical and managerial areas nevertheless do increase where employers adopt the merit system that puts more weight on job difficulty and performance of a worker in their wage determination schedules. Thus there is evident an increasing trend in the wage differentials.

For most of the worker population in Japan, however, the differences in wage payments are small. For example, in 2001 in the manufacturing industries the average monthly wages of men engaged in blue-collar work was 0.33 million yen and in the white-collar work 0.42 million yen, which is 1.3 times higher. In the United Kingdom and the United States the difference in wages was over 2.0, and it was 3 and 5

Table 3.8
Changes in percentages of workers in occupations

Year	Agriculture/ fishery	Manual labor	Security	Sales	Transportation/ communication	Professional/ technical	Managerial	Clerical	Services
1950	48.0	23.1	0.9	8.4	2.1	4.3	1.8	8.0	3.3
1955	40.6	24.9	1.1	10.6	2.7	4.8	2.1	8.2	5.0
1960	32.5	29.5	1.1	10.8	3.4	5.0	2.2	10.2	5.2
1965	24.5	31.0	1.2	11.7	4.3	5.5	2.9	13.1	5.8
1970	19.2	32.5	1.2	12.0	4.5	6.6	3.9	14.0	6.1
1975	13.8	31.9	1.4	13.3	4.5	7.6	4.3	16.7	6.5
1980	10.8	32.1	1.4	14.6	4.3	8.7	4.7	16.5	6.9
1985	9.2	31.6	1.4	14.3	4.0	10.6	4.0	17.7	7.1
1990	7.1	31.5	1.4	14.5	3.8	11.7	4.1	18.8	7.2

Source: Ministry of General Affairs, *Census of Population.*
Note: Blue-collar workers are classed here as manual labor.

times the blue-collar wages if we compare the wages with skilled white-collar wages. The fact that the occupational wage differences in Japan are small is because there are no significant differences regarded between white-collar and blue-collar workers. The concerned workers revere the egalitarian principle. The equal treatment of workers without differentiation according to class has led some critics to say that Japanese industrial relations are socialist in orientation. Although Japan may have a socialist outlook in its industrial sector, the country is by no means socialist but egalitarian in attitude. Further the idea of compensating with higher wages the workers who engage in dirty, dangerous, and hard jobs is supported by many Japanese.

Where no significant difference in wages by occupation is indicated in table 3.8, there was no large change in wage payments by occupation even if there occurred large changes in the occupational structures of workers. The most important occurrence since the 1950s has been the drastic decrease in agricultural workers, which has contributed to equalizing the income differentials between farmers and manufacturing workers, since the incomes of farmers were the lowest among the working population.

Inter-size Wage Differentials

The inter-size wage differentials receive the highest attention by economists when they investigate wage differentials in Japan, whether they are Marxian or non-Marxian. Inter-size wage differentials relate to the substantial differences in wage payments between large and small firms. Such differences are evident not only in wages but also in labor productivities, capital intensities, and rate of profits, for example. The difference are said to be due to a so-called dual structure. Marxian economists focus on the possibility of large firms (i.e., gigantic corporations) exploiting the subcontracting (usually family-run) firms, which is due to a parent-child type of relationship within a group conglomerate, while non-Marxian economists are interested in the enhanced wage benefits of these large firms.

How important is the inter-size wage differential in comparison with other factors such as gender, age, and occupation, in terms of nominal wage differentials? I have already emphasized that the male-female differential has been the largest. The following numbers may help elucidate these differences for the male regular employees: The wage of an employee aged 40 years old is about 1.7 to 1.8 times higher than that of an employee aged 20 years old, the wage of an employee with more than 1,000 coworkers is about 1.5 to 1.6 times higher than that of an employee with 10 to 100 coworkers, and the wage of a college graduate is about 1.2 to 1.3 times higher than that of a senior high graduate. Note that the difference is highest when age is considered, and lowest when education is considered. Because the size of a firm has significant impact on wages, Japanese economists are drawn to it in making labor economics investigations. This is in contrast to US economists who are not so interested in wage differentials among different size firms, but excluding Brown and Medoff (1989) and Idson and Feaster (1990). This is mainly because in the United States there is more interest paid to the effect of education level on earnings.

For Japan the inter-size wage difference of 1.5 to 1.6 due to firm size is a nominal figure, that is, without adjustments for other factors. The comparisons should be controlled for education, age, seniority, firm's market share, and so forth, since the larger employers have very low turnover rates. These employers are also usually able to retain their educated and experienced employees because of their high market power in the industry. One should be able to take out these effects, which raise the average wages in large firms, to obtain the pure effect of size of firm on the wage differentials. Such a comparison, from Tachibanaki (1996a), is shown in table 3.9.

From table 3.9 we have the following findings: First, with the controls the pure effect of size of firm proved to be weak. As with the nominal difference observed earlier, the wage differentials continued to be explained by the quality of work done by employees and the firm's market share, productivity, and so forth. Second, in the difference between gigantic firms (i.e., over 5,000 employees) and extremely small firms (i.e., 10 to 29 employees), the wage differential is found to be over 2.0. This difference in wages due to size of firm is substantial. Economists often talk of differences in wage payments among large firms (over 1,000 employees), middle-size firms (100 to 999 employees), and small firms (10 to 99 employees). In the size classifications of table 3.9 it is apparent that the wage differentials are much greater than are commonly understood when the differences due purely to size are considered.

Why can larger firms pay higher wages than smaller firms? There are several obvious reasons. First, capital equipment and machinery are of higher quality in larger firms, and thus employees have the operational capital with which to enhance their productivity. Second, because more and superior resources are available in larger firms for

Table 3.9
Wage differences by firm size (in percent)

Number of employees	1978 Before controls	1978 After controls	1988 Before controls	1988 After controls
5,000+	28.61 (7,448)	23.11	32.10 (8,647)	27.16
1,000–4,999	20.49 (7,356)	17.03	21.86 (7,091)	15.96
500–999	9.95 (3,552)	5.61	9.24 (3,667)	2.68
300–499	1.01 (3,235)	−3.31	−1.55 (3,038)	5.60
100–299	−7.54 (8,215)	−12.10	−11.93 (7,271)	15.37
30–99	−15.71 (10,382)	−19.90	−20.29 (9,330)	23.36
10–29	−21.24 (8,355)	−25.34	−25.34 (7,329)	28.78

Source: Tachibanaki (1996a).
Notes: Controls account for differing job functions. The number of firms are in parentheses. Minus signs indicate wages of the disadvantaged workers.

research and development activities, the products are more attractive and can carry lower price tags. Third, the higher equities of larger firms put them in a position to borrow more and absorb higher loans from banks, so these larger firms can readily invest in infrastructure and new machines. Fourth, larger firms have higher sales volumes and higher profits because they are able to sell through extraordinary advertising campaigns and thus improve their market share. Fifth, the best workers seek employment in larger firms, which is where the best working conditions in terms of wages, fringe benefits, and employment stability are found. Opportunities exist in larger firms for employees interested in training to develop new skills. Small firms are disadvantaged in these areas, and they are not able to pay high enough wages to attract the most qualified employees.

Fortunately or unfortunately, today the advantages of working in large firms are showing signs of decline. There are presently also some small firms, in particular, venture capital firms, that are said to pay very high wages, but the data on these successful venture businesses are not available to verify the wage figures. The recent serious recession has resulted in financial difficulties even for larger firms. More important, this phenomenon has caused many small firms to declare bankruptcies or lower their wages. We will have to wait out the recession to see its effects on the small number of currently successful venture firms and the balance of large and small firms.

Wage Differentials by Education

In Japan higher education has no significant effect on wage earnings. Take the example of the difference in the average monthly wages between male senior high graduates and male college graduates. The figure in 2001 for the senior high graduate was 0.35 million yen, while the figure for the college graduate was 0.43 million yen. The college graduate's wage was only 1.2 times higher. The advantage to obtaining a college degree in terms of wage payments was thus very low. The small difference between the two types of qualifications is small partly because a large number of educated people have come into the labor market. It is also partly due to the fact that in Japan the feeling is that higher educated people do not necessarily deserve much higher wages than less educated people.

Why is there such an attitude toward education? This is sharp contrast to most European and American countries where education is highly rewarded. For example, in 1979 college graduates in the United States and in the United Kingdom received respectively 1.51 and 1.65 times higher wages than high school graduates. The Japanese figure in 1979 was only 1.26. While the American and English college graduates could earn considerably higher wages than their high school graduates, their Japanese counterparts could enjoy only modest advantages.

There are several possible explanations. First, the Japanese are an industrious people who understand that college education does not necessarily increase skills or productivity. Job experience accumulated within a firm is more important than formal schooling. Human capital theory, of course, places value on both formal schooling and job experience as fundamental to productivity. On-the-job experience, however, is what matters more at least in Japan. It is the reason behind the Japanese idea to reward longevity of experience through the seniority wage system, as was explained previously.

Second, there is the egalitarian principle earnestly adopted by the Japanese people after World War II. Most of the population does not care for differential treatment to be given across the board to people who have educational beyond high school. Understandably this attitude may seem odd to Western cultures where people incur considerable education costs for the high rewards in the offing. Why do the Japanese people see the value of higher education differently? It is not possible to answer to this question definitively, but several speculations can be made.

For the Japanese the essential purpose of education appears to be not to provide higher earnings but to open the mind to the humanities. Knowledge in the humanities is not relevant to on-the-job capabilities. Although most people recognize that education can increase seriousness in the application to one's work tasks as a side effect, they tend to feel that this is not a sufficiently tangible result to reward with particularly higher earnings. So at least in response to the abstract idea of higher education the practice has been to diminish its importance in the determination of wages.

Another explanation has to do with the fact that higher education is still seen as the prerogative of sons of the wealthy and/or of educated parents as it was before World War II, as described in chapter 2. This was a form of elitism that is still resented by ordinary people. Possibly the higher educated minority among the workforce refrains from petitioning for higher wages in fear of strong resistance from the less educated majority. Today, to give higher educated people higher hierarchical position would smack of the days before World War II when, as we saw in chapter 2, wide differences in wages existed according to one's hierarchical position in a firm. Those people who experienced the changes after the war may still recall the importance placed on abandoning or minimizing this feature of the class-oriented society. Thus the simple way to achieve equality was to reduce the influence of education in determining promotions and wages, and Japan succeeded in its egalitarian mission by this means.

Another Egalitarian Feature and Why Egalitarian?

So far I have suggested that wage differentials by occupation and education are low due to an egalitarian principle prevalent among the Japanese. There are also the effects on wages of age and job tenure in a firm that support this interpretation. As was described earlier, the next important factor after the effect of gender (i.e., male–female wage differential) on wages is age and job tenure. Wages increase in proportion to employees' age and job tenure, and such a system is due to a seniority principle. The seniority principle is a form of egalitarianism for two reasons. All men and women age from year to year, and if they start their jobs at a company in the same year and at the same age and stay at this company, as they age they accumulate the same number of years of tenure. So no wage differentials should appear among these employees because their wages increase in proportion to their age and job tenure. This amounts to equal treatment for employees and a system by which over the years everyone acquires seniority.

It should be clear that the egalitarian treatment of employees has persisted in the determination of wages because age and job tenure is more important in the Japanese workplace than the job category and education. How is it that the Japanese system of wage determination is so egalitarian? I explained this in chapter 2 but will summarize the main points here. First, employers were afraid that low wages for the educationally disadvantaged, whatever their other qualifications, would result in low incentive to work. Second, the more productive and ambitious among the employees did not object to egalitarian treatment of their inferior coworkers because they expected that their own work would be recognized and they would be promoted to higher positions later in their company careers. Third, right after the war the economy was not prosperous, so it was not possible even to have wide wage differentials because the companies and all the wage earners were very poor. In sum, all concerned people—the employers and their employees whether or not productive or disadvantaged—agreed to an egalitarian principle in the workplace that would motivate all to work hard and revitalize the industrial productivity of Japan. The equality in income distribution that resulted was an effective force behind the higher economic growth of the immediate postwar period. The present circumstances and the future prospect appear to be very different (as will be explained in chapter 5). However, it should be recalled that over the years of postwar growth not all employees were treated equally. Women workers, part-time employees, and workers in small firms were excluded from an egalitarian principle.

Overall Wage Inequality

Again, in chapter 1 it was noted that two countries, namely the United Kingdom and the United States, have been showing a rapid increase in wage inequality. There were several reasons suggested for that wage inequality trend. Figure 1.3 showed that compared with other G-5 countries the wage dispersions in these two countries are significant. Two supplementary findings based on this figure are worth mentioning. First, the degree of wage dispersion in the United States was the highest in the 1990s, and it is still much higher than in other countries. Second, the unequal Japanese wage dispersions in the 1970s and 1980s showed small increases and then very minor decreases and after the mid-1980s climbed to an almost constant plateau.

It should be emphasized, again, that the wage inequality data used for Japan in the plot of figure 1.3 has limitations because the wages in the *Wage Structure Survey* are of only full-time employees in firms with more than ten workers. Part-time and small firm employees receive much lower wages. Because a very large number of Japanese workers fall into these two groups, the curve for Japan should instead be shown as substantially increasing. Today, as was discussed earlier in this chapter, the wage differential between full-time workers and part-time workers has even continued to widen.

Next there is the inter-size wage differential. As table 3.9 showed, employees in extremely small firms are seriously disadvantaged. So it is not easy to accept the wage data in figure 1.3 once this group of workers is included. Further the arrangement of data in table 3.9 involved enormous effort, and this task was particularly difficult because the data are scattered in many places.

In sum, it is likely that wage dispersions in Japan over the period covered in figure 1.3 was increasing as sharply as in the United Kingdom and the United States, although not as much.

3.4   Changes to the Household Structure

Changes within the Japanese family are one of the main causes of the increasing income inequality seen today. Consequently these changes are examined carefully here. The changes associated with the family unit are in (1) number of family members in a household, (2) number of income earners within a household, and (3) influence of single-member households.

Number of Family Members

In chapter 2 we cast income inequality in terms of equivalent scale incomes. We saw that the number of family members is the most important variable used in determining equivalent incomes. We depended on the simple concept of per-capita income, or per-capita consumption, to study the welfare of an individual household member.

Table 3.10 shows changes in the number of family members observed over the postwar period. Note that the number of family members in the early 1960s averaged around 4.0. This number has been steadily falling as single-member households have been substantially on the rise. Note that by the end of the 1990s the share of single-member households increased by about 5 percentage points. Four types of single households are possible: (1) young adults who leave home to attend universities or to take jobs outside the region to earn big money in order to marry, (2) widowed men and women, (3) divorced couples, and (4) individuals who never married. Note that in the table the increase in the average age of single-member household is huge, from about 25 years old to about 50 years old. The increase of single-member households among widowed women (husbands tend to die earlier than wives) is the first strong indication of change to the Japanese household structure.

The changes to the family unit started right after World War II. The change involved a shift from the extended family, in which adult children live with elderly parents, to the so-called nuclear families, in which adult children set up separate households from their parents. This is now a trend that has continued through the period of rapid economic growth to the present time. The impact on Japanese social and economic life has been enormous.

The main reason for the shift is that adult children are choosing to strike out on new career paths. Before the war and shortly after the war, adult children were expected to continue in the occupations of their parents. In the farming and small retail trade families, adult children lived with their elderly parents because they also inherited the family land, small shop, or small factory. Because agriculture, retail-trading and small manufacturing were the principal businesses in those days, adult children were not motivated to seek career improvements by moving away from their family business. With the rapid economic growth of the late 1950s and 1960s many job opportunities came open in manufacturing and service industries. Young adults from impoverished rural areas joined the blue-collar and white-collar employees on the factory floors in urban areas. Because these adult children had to settle near their jobs, they set up separate households from their parents, and sent a portion of their income to support their parents. So strong industrialization and regional labor mobility provide a purely economic reason for the change seen in the family structure and in the rise of single-member households.

Table 3.10
Changes in household structures

	1959	1964	1969	1974	1979	1984	1989	1994	1999
Two or more member households									
Number of family members	4.33	4.06	3.85	3.86	3.89	3.87	3.85	3.72	3.40
Number of income earners	1.46	1.56	1.59	1.53	1.56	1.62	1.65	1.71	1.55
Age of household head	39.7	40.2	40.2	40.8	41.0	42.2	43.5	44.9	51.4
Percentage owning homes	48.7	50.3	50.3	57.9	64.0	67.4	68.7	69.2	76.8
Average age of single member household	24.8	23.8	23.8	29.8	37.4	41.2	46.7	50.5	49.7
Percent of single member households among total households	17.3	17.8	17.8	18.2	18.3	19.4	20.0	21.9	23.6

Sources: Ministry of General Affairs, *National Survey of Family Income and Expenditure, and Comprehensive Survey of Living Standards.*

There is also another influence to consider that involves a change of attitude toward the social norm of an extended family. In the past the large family, or extended family, was a means that ensured that the aged would be cared for by their adult children who lived together with their parents, or sent money if they lived away from them. There were no well-prepared public pension programs at that time. Inter-family economic transfers were thus the norm, and family ties were strong willingly or unwillingly.

Individualism started to emerge among Japanese people during the period of the rapid economic growth. The prosperity due to rapid eco-nomic growth enabled young adults to become more independent of their families. In the urban areas young adults embraced the Euro-American culture, which was transmitted through books, movies, and television. The constant exposure through media to the American ideal of the individual charting his own course in a free society was un-avoidable. Young adults became enchanted with the individualistic lifestyle, and the diversions of urban life made this idea all the more possible.

A third influence is the introduction of the public pension system, public health insurance program, and other social security systems in the 1960s and 1970s. These systems were admired in the European style welfare state, and thanks to economic prosperity, such public in-surance systems could be financed through taxes. (See Tachibanaki 2000 for more on this historical development.)

In sum, because of economic changes the prewar family structure changed. Adult children seeking economic opportunities set up sepa-rate households away from their parents and that arrangement eventu-ally would challenge the social norm. With the coming of economic prosperity, the resettled adult children were happy to continue leading separate lives from those of their aging parents. The parents went on to live alone after the deaths of their spouses. This is the main explanation for the rise in recent years of single-member households, the largest among them being single households composed of widowed women.

What kind of effects on income distribution and welfare comparison can be expected from the decreasing number of family households and the increasing number of single-member households? The obvious effect due to the decreasing number of family household is increas-ing per-capital income—and thus welfare—provided that we ignore the immiserizing effect on the widowed women. Once we include aged widows, negative effects appear. First, this is because the public pension payment to a widow is reduced greatly when her retired husband dies. So widows experience a drastic decrease of their already low incomes. Second, if the husband's pension was through a pension program he was enrolled in as an employee of a firm, it is likely that the pension payments are discontinued when he dies, as this is the practice at most firms. Thus we can expect drastic drops in income to be experienced by today's very large number of aging single-member households. Some authors see the aging population as the cause behind income inequality. To the problem must be added the recent low rates of return on financial assets and the very low rate of interest. The rate of interest has been nearly zero for about several years in the Japanese financial market, and equity prices also have been staggered. Since most aged households hold large amounts of financial assets, the low rates of returns will further immiserize today's aging population.

Number of Income Earners
From table 3.10 it is evident that the number of income earners within households steadily increased over the past 40 years. The main reason is that in this period, and particularly in the 1980s and 1990s, married women joined the workforce. Their wages contributed to raise household incomes, although not very much because these women were mostly as part-timers, so their wages were very low. Nevertheless, those couples (husband and wife) that were employed full-time, had household incomes that were significantly high. Theirs was the situation of skilled labor, the white-collar workers. Several years ago, because of their lavish lifestyles, such rich couples were popularly referred to as "Dinks," short for "Double Incomes No Kids." Another reason for the rise of income is that in some households the young children living at home took jobs and contributed to the incomes of their parents.

There were three outcomes due to the rise of multiple income earners within a household. First, as noted above, the household incomes increased. In table 3.11 we consider the facts. Note the increase in the number of income earners from the first quartile income class (i.e., the lowest income class) to the fourth quartile class (i.e., the highest income class). There are considerable increases in the number of income earners within a household. By the fourth quartile the number of family members contributing to income is the highest, and with the number of income earners increased, so are household incomes. Because not all households can obtain higher incomes by

Table 3.11
Number of income earners and income distribution

	Average household members	Average number of income earners	Percentage employed
Total	3.07	1.47	48.0
First quartile	1.95	0.78	40.0
Second quartile	2.85	1.30	45.6
Third quartile	3.51	1.65	47.0
Fourth quartile	3.96	2.17	54.8

Source: Ministry of Welfare and Labor, *Comprehensive Survey of Living Standards*, 1998.

increasing the number of income earners, there will be household income inequalities.

Second, in accord with the above-mentioned increase in the number of income earners, there is the argument that because of the increase in the number of family members, it was necessary to raise the number of income earners. The causality goes from an increase in household members to an increase in the number of income earners in order to avoid a possible decrease in the living standard brought on by the need to spend money on the additional members. The first outcome and the second outcome thus complement each other.

Third, this outcome is not easy to measure quantitatively, but there is the possibility that households with multiple income earners had to allocate some of their earnings to housekeepers and child care because of the reductions in their at-home time. Therefore a household's welfare may decrease, even though the income increases significantly. That is to say, because household expenditures increase with the outsourcing of housekeeping and child rearing, the disutility of adding a member to the workforce must be high. It is important that the disutility of the additional wage earner to a household be appraised within an economics framework if the changes in household welfare are to be interpreted adequately.

Tachibanaki and Yagi (2003) attempt such an evaluation of household welfare changes. They take account of the disutilities of multiple household members participating in the workforce and arrive at the tentative conclusion that marginal improvements in welfare are possible, even if, overall, household income inequalities increase. This finding suggests the positive effect of a supplementary income to a household despite the negative effect each additional wage earner in a household has in broadening income inequality in a society. Because this is preliminary study, it cannot make any definitive claims. More studies are needed in this regard.

3.5   Role of Tax and Social Security Systems

Effect of Taxes on Income Re-distribution

Income taxes collected by the government at both national and local levels are mostly spent on public goods and quasi-public goods. The amounts of taxes paid by households, however, can vary significantly, depending on the tax bases used and how tax rates are computed, and so forth. For example, a program of progressive taxes can be used to redistribute income from high-income earners, who pay a higher income tax rate, to low-income earners, who pay a low income tax rate. Progressive income taxation can substantially lower the after-tax income inequality.

In general, governments avail themselves of three tax bases: income tax, indirect tax like VAT (value-added tax) or commodity tax, and corporate tax. Because the corporate tax does not have a direct impact on the redistribution of household incomes, it is ignored here. The income tax has the most direct effect on household incomes, and thus the highest attention is paid to this tax where income redistribution policies are the main concern. Any indirect tax, of course, has some influence on income redistribution. For example, the proportional VAT (called a consumption tax in Japan) is believed to be regressive because higher income earners and lower income earners pay the same amount of consumption tax under the proportional tax rate. It is possible for a tax to be progressive in its effect even as an indirect tax. For example, the zero tax on food products, educational supplies, and prescription drugs is prevalent in several Western countries. In my opinion, this feature should allow it to be termed a "progressive consumption tax," or a "progressive expenditure tax" to indicate where indirectly the lack of tax satisfies the property of progressivity (see Tachibanaki 2000 and Okamoto and Tachibanaki 2002 for more discussion).

There are two instruments used in determining the progressive tax: the minimum taxable income and marginal tax rate on increments of taxable income. The first is determined after all the various allowances such as for spouse and children reduce the income base. If the taxable income minimum is set at a high level, many households end up not

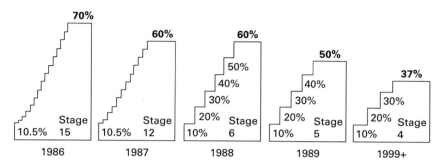

Figure 3.2
Changes in income tax rates. There has been a 20 percent reduction in the fixed rate since 1999. Resident taxes (i.e., local income taxes) are added to the income taxes.

paying income taxes, so income redistribution is high. The second case is easily understood because the marginal rates of the income tax serve to redistribute income.

Figure 3.2 shows the changes in the marginal tax rate on incomes. Before 1986 households at the highest income level had to pay a very high income tax rate, 70 percent. Right then the income tax rate for the highest earners began a decreasing trend, and by 1999 it had declined to 37 percent. Note in the figure that the tax rate was practically halved, which means a substantial, nearly 50 percent decrease. The next highest income level also shows a declining trend. From this there can be inferred that income redistribution by way of the income tax system was declining speedily at a constant rate, and rapidly widened the extent of after-tax income inequality. The income tax system of the Japanese government had clearly the sign of policy making aimed at raising income inequality.

The decreasing role of the income tax system in redistributing income is consistent with what was happening in some Western advanced countries, in particular, in the United Kingdom and the United States where the progressive income tax rate was lowered continually. This was because the Japanese conservative government was influenced by the tax policies of the Mrs. Thatcher and Mr. Reagan governments who advocated the importance of supply-side economics. Supply-side economics called for lower tax rates, and was beneficial in revitalizing the economy because the decreased taxes increased employment and productivity. The early successes of these two governments in re-vitalizing their troubled economies led the government in

Japan, in particular Mr. Nakasone, to adopt the UK and the US tax program. So the in the 1980s a line of Reagan–Thatcher–Nakasone neo-conservatism flourished.

Some other drastic reforms to the income tax rate were considered that would further weaken income redistribution. One example was a flat income tax rate. Such a tax system would preclude a proportional rate on all income levels and consequently any form of progressivity. Indeed, by 1988, both the United Kingdom and the United States had only two separate tax rates: 25 and 40 percent in the United Kingdom and 15 and 28 percent in the United States. Although these rates were not quite one single flat rate, the reduction in number of tax rates to two rates was a sharp difference from the multiple income tax rates previously observed for the various income levels. In other words, the tax rates in these two countries were near to a flat rate. It should be mentioned that both two-rate systems were enlarged in subsequent years.

Itaba and Tachibanaki (1987) compared the before-tax and after-tax income distributions (using density functions of income dispersion) and the shape of income tax rate schedule in both the United States and Japan. They presented the numerical difference in the progressive tax rates rather than the institutional tax rates. The United States was found to be less progressive in income tax than Japan. In other words, the Japanese income tax system had a stronger income redistribution program than that of the United States.

Income Re-distribution Effects of Social Security Systems

The social security system has two instruments that work to effect income redistribution. One is the contributions side whereby payments are made to the public pension, health insurance program, and unemployment insurance, and the other is the benefits side whereby the pensions, health care allowances, unemployment compensation, and poverty relief payments are distributed. Since the contribution side is withdrawn from income like a tax, it appears to have some income redistributing effect. However, there is no strong consensus that the social insurance system has or should have income redistributing power whereas there is no question that tax system redistributes income. The reason is that public pensions and health insurance programs are simple transfer programs that keep the government prepared for uncertainties. There can be, of course, be included the alternative idea that social insurance systems have some income redistributing effect.

Whether or not social insurance systems should contribute to income redistribution depends largely on a society's values, and thus the decision is customarily made by the majority rule principle in a democratic society. Nevertheless, there are two aspects of social insurance that have inevitable income redistributing effects. First, social insurance benefits are associated with disability and aging and the uncertainty of death. As a consequence, upon a person's death, the accrued public pension benefits and health insurance benefits have income redistributing effects. Of course, there cannot be dismissed the enormous difference in pension payments collected by a person who dies shortly after going on a pension and a person who dies at age 100. This does then amount to income redistribution. Something similar happens in health insurance programs where the costs of treating persons who are frequently sick are compensated by payments from persons who are never sick.

Second, tax revenues are the principal source of the poverty relief payments to disabled or injured persons, so there is an income redistribution effect present here. Clearly, people who receive such financial aid do not contribute money to the system. The income transfers come from people who pay taxes. This is a pure case of income redistribution.

However, poverty relief as a form of income transfer to disabled people requires some discussion. Although many people contribute payments and support the notion of benefits to the truly needy, the system in Japan is weak. Primarily only a small number of people or households actually receive poverty relief. Simple figures show this best. In 1970 the percentage of people receiving economic assistance from the government in Japan was only 1.3, while it was 7.7 percent in the United Kingdom. This is a big difference in poverty relief payments. Today this difference between Japan and the United Kingdom has remained much the same.

How is it that poverty relief payments continue to be so low in Japan? More important, why doesn't the rate of people who receive financial relief payments reflect the rate of people who are entitled to receive financial relief by the law? That is, the very low payout rate simply shows that only a fraction of the people with incomes below the official poverty line receive financial assistance. While the payout rate in Japan did rise to around 10 percent in 1993, some comparable international figures of that time are around 48 to 54 percent in 1985 in the United Kingdom, 24 to 36 percent in 1986 in Australia, and 64 to 70 percent in 1991 in the United States. Again, the Japanese payout rate showed very low. This is unfortunate.

It is necessary to explore the reasons why the poverty relief payouts are so low. First, there is a law that stipulates that families must help their poor relatives economically if they are natural citizens. Economic aid to the poor is therefore obligatory from relatives who are better off. This is in accord with East-Asian tradition. Most poor people thus receive financial assistance from their families and relatives. Second, poor people applying for poverty relief must meet very stringent requirements. For example, they can have no personal savings. Also, if a needy person is found to be physically and mentally able to work, financial aid is denied even if there are no job opportunities. Third, there is a feeling of shame or stigma among Japanese people when they receive financial aid from the government. These three factors have combined to lower the payout rate significantly. It should be noted, nevertheless, that once a person qualifies for financial aid, the amount of payment is sufficiently high. Clearly, Japan needs to ease the very severe restrictions on poverty relief payments, and raise the payout rate substantially while lowering somewhat the payment amounts.

Today, besides the very low income redistribution through the poverty relief program for the reasons cited above, family ties have been showing a rapid decline. It is especially critical to strengthen the poverty relief program before the number of poor people overwhelms Japan. Recall from table 1.11 that when compared internationally, Japan's poverty rate is now very high.

Combined Effects of Tax and Social Security Systems

Recall tables 1.1 and 2.5 where the changes over time were presented for the income tax and social security systems. Redistribution coefficients were used in these tables to indicate the extent of redistribution from the various combined effects of income tax and social security contributions, tax policies, and social security benefits. The several important observations made from the data in these tables are as follows: The redistribution coefficients in 1975 to 1978 were lower than in the surrounding years. Because this was around the time of the oil crisis, the statistics are incongruous because of the very high inflation rate. Thus these years can be ignored.

First, both tax and social security contributions have been increasing, by which it can be inferred that the income redistributed by these systems has been increasing. Second, although contributions to both sys-

Table 3.12
Income re-distribution policies by tax and social security programs

	(A) Pre-distribution Inequality (Gini)	(B) Post-distribution Inequality (Gini)	(C) Difference (A) − (B)
Italy	51.0	34.5	16.5
United States	45.5	34.4	11.1
Australia	46.3	30.6	15.7
Germany	43.6	28.2	14.4
Belgium	52.7	27.2	25.5
Japan	34.0	26.5	7.5
Netherlands	42.1	25.3	16.8
Finland	39.2	23.1	16.1
Sweden	48.7	23.0	25.7
Denmark	42.0	21.7	20.3

Source: OECD study (see also Oxley et al. 1997).

tems have been on the rise, the role of the social security system in income redistribution has been increasing whereas that of the tax system has been decreasing. Third, in more recent years social security has had far more importance than taxes in income redistribution, with taxes having practically no effect.

Table 3.12 shows the redistribution effects of the tax and social security systems in Japan compared with those of other advanced countries. The Gini coefficients for all ten advanced countries are computed for both the pre- and post-distribution income inequalities in 1995. Note that Japan alone has the highest equality at the point of pre-distribution but at post-distribution ranges in income equality in the middle among the ten countries. This is an indication that the income redistributing effect of both its taxes and social security contributions is considerably weak. Neither the tax system nor the social security system works well as income redistributing mechanism when compared internationally. All the other countries have much stronger income redistribution programs. These differences are clearly evident when the figures in column A are subtracted from those in column B. Column C gives the result. The Japan's decrease of inequality is a low 7.5. Largest is 25.7 by Sweden, and conversely, closest is 11.1 by the United States. Both Japan and the United States show the weakest income redistribution programs through taxes and social security contributions, whereas the strongest are by Sweden, Belgium, and Denmark.

The results in table 3.12 provide some insight into the income redistribution policies in use among advanced countries. First there is Sweden to consider where the pre-distribution income inequality is very high and the post-distribution income inequality is very low, as mentioned. The interesting point is the substantially high pre-distribution income inequality. Swedish people do not care about the fact that pre-distribution income inequality is so high; they depend on their tax and social security systems to maintain a strong income redistribution program. Consequently post-distribution income inequality is far lower, amounting to the lowest among advanced countries. However, unlike Sweden, the pre-distribution income inequality is already very low in Scandinavian countries like Finland and Denmark where also the post-distribution income inequality is very low. The degree of income redistribution by tax and social security systems is therefore not great but about the average.

These two different approaches among equality-oriented countries where post-distribution income inequality is very low (i.e., very high equality) show that it is possible, on the one hand, to admit a substantially high pre-distribution income inequality, as long as strong income redistributing policies are adopted through the tax and social security systems (call this strategy 1), and that, on the other hand, to sustain substantially low pre-distribution income inequality while not committing to strong income redistribution policies (call this strategy 2). In each of the two strategies the objective is to have high post-distribution income equality.

The two strategies can provide economists attractive alternatives. The efficiency factor that will make a difference as to which strategy to achieve high equality is preferable is higher economic growth. With this as a simultaneous goal, we have the case of trade-off between efficiency and equity as was argued in chapter 1. I will confine the argument here to the choice between strategy 1 and strategy 2, although it is possible to consider a strategy 3. This is the country that, despite fairly high pre-distribution income inequality, does not seek high post-distribution income equality and thus admits only a small effect of income redistribution policies. Typically this strategy is adopted by Italy. Yet a further strategy, which may be called strategy 4, is to have modestly high inequality in both pre-distribution and post-distribution incomes like Germany and Australia. Both strategies 3 and 4 do not seek strong income redistribution policies. A discussion of all four strategies is deferred to chapter 5.

A further note about table 3.12 must be added. The statistical source for Japan was the *National Survey of Family Income and Expenditure*, which does not represent all the people in Japan as was emphasized several times above. Also the measurement of annual incomes is in question because the figures come from only three months' wages and estimated bonus wages are added in order to compute the annual incomes. Thus the Gini coefficients estimated for Japan in table 3.12 must be taken with some reservation. However, the relative position, or the difference between pre-distribution income and post-distribution income is not greatly affected. Table 3.12 is provided only for the general purpose of showing the relative rank of Japan among tax and social security income redistribution systems internationally.

4

Wealth Distribution and Intergenerational Transfers

4.1 Real Assets and Financial Assets

Real Assets

Chapter 1 presented the empirical evidence that wealth distribution was considerably skewed during the period of the bubble economy in the late 1980s. The large rise in both stock prices and land prices widened wealth inequality between wealth holders and non–wealth holders enormously. The collapse of the bubble economy in the early 1990s, however, lowered both stock prices and land prices considerably, and these prices returned almost to the pre-bubble level recently. Prices are expected to drop even more if the current asset deflation (i.e., a decrease in the prices of lands and financial assets) continues. While current prices of lands and assets are nearly the same as in the pre-bubble years, the wealth inequality due to the bubble has not disappeared. In fact, by excluding the bubble years of 1985 to 1990 when the economy experienced abnormal growth, we can see that the price increases of both lands and equities have been moving at a constant and steady pace over the entire postwar period, amounting to over 50 years. Consequently it is possible to say that wealth inequality gap has been slowly, but constantly, widening since the Second World War and was exacerbated in the period of the bubble economy.

Broadly speaking, there are two types of wealth or assets: real and financial. The values of both are measured not as flows of income over a certain period, like wages and interest, but only at one-shot when they are sold, which is why they are called assets. Measurements of these assets are therefore not as easy as those made of income flows. In other words, there can be substantial measurement errors.

How do the measurement difficulties arise? First, real assets are of two types. One is land, and the other is the residential house. So there are two prices, a land price and house price, that determine real estate

value. More precisely the total value of a real asset is derived from a
square meter price for the land area and the house. It is understandable
that the total value of real assets can fluctuate because both land and
house prices fluctuate. An important component of house price is the
depreciation value because houses deteriorate over time. In Japan, the
older the house, the higher is the depreciation, so the real (net) asset
value of the house becomes smaller. Because the appreciating land
price must be accounted for along with the depreciating house price,
the measurement of a real asset is complicated, and measurement
errors are unavoidable.

Yet another difficulty in measuring real assets in Japan is that there
are three ways of pricing land. The first is the registered (or public)
price reported by the public authority, the second is the route price
reported by the tax authority, and the third is market price available at
various real estate agents. The second is used for the determination of
inheritance values and thus inheritance taxes. The market price seem
to be the best choice to assess the real asset value because this price
reflects the actual price paid in transactions of land and houses. However, the difficulty here is that transactions of land and houses is obviously not frequent, since a large number of land and house owners
keep their real assets for a long time, and do not readily commit to
making such transactions. So in these cases no market prices are available, and some other methods have to be used to assess the value of
real assets. Again, the various difficulties in pricing land suggest that
measurement errors are unavoidable.

Financial Assets
There are many forms of financial assets: cash, deposits (demand
deposits, time deposits, and transferable deposits), commercial papers,
bonds (both public and corporate), equities, and so on. In a broad
sense life insurance, casualty insurance, public pensions, and business
pensions are also financial assets. Each financial asset has its own price,
both book value and current (market) value. In principle, it is not hard
to determine the value of a financial asset because each asset has a
price. The difficulty, however, is due to the following reasons: First,
there are an extremely large number of financial assets that are sold
and bought—transacted—very frequently by many participants who
do not necessarily report the asset values correctly. Second, almost all
financial assets produce interest rates, dividends, and capital gains (or
losses). Since some of these fluctuate so much that it is not easy to iden-

tify the returns. Also there is the issue that financial asset values should be measured and reported either without taking into account the above various returns or with these returns. Third, taxes are normally levied on interests, dividends, and capital gains. The question is whether the financial asset values should be assessed before taxation or after taxation. These various measurement difficulties have conceptual and empirical implications for the use of measurements of financial asset values.

In summarizing the above, it may be useful to assemble the main criteria that distinguish between real and financial assets. First, the frequency of transactions of real assets is normally small, and thus the durations of real asset holdings are longer, while the frequency of transactions of financial assets is large, and the durations of financial asset holdings are short. Nevertheless, there are certain exceptions. For financial assets, there are intercorporate share holdings that are particular to the Japanese capital market. In Japan the keiretsu firms, or parent subcontracting firms, each hold their counterparts' shares, excluding any long-duration national bonds and corporate bonds. For real assets, the transaction cost of land or houses is much higher than the transaction cost of a financial asset because the unit of buying or selling is large, and the buyers and sellers are harder to find. Third, we cannot ignore the effects of taxes when we consider the volume of transactions and asset values in both real assets and financial assets. There are, for instance, inheritance and bequest taxes, real asset holding taxes, interest and dividend taxes, and capital gains taxes. Since total assets can be allocated into various different assets, transactors can minimize such tax payments by their portfolio behavior. A particularly important tax in regard to wealth inequality is the inheritance or bequest tax because it substantially affects the amount of intergenerational wealth transfer. Inheritance taxes will be considered later when intergenerational transfers are discussed.

Factors That Determine Wealth Distribution
What determines the allocation and value of an asset? Because the use of assets can address the state of wealth distribution to a considerable extent, this is what is examined here. The mathematics is not technical but more or less intuitive.

The following equations are based on the notion of an individual's asset holdings having a life cycle of one year. The value of holding an asset in a single one-year period, t, is

$$W_t = W_{t-1} + S_t$$

$$S_t = Y_t - C_t$$

where W_t is wealth (i.e., asset value) at the end of year t. S_t is saving, Y_t is income, and C_t is consumption during year t. W_t and W_{t-1} are stock values, while S_t, Y_t, and C_t are flow values. Note in these two equations that the smaller is C_t, the larger are both S_t and W_t. In words, when people save much (consume less), their value in asset holdings at the end of the year or the beginning of the next year is larger.

Stock value is expressed as the unit price of an asset multiplied by the volume of holdings. Likewise equity, it is expressed as the equity price multiplied by the volume of equity holdings. The same goes for land holdings. Therefore the increase in wealth (i.e., due to an asset) is expressed by the increase in asset price and/or volume of holdings.

In sum, there are three explanations for an increase (or a decrease) in wealth (i.e., asset) value: (1) an increase (or decrease) in quantity, (2) a change in unit price such as interest, rent, and land price, and (3) a change in the amount of savings (i.e., income minus consumption). It is useful to examine which of these is the most important determinant of wealth holding for a household, and a society's wealth inequality when all households are considered.

4.2   Owning Homes, Choosing Safe Financial Assets, and Maintaining High Personal Savings

In the preceding discussion we saw that the assets used by Japanese people to accumulate wealth are homeownership, financial investments with low risk, and high personal savings from disposable household income. On the larger societal scale these components combine to raise wealth inequality in some instances and lower it in other instances. In this section we turn to evaluate this larger meaning of wealth accumulation, and to examine the direction in which each element leads a society toward more or less wealth inequality.

High Homeownership
Recall from table 3.10 the rising rate of homeownership from the late 1950s to the present time. Today homeownership is nearly 70 percent, which is quite high. From this high rate it is evident that only about 30 percent of people rent their living quarters. Why is the rate of owning a

home so high? Why do people prefer to buy rather than rent? There are some good reasons.

First, the largest share of the professions and occupations before the Second World War, and in the ten to fifteen years shortly following the war, consisted of farmers, small retail traders, and small family-type manufactures. The tradition of these households was to live where they could farm their own land and keep near these living facilities small shops or small factories. This tradition of people operating small industries out of their own homes can in fact be found worldwide. Because the oldest son, and in rare cases the oldest daughter, inherited the home, agricultural land, small shop, and small factory, the high rate of homeownerships persisted from generation to generation. Simply put, intergenerational transfer of familial occupations is the most important reason for the large percentage of Japanese owning their homes.

Second, the tradition of intergenerational transfers helped generate the myth that land is the most reliable asset to hold. For the Japanese people homeownership was cherished as a symbol of culture and prosperity. In other words, and to some extent this is an exaggeration, those people who could not afford to buy their homes were regarded as outside the cultural norm, as social misfits. Thus it was thought by most people that to be respectable one had to live in one's own home.

Third, because in the 1960s through the 1990s land prices increased along with the rise of homeownership, people could believe that there were certain capital gains from holding land. The myth of owning land was bolstered by the conviction that land prices could rise without end. Land rose in value from generation to generation and thus became the most important source of wealth in intergenerational transfers.

Fourth, Japanese law on inheritance and gift taxes is much more favorable to land than to financial assets. People can save on taxes enormously by leaving their land assets to their offspring. If in addition the offspring were amenable to continuing the occupations that went along with the inherited land, be it farming, retail trading, or small manufacturing, the tax law was particularly favorable. This way society encouraged intergenerational occupation transfers and thus land transfers.

Fifth, as was mentioned previously, no income tax is levied on imputed rents. In other words, income used to pay rent is taxed. It is natural for households to desire the tax relief that comes with buying homes. Those homeowners who have never had to pay rent for their living quarters probably are not aware of this benefit, but tax payments are a real fact of life for home renters.

Sixth, most Japanese dream of living in a house with a garden in the suburbs, even if the house and the garden are very small. This is due to the social phenomenon mentioned in chapter 2, the rise of the nuclear family. This is a family that consists of a husband, a wife, and a few children. In this dream the house is small and the wife does not work outside the home and is highly appreciated as a good wife and mother. A husband holds a white-collar job in the city. (See the discussion on familial life in Japan in Tachibanaki 2003.) Owning a house in the suburbs is therefore a way people act upon this dream.

It should be nevertheless emphasized that only a small number of families can achieve this dream because at today's high prices it is not easy to buy a house with even a small garden. The extremely high prices of houses have caused most people to resign themselves to buying condominiums. In the 1970s and 1980s the condominium became a popular concept, and today it has displaced owning a house. Thus for some people the condominium is the only way they can own their home.

Seventh, rent control is very strict. So homeowners with land suitable for building are reluctant to enlarge their homes in order to create rental units. Why is there strict rent control? The reason is that it is important to protect the tenants who are supposedly in a weaker position financially compared to that of landowners.

Choosing Safe Financial Assets

Safe assets are cash and savings deposited at banks and post offices. Most Japanese households prefer these safe assets to investing in bonds and equities. The prevalent allocation of savings in safe financial assets produces relatively low average rates of returns with small variances. Thus the vast majority of the Japanese choose to forgo relatively high average rates of returns with large variances from risky assets.

Figure 4.1 gives a comparison of household financial assets allocation in Japan with that in the United States. As the figure shows, the share of time deposits is largest in Japan but fairly low in the United States. The difference between the two countries even widens if cash and demand deposits are added to the time deposits. In the area of bonds and equities, the outcome is completely different: the sum of the two assets in the United States is largest but very low in Japan. Likewise, because Japanese households prefer safe financial assets to risky

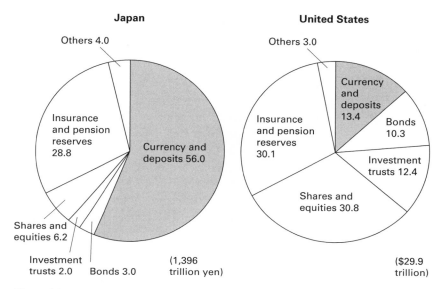

Figure 4.1
Allocation of household assets: Japan versus United States. Shares are percentages of total assets. Source: Bank of Japan, *Flow of Funds: Japan and US Overview* (2002)

assets, the shares and equities are substantially different for the two countries, whereas the reserves of insurance and pension are about the same.

Why do Japanese households gravitate toward safe assets? The reasons are many, but several are important to the discussion here. First is that the Japanese household is relatively risk averse in determining its financial assets allocation. Asano and Tachibanaki (1992, 94) were able to draw out the econometric evidence that shows the high risk aversion of the Japanese reflected in the low share of risky financial assets among households. The parameter value of relative risk turned out to be high in Japan, confirming that Japanese households are largely risk averse.

Second is the fact that the bonds and equity markets are underdeveloped in Japan. Conversely, banks and postal savings are quite eminent. In particular, banks and postal offices are very aggressive in encouraging households to deposit their funds with them. They have very impressive sales campaigns and large advertising budgets. Security houses' activities, however, are unknown to most households, since the domain consists mainly of interfirm share holdings committed to incorporated firms. Unfortunately, there have been a number of scandals involving insider-trading and unlawful compensations to certain investors who encountered huge capital losses. Simply put, security houses that deal in equity and bond transactions are regarded as unfair and shady businesses by many people. This understanding of security house practices in Japan may be an overstatement, but it is true that as a rule, Japanese households do not trust security houses.

Third is the Japanese type of indirect financing. In the 1960s to the 1990s the funds deposited in banks by Japanese households were commonly lent to nonfinancial firms. The overwhelming result of such indirect financing, instead of direct equity or bond financing, however, was that it did not promote the development of the capital market. A related attempt was that of the government to collect funds from households in the form of postal savings in order to fund several government investment activities. Households were encouraged to deposit their savings at postal offices. Bank deposits and postal savings were considered secure because of strong government regulations protected the banking sector and postal offices from bankruptcy (recently some bankruptcies of banks have nevertheless occurred).

Finally, there is the very high personal savings rate itself that indicates Japanese households to be risk averse, since personal savings are considered to safeguard the household against future uncertainty. A people's inclination to allocate a large share of their financial assets to savings in order to be prepared for future uncertainties such as unemployment, sickness, and physical disability does tell of their precautionary nature. By some statistics the precautionary motive was as high as 80 percent of the respondents reporting it as the important reason for savings. When respondents were asked to choose only one reason among several in multiple-choice questionnaires, about 30 percent chose the precautionary savings motive. Again, this was the largest share among various savings motives.

The Japanese households' unique preference for safe assets has been, quite simply, responsible for low wealth inequality. The financial assets of the great majority of people are low because the rates of returns to safe financial assets are low. This is the main reason behind the widening inequality of financial assets, as wealth is due to wide portfolio holdings. This is in contrast to the past when the size of income inequality was low, and it was hard to believe that financial assets inequality could be high unless the difference in personal saving rates was higher among households.

Thus, unlike the great majority of households that preferred safe financial assets allocations, there are the few households that invested in risky financial assets. Their excellent portfolios are ensuring them further accumulations of financial assets. Also the initial financial asset holdings of these households are usually large and thus handled by top financial managers. These portfolios are bound to continue growing and widening the financial assets inequality.

High Personal Savings Rates
According to Harrod-Dowar growth theory, high personal savings can help the economy grow and not necessarily cause wide disparities in wealth to arise if the majority of households have a common savings rate and their incomes are fairly equal and high. Therefore total household wealth, in particular, financial assets, must be high under these circumstances. The current account is today about 1,400 trillion yen. It is interesting to see where the aggregate savings go. Reportedly domestic savings go abroad to buy government bonds in the United States and other countries, go to the government in Japan to finance the huge public debt, and go to firms mainly in Japan and sometimes in other countries. It is well known that Japan was the largest net exporter of capital abroad in the late 1980s and 1990s.

It used to be thought that the very high personal savings rate of the Japanese was a positive phenomenon. It was a subject that received much attention by academics and the news media. Some of the main points are summarized here. Interested readers can refer to Tachibanaki (1996b) and Hayashi (1997).

First, in the 1960s and 1970s the younger generation had a high propensity to save, so the personal savings rate was naturally very high, especially because this generation was concerned about saving money for their retirement years. The demographics of those years are crucial to understanding the high aggregate domestic savings. Over time the demographics have changed. In the present day there are fewer young people and many old people. The population of Japan today is in fact that population that has saved for their retirement years and is ready to put a negative effect on the aggregate domestic savings. Thus it is largely because the aged do use up their savings that the current account in Japan is on the decline, even though not yet substantially because the Japanese saving rate is still high by international standards.

Second, related to the matter of the larger population at the point of retirement is the weak social security system. The personal saving rate has been high because the social security system is deficient. If public pensions, medical insurance, and unemployment compensation were guaranteed, people might feel less of an incentive to put all their financial assets into personal savings because they could depend on benefits from social security system in times of bad luck. Further, in support of this argument, the several Scandinavian countries whose social security systems are very developed show personal saving rates that are very low, and even negative in some years. Simply put, there is a substitution effect between the savings rate and the effectiveness of the social security system.

Again, as was noted earlier in this book, the Japanese social security system is underdeveloped because families and firms, in particular, large firms, have taken the responsibility to provide welfare services. So the public sector has not been charged with much of a role in this regard (see further Tachibanaki 2000). In 1973 the Japanese government toyed with the idea of a European type of welfare state, which it admired. Almost immediately after it declared for the welfare state the dream was shattered mainly because of the two oil crises. The oil crises of the 1970s forced the Japanese economy to grow at a slower rate, and thus the revenue could not be raised to finance social security. Secondarily by the 1970s it was already evident that population growth was beginning to slow and that a large young population choosing not to start families could not be sustained in their old age by any government social security plan.

The government therefore worked with corporate groups to find an alternative system of welfare. The corporate firms consented because they could avoid high social security contributions. Because of the aging trend of the population, however, the idea was to cut the benefits side of social security payments and increase the contributions side. (Chapter 6 is devoted to the issue of desirable policy reform in social security systems.)

In sum, the inability of the Japanese government to develop a social security system over the postwar period has been instrumental in raising the aggregate domestic savings rate. In effect, the personal savings rate in Japan has always been high only because the social security system has never been fully developed.

Third, in the late 1980s and 1990s household incomes rose as high as 3 to 5 percent a year. Households accustomed to maintaining high personal savings did not adjust their consumption in response to the increase in household incomes. In the aggregate, the circumstance of underconsumption led to a demand deficit in the economy. Government had to use both fiscal and monetary policy in order to compensate the underconsumption and meet the needs of high growth of the macroeconomy. Obviously the underconsumption fed the already high personal saving rate.

Fourth, for the great majority of employees in both the private and public sectors there is a bonus wage system that pays extra wages twice a year. It is not a reward paid to extraordinary workers who exceed in production or sales activities but is paid to nearly all employees. The amount of the bonus is, however, marginally influenced by the performance and capabilities of the employees, and by the profits of the firm. Employees expect, nevertheless, to receive the bonus regularly even when there is some fluctuation in the economy. Therefore the bonus system is regarded as semi-steady income from employees' point of view. Some economists do regard it as steady income, while some others regard it still as pro tem income. There is a debate about the exact nature of the bonus payment.

Ishikawa and Ueda (1973) investigated the effect of bonus payments on personal savings, and found that it definitely raised the personal saving rate, although all of the bonus payments do not go into saving accounts at banks or postal offices. Consequently it was concluded that the bonus is pro tem to a certain extent, and that it contributes to the rise of the personal savings rate.

Fifth, home mortgage loans are insubstantial, requiring fairly large downpayments. Considering that buying a home is regarded as a lifetime dream, it is natural to believe that households save also for downpayments on a home. The same can be said for durable goods like electrical appliances, cars, furniture, vacation homes, and so forth. Saving for marriage, one's children's education, one's children's marriage, for major travel, and so forth, can be also a reason for high savings. The motivation for savings thus often has to do with a spending objective, or a money target.

In effect, because of the imperfect capital market for home buying, personal savings have to be kept high. The capital market for mortgages developed slowly but constantly in the 1980s and 1990s for some good reasons. Banks had to find new borrowers, and turned eventually to households when the demand for debt-financing from nonfinancial firms drastically fell in the late 1980s. Households soon discovered the convenience of purchasing many goods, including houses and durable goods, on credit. This development in the capital market nevertheless contributed marginally to lowering the personal savings rate of households.

Sixth, there is a strong inclination to bequest property among the Japanese, as has been studied by many investigations, including Ohtake (1991), Tachibanaki and Shimono (1991), Tachibanaki and Takata (1994), and Horioka (1996). It is important to distinguish intended bequests and inheritances from unintended ones. Unintended bequests occur when people die intestate, usually unexpectedly. Intended bequests relate to accumulated wealth from people able to will it to their offspring. Although it is not easy to separate these two forms of bequests statistically, accumulated savings are often left as bequests or inheritances. In general, where there is a large bequest motive, the personal savings rate is large.

Seventh, the number of self-employed workers in the total labor force has been high. In the 1950s and 1960s the rate was about 20 to 25 percent. The household incomes of the self-employed, which are mostly farmers and small retail-traders, can fluctuate substantially. As a result their personal savings rates are normally very high, in addition to the funds they have saved initially to be able to open a business. This has contributed to raising the aggregate domestic savings rate. Since the 1960s the percentage of self-employed workers has steadily declined; by 2001 it was halved at about 12 percent. The declining number of self-employed workers has showed in a lowering of the aggregate savings rate. The 12 percent rate nevertheless is still marginally higher than that in other advanced countries. So even today the contribution of the self-employed to raising the savings rate is still somewhat applicable.

Eighth, in line with the fifth point I made above, is that the credit market was imperfect. Households cannot borrow from banks, or other financial institutions, without large downpayments. In the United States equity loans and other forms of credit were available, so the American household is not faced with making downpayments to buy durable goods. Japanese households thus have to save also because of the lack of personal credit markets.

Additionally, whereas in the past, namely during the period of the rapid economic growth and the subsequent years of a stable economy, the primary interest of banks and related financial institutions was to lend to nonfinancial firms because there was high demand for corporate financing from the nonfinancial sectors. This system helped build a policy of support for industrialization. In the 1990s, as the Japanese economy entered an era of recession, the demand for corporate financing greatly declined. Banks and other financial institutions had to find other borrowers during this serious recession. The credit market for households therefore rapidly developed, and the capital market for households seems to be no longer so imperfect. The trend to use credit for durable goods has obviously reduced the personal savings rate.

Ninth, it is necessary to explain the influence of tax policy on the savings rate. Before 1988 there was a special tax-free allowance for personal savings accounts. Also government bonds and some other special financial assets held up to a certain amount were tax free. In general, savings under 16 million yen were tax free, meaning no interest incomes on this amount was taxed. The main motivation for this generous tax-free arrangement was to raise household savings, and to transfer these funds to the industrial sectors. Tachibanaki (1996b) concluded that in the aggregate the effect of this tax break on raising savings turned out to be not so great as the government had hoped, but it was enough to generate funds to be allocated for various capital investments.

The generous tax policy on interest and dividend income was adjusted from time to time. For example, today only the aged can apply for a tax-free saving account up to a certain amount of savings. Also interests and dividends are now taxed. The tax policy that worked to boost up personal savings is in fact a thing of the past. Currently receiving attention is the huge I–S imbalance (I: investment, S: saving) in the macroeconomy, for which the policy goal desired is more consumption (and thus less savings). The debate is whether government should lower taxes to encourage consumption and discourage savings in order to reduce the current I–S imbalance. However, as I have already mentioned, tax policies do not seem to change a people's nature. I doubt that any tax policy in Japan can lower savings.

Tenth, the banking and financial sectors were strictly regulated. The government regulates interest rates; the separate businesses of banks, security houses, and life insurance companies; the number of branches they can open, and even what financial products they can offer. The entire purpose of the regulations is to protect banks and financial companies from bankruptcy. No bankruptcy of financial institutions was seen before the mid-1990s, thanks to government regulations. Households therefore felt secure in depositing their savings in banks, buying securities at security houses, and life insurance policies at insurance companies. It is reasonable to assume that this kind of safe feeling about financial institutions marginally raised the personal savings rate.

All changed completely in the mid-1990s. Several banks, security houses, and life insurance companies filed for bankruptcy in the financial crisis that has continued until now. Households are now careful about which financial institutions to use for transactions. Although I do not claim that the current financial crisis has lowered the personal saving rate substantially, it has had some small influence nevertheless.

Again, it should be emphasized that it is the relatively high risk aversion of Japanese people that can explain their preference for personal savings. The ten explanations above provide the background for understanding the safety-minded behavior of the Japanese.

Savings and Debts by Income Class
One of the differences in savings by different income classes is that the amount saved is higher, the higher the income class. Table 4.1 shows these differences in savings by income class. Note that the super rich having annual incomes over 20 million yen can save about 18.7 million yen on average. However, the percentage of super rich in the total population of households is very small, a mere 10 percent. Therefore the very few very rich households manage to save very large amounts. Note also that the amount of annual savings decreases considerably as the annual incomes decrease. Households whose annual incomes are lower cannot save large amounts. This is, of course, not a surprising outcome.

Nevertheless, we have to consider the implication of this outcome, that those with higher incomes can have higher savings. Although

Table 4.1
Savings by income group

	Annual income (million yen)	Average saving (million yen)	Savings–income ratio
Super rich	20.00+	18.67	1.718
High income	10.00–20.00	12.19	1.511
Middle income	7.00–10.00	7.42	1.066
	5.00–7.00	5.67	1.115
Lower than middle	−5.00	4.11	2.126

Source: Ministry of Welfare and Labor, *Comprehensive Survey of Living Standards*, 1998.

table 4.1 provides only the annual figures for 1998, we can infer that if the observed income and saving are continued over many years, every year the financial assets of the high-income households, here amounting to annual savings, will increase more rapidly than those of low-income households. Unlike the high-income households that can obviously save a lot, within the middle-income households we can expect the annual incomes to fluctuate such that a household receiving high income this year may receive less income the next year. In the two extremes, however, it is not an exaggeration to say that the probability of receiving high (low) income next year is high for a high (low) income household this year. It is likely for savings to continue in this way over many years.

The implication for wealth distribution is that the gap does widen as time goes on. First, there is the fact that higher income households can accumulate financial assets much more rapidly than lower income households because they have more savings to put away than lower income households, and second, there is the fact that the savings build over many years and become a source of the widening gap. (The numerical dynamics are covered in Tachibanaki and Shimono 1991.)

Not possible to observe in table 4.1 is the rate of household savings by income class. In fact it is interesting that although the different income classes save different amounts, the rate is nearly the same. The source that shows the household saving rates for each quintile income class rate is the *Family Saving Survey*. In it the saving amount and income amount are calculated as average saving and average income within each quintile class based on individual saving and income figures. For example, the household saving rate reported in 1996 for each quintile income class was as follows: income class I (super rich), 13.4 percent; II (high income), 15.5 percent; III (upper middle), 12.8 percent; IV (lower middle), 15.1 percent; and V (low income), 15.1 percent. All saving rates were within a 12 to 15 percent range. Of course, minor differences are possible in the household savings rates by income class. Nevertheless, the savings rate is quite close. So, although the *amount* of savings may appear to be considerably large or small according to the income class, the saving *rate* is nearly the same in each case.

Finally, the debt amounts by these same income households are examined briefly. Debts are the opposite of savings. Debts contribute to wealth negatively, whereas savings contribute to it positively. Table 4.2 shows the differences in the household debts by income group. Note from the amount of debts and the ratio of debts over incomes off1off1off1

Table 4.2
Debt by income group

	Annual income (million yen)	Average debt (million yen)	Debt–income ratio
Super rich	20.00+	10.86	0.543
High income	10.00–20.00	8.07	0.807
Middle income	7.00–10.00	6.96	0.995
	5.00–7.00	5.08	1.016
Lower than middle	−5.00	1.93	0.386

Source: Ministry of Welfare and Labor, *Comprehensive Survey of Living Standards*, 1998.

that the picture has considerably changed from that of table 4.1 on household savings.

Clearly, the household debt gets higher along with household income. The richest household with an annual income of more than 20 million yen borrows the most, 10.9 million yen, while the lowest income household with less than 5 million yen borrows only 1.9 million yen on average. So the higher is the household income, the higher the amount of debt. However, while this result reflects that of savings by income household, a different story emerges when we compute the ratio of household debt over annual income. Then the highest ratio, 1.016, is due the lower-middle income household (annual income between 5 and 7 million yen). The ratio decreases as household income increases, and for the super-rich it is only 0.543. Interestingly the lowest ratio of 0.386 is that of the poorest household group. The lower income households are likely to be unable to borrow from financial institutions because of borrowing constraints (i.e., a capital market imperfection) on lower income households or because they have very weak intention of borrowing. The inference that can be made about the highest ratio of debt over income being that of the lower middle income households is that this group has relatively low living standards, since they have to bear considerably high interest payments and repayments.

4.3 Effect of the Bubble Economy

Bubble
The Japanese bubble economy occurred in the late 1980s. The prices of both land and equity went up drastically. For example, in the six largest cities, chief among them Tokyo and Osaka, the price index rose

from about 7,000 in 1985, evaluated at the 1955 price level, to well over 20,000 in 1988 to 1989. The land price almost tripled in only three to four years. Equity prices showed a similar trend. The equity price index in 1985 was about 1,000, evaluated at the 1955 price level, and it increased up to 2,500 in 1988 to 1989. Then abruptly in late 1989 the enormous increases in both the value of land and equity collapsed, and by early 1990 prices started their steep decline. Prices fell to the pre-bubble level around the mid-1990s. Consequently today the Japanese economy suffers from asset-deflation, since the market value of both land and equity is still at a very low level.

A bubble is a mechanism that cannot be explained by rational economic behavior. Extremely large fluctuations of land and/or equity prices are not said to be due to a "bubble" economy if the rational economic behavior or scientific economic theory can adequately explain their cause and the effect. The bubble economy of the late 1980s was in fact the product of irrational behavior.

Among the causes or events that trigger a bubble are large numbers of people deciding to speculate in the financial markets. Usually a calamity occurs and sends a sudden shock to the market. The most famous bubble in modern history is the tulip mania bubble of the 1630s that took place in the Netherlands. Rare new varieties were developed to in attempts to meet extremely high demand for the tulip bulbs. Tulip bulbs prices shot up drastically. The collapse of the bubble was a huge blow to the economy. The Dutch tulip mania, because it seems bizarre by today's standards, is one of the most quoted bubbles in history. However, we will not pursue the reasons why this or any other bubble has occurred in the real world. We will instead turn to a more attractive subject of the bubble's effect, in particular, on income and wealth distribution.

Wealth Distribution
We saw in chapter 1 that Japan's bubble economy had an enormous impact on wealth distribution. The gap in wealth distribution widened considerably. Particularly affected were the households that did not own their homes. Recall from chapter 1 that the Gini coefficient increased by about 0.7 to 0.8 percentage points between 1986 and 1988. There are not many instances of bubble economies where the increase in Gini coefficients is so large within the space of two or three years.

As the bubble started to burst in late 1989 the prices of land started to plummet to where they are today at nearly the pre-bubble level.

However, wealth distribution did not shrink in kind. So it is apparent that the extent of wealth inequality, in particular, the real assets inequality, will not move below where it is now. The reason for this is that the wealth inequality has been on the rise over the entire 58 postwar years. That is, if we eliminate the period of 1985 to 1995, land prices will show an increasing long-term trend. The occurrence of the bubble economy was really an anomaly that magnified the upward movement of land prices. Therefore we can expect wealth inequality to proceed along the same line of gradual increase in land prices, excluding the recent bubble economy.

A sharper result than that of land prices appeared in equity prices during the bubble economy. Equity holdings rose dramatically as we saw previously. The impact on wealth distribution of holding equity was much larger than that of holding land because the concentration of equity among individual households was greatly skewed. In the period of the late 1980s when the bubble economy was at its height, the following statistics record the extremely skewed distribution of equities: The first quintile (i.e., the lowest income class), 6.3 percent; the second, 8.0; the third, 12.4; the fourth, 18.3; and the fifth (i.e., the highest income class), 55.0. Held by the highest income class were more than half the total equities. This extremely skewed distribution suggests that equities are financial assets meant only for rich households.

A more dramatic result on equity holdings is that only around 10 to 15 percent of individuals hold equities, so the remaining 85 to 90 percent of the population have no dealings in equities. Only a very small number of individuals live in a world of equity trades, and thus the equity market; the vast majority of Japanese individuals have nothing to do with equities. Then, who holds the majority of equities? It is the enterprises that hold other enterprises' equities and shares. About 70 percent of shares in Japan are currently held by enterprises, and such a system is called inter-firm mutual share holdings.

In sum, shareholders in Japan are an extremely small group of rich individuals, and a large group of enterprises. These two groups receive all the benefits of share holdings. Let us examine the case of the rich households. Table 4.3 shows the increases in financial asset values due to the increases in equity values (i.e., capital gains from equity holdings) by income group. Note that the fifth quintile group gained about 24.4 trillion yen, which is much larger than that of any other group. The richest households thus scored enormous gains while the poorest gained little or nothing at all.

Table 4.3
Rising wealth due to rising equity values by income group in 1987 (billion yen)

First quintile	2.8
Second quintile	5.5
Third quintile	5.1
Fourth quintile	8.3
Fifth quintile	24.4

Source: Economic Planning Agency, *White Papers on the Economy*, 1988 (in Japanese).

Table 4.4
Changes in average equity values

	Households with equities		All households	
	Equity values (million yen)	Gini coefficient	Equity values (million yen)	Gini Coefficient
1979	0.307	0.659	0.049	0.945
1982	0.367	0.634	0.067	0.934
1985	0.529	0.622	0.084	0.940

Source: Tachibanaki (1989).

Table 4.4 focuses on the increase in equity values for two house-hold classes: first, households that hold equities and, second, all house-holds whether they hold and do not hold equities. Clearly, households that hold equities increased their share values from 3.07 million yen in 1979 to 5.25 million yen in 1985 on average. This is a very large increase. If we are concerned with inequality in equity holdings, the Gini coefficient for households holding equities was about 0.64, and it is about 0.94 when we include households not holding equities. Since the figure 0.94, is close to unity, the implication is near perfect inequality. Therefore inequality in equity holdings is unbelievably high in Japan.

What can be deduced from this description? The large share of increases is due to increases in equity prices during the period of the bubble economy. Rich households gained a lot. Since trade in equities is liberal economic activity, thus open to all individuals, it is not right to accuse rich households of amassing great fortunes due to rising share prices. These households also have to face the risk of declining share prices. The only cynical remark that a poor individual may be entitled to make is that the very rich can live off the capital gains of their equity holdings.

4.4   Role of Intergenerational Wealth Transfers

Bequests

Recall the three factors that determine how wealth is distributed: (1) income, (2) asset prices and quantities, and (3) savings rates. To these there may be added an important other factor: intergenerational transfers from parents to children, or to offspring in the form of gifts and bequests. The initial state of wealth passed from generation to generation is a critical factor in the determination of current wealth. There are several forms of intergenerational transfers. They are distinguished in terms of the timing of receipts, tax elements, intentions of past generations, and so forth. Thus there are several terminologies for intergenerational transfers such as bequests, gifts, and inheritances. In this book we will use the term bequests to represent all intergenerational transfers.

The problem with bequests, however, is the measurement error, for the following reasons: First, nearly all statistical sources on bequests rely on self-reporting amounts by responders to questionnaires. Responders are often unable to give an accurate amount of a bequest, or of their wealth in general, since they do not know the current prices of both their financial and real assets. Second, tax factors play an important role in the real world of bequests. Tax avoidances and evasions are common. Thus self-reporting cannot avoid some, occasionally serious, measurement errors. This is, in particular, true in the statistics reported by tax authorities. Since it is impossible for us to adjust or modify these measurement errors unless we make a special effort, we will depend on the figures of reported bequests.

Why do people leave bequests? This question is important for the various issues concerning wealth distribution, the economics of government debts, and so forth. The question may be more concisely treated under the topos of "bequest motive." Before arguing bequest motive, it is important to recognize the distinction between intended bequests and unintended bequests. The unintended bequest arises upon sudden death of a person without a bequest motive. Statistics on bequest amounts do not make this distinction. Therefore we should address the various bequest motives in questionnaires to people who are alive.

There are, broadly speaking, three representative bequest motives: (1) life-cycle motive, (2) altruistic motive, and (3) exchange (or strategic) motive. For those with a life-cycle motive, we can assume that they want to use up all their financial resources, including capitalized real assets, in their own consumption. Consequently they have no intention of leaving any bequests to their next generations. In reality, however, they leave bequests because they die before they use up all their financial reserves. Bequests are largely therefore unintended, and this circumstance arises because of uncertainty of death. Because of the lack of intention to leave a bequest, we call it a "life-cycle motive."

Individuals making altruistic bequests can be assumed to feel utility from leaving bequests to their offspring, and not to expect any act in exchange from offspring. They simply leave the bequest out of love for their offspring, and feel the satisfaction of bringing happiness to their offspring. This is thus pure altruism. For the exchange (or strategic) motive, the third case, we can assume that the individuals making the bequests expect some benefit from offspring in return. Typical examples in Japan are the living accommodations adult children provide in their homes for their elderly parents (in an extended family), or else tend to their financial security and nursing care. Offspring are expected to support parents thus economically or in various arrangements involving living together, taking care of their needs, and so forth. This is the reasoning behind the exchange motive.

It is interesting to note the relative importance Japanese people assign these motives. There are two sources that give this information. The first is the *Survey on Financial Asset Allocations*, by Ministry of Postal Bureau, 1991, and the second is the *Survey on Living Standards of Middle-Age and Old People, and the Function of Social Security* by National Institute of Social Security and Population, 1997.

The 1991 survey is a brief report. From it we learn, first, that 56.7 percent of individuals are interested in making bequests to their children, and 40.3 percent have no intention to make bequests. While most individuals hope to leave bequests, it is not the great majority. The 40 percent figure for people not intending to leave any bequests is rather high. In terms of intention versus no intention for bequest motives being 57 versus 40, it should be emphasized that in reality, of the 40 percent with no intended bequest motives, the greater part of their wealth is left as unintended bequests because of the uncertainty of death, as was explained previously.

Second, we learn from this survey the interesting way the question of bequest was posed to responders: "Is provision of some help to parents a pre-condition for leaving bequests?" The ratio of "yes" answers was 43.1 percent, while that of "no" answers was 37.9 percent.

Although these two figures are identified as almost equivalent, the exchange motive (i.e., yes) is somewhat higher than the no exchange motive, which may be roughly equivalent to an altruistic motive.

Third, we have some data on the bequest value, and it is about 66.49 million yen on average. We have to discount this value substantially because it was reported just before the end of the bubble economy. A more interesting and useful figure is the instrument of leaving bequests. 86 percent of individuals say that they leave land and house, and 41 percent that they leave financial assets. Since there are individuals that leave both land and financial assets, the sum of 86 and 41 is over 100. It is concluded that the principal instrument is land and house.

Finally, it is reported that only 20 percent of the individuals received bequests from their parents. This is a very low rate, and there are several explanations for it being low. Traditionally families were large. So few children received bequests, usually only the eldest son. There was no custom of equal allocation of bequests among offspring. This is not unlike the custom in many other countries. Today, because the sizes of families have been decreasing, and the number of brothers and sisters is not large, the number of recipients of bequests within a family is bound to increase.

The 1997 survey by the National Institute of Social Security and Population is now examined. This survey included a number of further details. In particular, on bequest motives concerning "To whom you will leave the bequest," there are five possible answers: (1) Life-cycle type I, (2) Life-cycle type II, (3) Altruistic, (4) Exchange, and (5) Inheriting Business. The way to allocate had six possible answers: (1) The eldest son, (2) A child who took care of parents, (3) Equal, (4) A child who inherited business, (5) Only one child, and (6) Children who have lower incomes. The difference between life-cycle type I and type II appears in the following way: type I says no strong intention of leaving bequests but admits unintended bequests, while type II says that it is not necessary to leave any bequests. Inheriting business means that the children must continue to carry on the businesses of their parents. The eldest son has a peculiar position in East Asia. The social norm is that the eldest sons are entitled to bequests but must in return take care of their parents.

Table 4.5 presents a sample of the Japanese peoples' choices regarding bequests and inheritances. Note that the most important bequest motive is life-cycle type I, which signifies no strongly intended bequest

Table 4.5
Bequest motives and methods of allocation in 1990s (in percent)

	Life-cycle[a]	Life-cycle[b]	Altruistic motive	Exchange motive	Business motive	Ratio
Eldest son	10.82	10.53	30.37	10.09	25.01	17.80
Child who took care of parents	19.20	10.53	16.49	48.62	8.33	20.78
Equally to all children	52.01	47.37	33.77	25.69	12.50	42.19
Child who inherited business	1.40	0.00	3.14	1.83	41.67	2.89
Single child	13.96	31.58	13.87	12.84	12.50	14.09
Children who have lower incomes	2.62	0.00	2.36	0.92	0.00	2.26
Total	100	100	100	100	100	100
Ratio	51.76	1.72	34.51	9.85	2.17	100.00

Source: National Institute of Social Security and Population, *Survey of Living Standards and Social Security for Middle-age and Older People*, 1997.
a. Life-cycle type with no strong intention of leaving bequests but admits unintended bequests (called life-cycle type I in the text).
b. Life-cycle type not seeing necessity to leave any bequests, (called life-cycle type II in the text).

motive but nevertheless admits unintended bequests, and the next important is the altruistic bequest motive. The exchange motive is not so favored, with only about 10 percent responding in the affirmative. If we consider next the way the bequests are allocated, we see that the highest share, about 42 percent, is the equal allocation to all children. The second in importance is to the child who takes care of the elderly parents, and the third is to the eldest son. In the case of only one child, the first and second allocations would apply as well. Thus the figures for with first, second and fifth allocation cases may be inexact, since these cases overlap. Nevertheless, overall, the largest share is a combination of life-cycle type I and equal allocation, 26.9 percent, and the next largest one is a combination of altruistic and equal allocation, 11.6 percent.

From these two surveys what inferences can we make regarding bequest motives, despite the somewhat different results obtained between them? First, strong intentional bequest motives, and no intentional bequest motives but admitting some unintended bequests, are roughly at the same level. Equal allocations to offspring are the most popular. The exchange (i.e., strategic) motive is not particularly strong even though it is frequently mentioned. So some nonnegligible influence of the exchange motive must still be present.

Finally, we should briefly mention the relationship between bequests of financial or real assets and investments in education. Such a model is covered in Tachibanaki and Takata (1994), in which a distinction is made between bequests of assets to children and investments in children's education. Tachibanaki and Takata found, at least for Japan, that parents prefer to invest in their children's education if they find that the children are inclined toward higher learning, and to leave land and houses if that inclination is lacking. Bequests are thus left children who do not achieve in school, and it is interesting that these are the children that demonstrate a strong inclination to take care of their elderly parents. Children who received high investments in education from parents generally are not able to take care of parents when they become aged because they work as administrators and managers in large urban centers away from their parental homes. These children, of course, earn their high salaries, thanks to their parents' investments in their education. They nevertheless do not feel obligated to provide for their parents in return. Is it therefore better for parents to leave bequests, or to invest in their children's education? This is no doubt a delicate question that cannot be easily answered.

Effect of Bequests on Wealth Distribution
Bequests endow individuals with a financial advantage. Often bequests are not received until the ages 30 to 60, because these are the ages reached when parents die. Thus most children receive bequests after they have completed their formal education and have begun their work or economic life. It is nevertheless possible to compute the discounted value of bequests to the starting age of economic life, which is technically at age 18, or 22 for higher educated individuals, even if the bequest is received at age 40. Let us call this discounted bequest value "initial wealth holding," which is what it is conceptually.

People who receive bequests from the preceding generation are well positioned for wealth accumulation because their initial wealth holdings are positive, and usually large. People, who do receive bequests in future, thus have zero initial wealth holdings. Distinctions between positive initial holdings and zero initial holdings are crucial when we are interested in investigating wealth distribution.

It is useful to see how these facts correspond to statistical data. Table 4.6 shows the contributions of bequests to household wealth holdings.

Table 4.6
Share of bequests in total household wealth (million yen)

	Average household wealth	Households receiving bequests		Percent of assets to total bequests
		Percent of total households	Average bequest	
Financial assets	105.12	4.3	11.5	4.7
Real assets	519.63	23.7	115.0	52.6
Total	624.75	24.6	105.3	44.5

Source: Tachibanaki and Takata (1994).
Notes: Assets are evaluated at current prices. Bequests are the sum of financial and real bequests.

The totals include financial assets, real assets, and bequests received, on average, and in relation to total wealth. It is evident that the contribution of bequests to total wealth holdings is 44.5 percent. Interestingly financial assets comprise only 4.7 percent, whereas real assets are a high 52.6 percent. Inheritances thus seem to consist mostly of real assets.

Is the 44.5 percent figure high or low? This figure differs from that in the United States, which Kotlikoff and Summers (1981) show to amount to about 80 percent of wealth coming from intergenerational transfers. Several authors have commented on the 80 percent figure being too high, and countered with much lower figures, among them, Modigliani (1988). The distinction appears to be between life-cycle savings, which are accumulated during an individual's lifetime, and bequests, which are received at the start of an individual's economic life. Modigliani observed the contribution of life-cycle savings to be quite high in comparison with that of bequests (i.e., intergenerational wealth transfers). Kotlikoff and Summers (1988) gave a rejoinder. The consensus among American economists regarding this controversy is that the estimate of Kotlikoff and Summers on bequests was somewhat inflated.

How about the percentage of bequests in Japan? Takayama and Arita (1996) obtained a figure of about 60 percent, which is the highest contribution of bequests to total wealth holdings among several studies. There are some studies that bring the figure down to about 30 percent. In my estimation, the 44.5 percent is reasonable because it falls between the lowest and the highest figures considered thus far.

For Japan it suggests that slightly less than half the wealth holdings over total wealth holdings can be accounted for by bequests (i.e.,
intergenerational wealth transfers). As we accumulate more empirical
studies, a more definite and reliable figure will emerge to tell the full
story of wealth in Japan.

There are other surprising features to note in table 4.6. Most important, observe that only 4.3 percent of households receive financial
assets as bequests, but 24.6 percent receive real assets as bequests. This
is a low rate of inheritance of financial assets, and also a considerably
low rate of inheritance of real assets. The low figures suggest that the
great majority people receive no bequests. Only a small number of
households are in a position to receive bequests, and the great majority
is on the outside of intergenerational wealth transfers. This fact has an
important implication for wealth accumulation and distribution because it suggests that an individual or a household able to receive a bequest will receive a fairly large one that gives a powerful boost to their
economic life.

The idea is confirmed by table 4.7, which presents relative contributions of bequests to total wealth inequality. The wealth figures in this
table are discounted at the measurement period. The following observations can be made based on these figures: First, the relative contribution of bequests of financial assets to total financial wealth inequality is
practically zero, which indicates that such financial bequests play no
role in the determination of financial assets inequality. Second, the role
of relative contribution of bequests of real assets to total real assets inequality is about 40 percent. This is a rather high contribution. Further
its contribution to total assets inequality is about a third, which is again
considerably high.

Table 4.7
Effects of bequests on wealth inequality (in percent)

	Due to bequests[a]	Arising from other means[b]
Financial assets	0.4 (1.4)	28.1 (98.6)
Real assets	25.1 (31.9)	46.2 (68.1)
Total	25.6	74.4

Source: Tachibanaki and Takata (1994).
a. Gini coefficients for contribution to total wealth inequality are in parentheses.
b. Difference between assets due to bequests and due to other means are in parentheses.

From the combined results of both tables we have total wealth inequality explained largely by bequests of real assets. Put plainly, individuals with real assets as bequests show high wealth holdings, whereas those without real assets as bequests show low wealth holdings. So whether or not individuals receive real assets as bequests does matter in regard to total wealth figures. Recall from chapter 1 that this result is the most important element used in determining total wealth inequality: whether or not individuals own real assets. Therefore the most important contributor to total wealth inequality is whether or not individuals received real assets as bequest from the past generation. Intergenerational wealth transfers, in particular, real assets transfers, lead to intergenerational wealth inequality.

The intergenerational transfers of wealth nevertheless do not tell the whole story of wealth accumulation, or wealth inequality. There are those individuals among the population that inherits nothing from the preceding generation that accumulate enormous wealth and thus join the ranks of wealth holders. These individuals are able to earn high incomes during their economic lives and/or save a lot during this time. However, the vast majority is not so able to accumulate wealth, have low incomes during their economic lives, and thus low savings.

In sum, the three factors that determine wealth accumulation and consequently wealth inequality are (1) intergenerational wealth transfers, in particular, bequests of real assets, (2) economic lifetime incomes, and (3) life savings. However, it is namely bequests of real assets that have the largest impact on wealth inequality.

Policies on Bequests

In this final section of the chapter we turn to Japanese economic policy on bequests, in particular, on real assets, since this is the most important component of wealth accumulation and thus wealth inequality. The main instrument here is the delicate issue of the inheritance tax or gift tax on intergenerational wealth transfers. The two extremes are all of the wealth transfer being intercepted by a 100 percent inheritance tax, and no intervention in such transfers of wealth, meaning a 0 percent tax rate.

Is there an optimal inheritance tax rate? There is no simple answer to this question despite the optimum income tax argument given, for example, by Mirrlees (1971). There are several reasons why there can be no optimal tax rate on inheritance. First, value judgments are involved. For example, some people may prefer to abide by the equal opportunity principle. Equal opportunity is not possible in a society where some citizens are advantaged from the start by initial asset holdings due to bequests while others receive no bequests and are economically handicapped from the start. Some other people may prefer to regard humans as inherently altruistic and so accept the notion of bequests as a natural human motive. Whether the former or the latter is considered more appropriate will depend on the values of the government in office. Second, it is not as easy to measure the economic effects of the inheritance or gift tax on economic growth, labor supply, resource allocation, and wealth distribution as it is the economic effects of income taxes or corporate taxes. So it is not possible to decide on a tax rate system that can please all people. Third, if the inheritance tax is made too large, to compensate for the fact that some individuals receive huge bequests while other individuals receive none, sedition may arise, as explained below.

In effect in Japan there are two policy positions on the inheritance tax: either lower the inheritance tax burden in order to protect intergenerational wealth transfers, or raise it in order to ensure equal opportunity and thus equal economic starts for all individuals. Obviously rich households support lowering the inheritance tax, but so do self-employed people such as farmers, small retail-traders, and small enterprise owners who wish to transfer their business activity to offspring. The support of farmers and small business owners gives this side a considerably large voice. Politicians are willing to listen because these are the people who elect them. The 100 percent inheritance tax policy has received only minority support (including myself). Therefore the burden of the inheritance tax rate has shown a declining trend historically. As a result inheritance continues to work as a widening

Table 4.8
Inheritance tax rates on bequests equivalent to 300 million yen for G–5 countries (in percent)

United States	0.00
Germany	2.54
Japan	6.67
France	8.56
United Kingdom	13.56

Source: Japanese Ministry of Treasury data.

force in wealth distribution, and the extent of inequality in intergenerational wealth transfers continues to increase.

Let us consider the reasons why a high inheritance tax rate is good policy despite its rejection by the majority. The primary point is, of course, the equal opportunity principle, which purports the basic human right that everyone is entitled to an equal economic start in life. Japan's large differences in bequests work against this principle. The second point is that equality of opportunity can provide everyone with a work ethic and thus a strong incentive to put in more effort at work. High work incentives benefit the economy in general. The third point is that the widening wealth inequality, due to the large bequests, is a disincentive to those in impoverished circumstances who instead of embracing a work ethic become dependent on the altruism of society. As a final point there is the admonition made by the wise Mr. Takamori Saigo, a famous revolutionary politician during the Meiji Restoration period, about one hundred years ago: "Do not leave beautiful and fertile land to your offspring." The meaning has to do with the natural inclination of youth, as historically youth have proved themselves to become lazy if they can depend on large bequests.

Last, to see how Japanese policy on the inheritance tax compares internationally, we have in table 4.8 a summary of the tax policies of the G-5 countries. Japan's rate is 6.67 percent, and this puts it almost half way among the G-5 countries. The Japanese rate used to be very high, as much as 20 percent in the past. The decreasing trend, however, is not only peculiar to Japan, many countries are observing the same. How can we interpret the 6.67 percent inheritance tax rate? Currently there is strong demand to lower the inheritance tax burden, as was mentioned previously. I do not endorse this view because it violates the principle of equality of opportunity. However, it seems to be the direction in which Japanese policy is moving.

Equality of Opportunity
                                              and Equality of Outcome

In chapters 1 through 4 we examined income and wealth distribution
mostly as an economics issue. We were concerned about the equity
(or inequality) of outcome (or consequence). We saw that the state of
income and wealth distribution is determined by the outcome of individual households' economic activity. Equality (or inequality) of opportunity is a question whether or not every individual can commit to
an economic activity fairly and freely without barriers. Equality of opportunity is measured by many criteria and variables such as education, occupation, position, employment, and earnings. If some barrier
or discrimination is observed for any individual who wishes to attain
a certain level of education, position, employment, and earnings, this
individual is then denied equal opportunity. The great majority of people might disagree with the idea of inequality of opportunity. The difficulty is where to insert such factors as ability, effort, and luck when
we argue for equal opportunity. Ethnicity, meritocracy (or educational
achievement), religious beliefs, social as well as economic strata, all
have been argued on this subject. I do not pretend to be knowledge-
able in all these different areas, but I will argue below as best I can for
the case of Japan.

5.1   Class, Education, and Occupation

Class (Stratum)
Sociologists are concerned with individuals being categorized by their
occupations such as manual laborers, white-collars, or sales workers.
An occupation can tell much about the level of an individual's attainment in a social order. A prime minister or president of a country, or
a supreme-court justice, is an example of a very esteemed occupation, or a member of the upper class in a society. The power, authority,

responsibility, and difficult decision making in such achievements are high. Thus people tend to see these occupations as very prestigious. There are a countless number of occupations in any society, from prestigious to lowly.

Why are sociologists and other specialists interested in occupations? There are several reasons to consider. First, each occupation tends to fit into a hierarchical structure, according to the educational requirements, responsibility, rank, earning power, social respect, necessary intelligence, and so forth. In the Japanese case there are eight occupational classes that are commonly considered in order of prestige to accord with these criteria: (1) professional, (2) managerial, (3) routine clerical, (4) sales, (5) skilled manual (blue-collar), (6) semiskilled manual, (7) unskilled manual, and (8) farming.

Second, certain job categories require more educational attainment. The typical example is the medical doctor, who besides a university level education must engage at several levels of internship and pass a national qualifying exam. Because educational attainment is determined by such factors as intelligence, ambition, determination, and parental economic stratum, occupation, and educational attainment, it is useful to investigate their full effects.

Third, jobs demanding intense performance, jobs with high educational prerequisites, scarce jobs, are among the ways earning capacities are further differentiated within occupations. So it is as interesting to include the variances within occupations in earnings differentials.

In short, there are many interesting ways to treat occupational differences. At least in Japan, a social class is defined by a bundle of occupations that have some similar qualifications and characteristics for each of the eight categories presented above. The usual definition of upper, middle, and lower classes is used in many European societies. In the United Kingdom there is further the popular reference to the "working class," and in France this same group goes under several names, most often *cadre* and *class travailleur*.

In Japan, as well as in several other countries, the term "class" is still laden with Marxian connotations. Marxist theory sets capitalists against workers and landowners against tenants. However, the distinction of owning land within the class system is important in Japan. The landowning class, of course, has power over the tenant class, and may even "exploit" them, if that is the correct word to use in expressing the relationship between these two respective classes. Because Marxian economics and sociology was also disseminated in Japan in the past, for a long time the word "class" reminded the Japanese of the crude oppositions of capitalists versus workers and landowners versus tenants. In the West there remains a tradition of economic and sociological Marxian literature continuing this distinction, such as by Bowles and Gintus (1976) and Wright (1978, 1997).

Thus, as Marxian dialectics started to lose ground in the 1970s in Japan, it became no longer appropriate to treat the word "class" as a reference to a social hierarchy that invokes the "exploitation" of the lowly or the dialectic of capitalists versus workers. Class is now used to signify a bundle of occupations, or a single occupation. There is a word "stratum," from which obtains the word "stratification." This word has no direct relation to Marxian ideology, so stratification is used frequently in the Western sociological literature. I, however, do use class and stratum interchangeably.

Intergenerational Social Mobility

Sociologists were concerned with (intergenerational) social mobility. Such investigation centers on the relationship between father's occupation (or class) and son's occupation (or class). If the influence of the father's occupation is negligible for the determination of the son's occupation, social mobility is considered to be high. Mobility here may be interpreted as equal opportunity because a son can choose his occupation freely without any constraint or benefit arising from his father's occupation. Of course, the son's education is a determining factor in his choice of occupation. We will, however, ignore for the moment the level of the son's education and concentrate on the relation of the father's occupation to that of the son. The mother and daughter connection to occupations outside the home is more unique. This is because in the past most mothers did not work outside the home, but the increasing rate of female labor force participation in Japan as well as in many countries will make this subject an interesting one to investigate in the future.

There are many hypotheses pertaining to social mobility. A good number of these hypotheses have been confirmed or refuted in empirical studies by sociologists and presented internationally. Only the three most relevant hypotheses to our purposes are described here. First is the Lipset-Zetterberg hypothesis (1959), which considers the effect of industrialization and economic growth on the extent of social mobility in a country. Lipset and Zetterberg were able to show that the extent of social mobility is roughly comparable to a certain reached level of industrialization. Second is the Treiman hypothesis (1970), which includes many interesting correlations. The most applicable for Japan's strongly industrialized society is the correlation between higher educational attainment determining occupation—or "exchange" mobility—and the pure social mobility simultaneously possible due to occupation. Correspondingly education and occupation levels affect earnings either positively or negatively. Third is the Featherman-Jones-Hauser hypothesis (1975), which suggests a cyclical pattern of mobility in that for nearly all industrialized countries, the available occupations change over time.

Exchange, pure, and cyclical mobilities are concepts representative of intergenerational social mobility. In disregarding the contribution of the occupation of fathers, in time and with increased industrialization the occupations in any society change. One example seen over the past century was the decrease in farming positions in industrialized societies and the increase in professional white-collar jobs. From time to time it may be even necessary to discard certain occupational positions, frequently called enforced mobility, in order to achieve some sense of pure social mobility. In this instance, absolute mobility, or observed mobility without any adjustments, would be prevalent before enforced mobility is commenced. Thus pure mobility (or relative mobility) is equal to absolute mobility minus enforced mobility.

Which is better, pure (or relative) mobility or absolute (or observed) mobility? And, should we pay much attention to social mobility? Technically pure mobility may appear to be better because certain disturbing constraints are absent, as it has occurred internationally at various time periods in many countries. Absolute (or observed) mobility has some positive value for most peoples because they can experience mobility between occupations and witness changes in occupational structures. Sociologists, of course, like to focus more on pure mobility than absolute (observed) mobility.

What empirical findings have been obtained regarding social mobility in Japan? Although a large number of findings have emerged from studies by sociologists, we will consider here only the most important ones. First, pure mobility is a phenomenon of the postwar period; it did not exist in the pre–World War II period, as shown by Seiyama and Naoi (1991). This is natural outcome the postwar social and economic reforms described in chapter 1, which were influential in creating in Japan a more open society.

Second, turning to changes in the postwar period, we can say that the openness of society enabled both pure and absolute mobilities to take off, on an increasing trend from 1955 to 1975 but on a decreasing trend from 1975 to 1995. Thus sons were eager to choose different occupations from their fathers' in the first half of the postwar period, but the next two generations, coming of age in 1975 to 1995, upheld the status quo, as shown by Hara and Seiyama (1999). The decreasing trend in absolute mobility obtained by Hara and Seiyama, in particular, runs contrary to the openness of society from 1985 to 1995; that is, in these years there are signs of inactive social mobility. Sato (2000) obtained a similar finding for upper-class white-collar workers. The probability that sons of upper-class white-collar father attain the similar job status was much higher than in other occupations, so evidently social mobility became inactive for upper-class white-collar employees in the more recent period. Sato's finding caused quite a sensation because it implied that besides the condition in Japan of inequality of opportunity, there was now evidence that Japan had become a closed society in terms of social mobility.

Third, there are many indications of inequality of opportunity relating to occupational attainment, as described above, there are studies that deny that there were significant changes in social mobility over the postwar period. Two such representative studies are those by Kanomata (2001) and Ishida (2002).

Ishida's results are briefly described in table 5.1. Note the changes in pure (relative) mobility from 1955 to 1995. The three possible patterns of change illustrated in figure 5.1 are obtained by log-odds ratios. They show the considerable ease with which the population moved from one social state (i.e., based on father's occupation) to another social state (i.e., due to change in son's occupation). The first pattern

Table 5.1
Time-series changes in log-odds values

Social mobility	1955–65	1965–75	1975–85	1985–95
First pattern	54%	44%	34%	49%
Second pattern	31	41	45	35
Third pattern	15	15	21	16
Overall parameter values	−0.016	−0.004	0.114	−0.137
Standard error	(0.065)	(0.069)	(0.072)	(0.080)

Source: Ishida (2002).

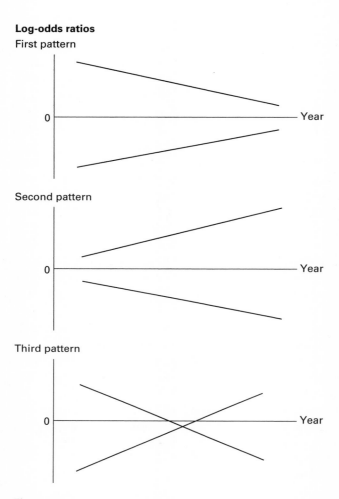

Log-odds ratios
First pattern

Second pattern

Third pattern

Figure 5.1
Patterns of change in social mobility based on log-odds ratios.

shows a convergence of the log-odds ratio to zero, meaning that the probability of an upward move has declined. That is, there are barriers to social mobility and thus sons hoping to change their occupational status from those of their fathers' face great difficulties. The second pattern shows a complete reversal, in the case of no barriers or pure social mobility. The third pattern is a mix of the previous two cases, and thus shows both increasing and decreasing social mobility depending on the openness of society to change from fathers' occupations.

Table 5.2
Log-odds ratios of sons following in fathers' occupations

	Upper level white-collar	Lower level white-collar	Self-employed	Farming	Upper level blue-collar	Lower level blue-collar
1955	2.085	1.267	1.270	2.697	1.760	1.791
1965	1.580	0.937	1.294	2.340	1.093	1.003
1975	1.390	0.130	1.055	2.536	1.089	0.602
1985	1.343	0.834	1.193	2.931	0.781	1.360
1995	1.295	0.622	0.965	3.236	0.699	0.613

Source: Ishida (2002).

By way of table 5.1 we can make the following observations about the results in figure 5.1: The years 1955 to 1965 are when Japanese society begins to move toward openness. In these years sons first realize the possibility of rising above the occupational levels of their fathers. From 1965 to 1975 the pattern is the same despite the change in direction, which indicates that this period, from 1965 to 1975, is characterized by no change in social mobility. The period 1975 to 1985 was a time when society experienced low economic growth, which consistent with Japan's move toward a closed society, as is observed in the largest share (i.e., 45 percent) being due to no change. However, because this share is below 50 percent, the effect is not particularly large. Finally, for the more recent period, 1985 to 1998, as the third pattern shows, there is again a move toward openness but not with much more force than 49 percent. As is evident in the lowest panel of the figure, the opposite shifts between open and closed social mobility cross. So it is not possible to find any clear, strong trend toward more or less social mobility.

Another notable result due to Ishida (2002) is the persistence with which sons follow fathers' occupations. Again, we have the relevant numbers in log-odds ratios. Table 5.2 can show how the rate of change in father-son occupations has occurred over time. The most interesting result among the various occupational groups is that farmer and professional white-collar jobs showed relatively consistent high retention rates. So these are occupational categories where sons are inclined to engage in occupations of their fathers. The trends are not, however, clear and simple (i.e., always increasing or decreasing) for all occupational classes; besides the professional white-collar group and farmers, the skilled blue-collar group also shows relatively weak decreasing trends. Consequently the openness in these occupations has increased only marginally.

In the case of the professional white-collar group, the considerably high rate of sons maintaining the status quo has continued up to the present day. This same result is discussed more recently in Sato (2002). The sign is thus from these two studies that the Japanese society is no longer experiencing intergenerational social mobility.

In sum, the state of social mobility in Japan based on the empirical studies examined above is as follows: Social mobility in its pure (or relative) form can be computed in terms of a marginal increase by subtracting enforced mobility from observed (absolute) mobility. The computations we reviewed show that in 1955 to 1965 Japan moved toward an open mobility that was obvious and large. A small U-turn next occurred, indicating a trend toward no mobility. The equality of opportunity inherent in open mobility, as associated with the occupational attainment of fathers rising in sons, has showed a decline in recent years.

There are several explanations for the declining trend, and they are more or less consistent with the observations of Ishida (2002). Most of the population is not interested in the numerical values of pure (relative) mobility computed by sociologists. Rather, they judge a real world with their own eyes as they see daily intergenerational occupations not to change. Farmers' sons become farmers, and in particular, sons of white-collar professionals step into the same professions. That is, most sons of medical doctors become medical doctors, about a third or even half of the seats of parliament are held by families and relatives of parliamentary members, and many popular artists and television talents are children of famous artists and television talents. Among the recent four prime ministers, three are sons of parliamentary members. The example of prime ministers coming from high ranks of society sends a message of low social mobility that reinforces what the general populace observes day to day in the large number of children engaging in the same occupations as their parents. These facts lead people to believe that social mobility is closed to them.

Another explanation has to do with the limited span of pure (relative) mobility. Sociologists measure pure mobilities every ten years, and argue whether pure mobility increased, decreased, or fluctuated. The age difference between father and son is usually 25 to 45 years, which significantly spans more than ten years, the difference in observation years. If social mobility were examined for longer periods such as 40 or 50 years, the empirical result might be more meaningful. Ten-year fluctuations or changes seem to be too short to allow appropriate inferences to be made about social mobility. In other words, significant changes in social mobility cannot occur within ten years given the fact that the age differences between fathers and sons are much larger than ten years. If there were some changes in social mobility within a ten-year period, they may be due to statistical measurement errors or methodological issues associated with the complex estimation methods used. This last concern, however, does not necessarily disavow the sci-entific value of measurements of pure (relative) mobility put forward by sociologists.

In the end, it is equality of opportunity as indicated by the small re-cent erosion in intergenerational social mobility that must concern us most.

Sociology of Education
Blau and Duncan (1967) produced a path-breaking study on social mobility. They examined the role of parents' socioeconomic status, the effect of children's educational attainment, and the outcome of the children's first job in terms of the current job along the line of a life cycle or lifetime. In other words, personal history was traced from a parent's to a child's succession of jobs. The β-coefficient approach, or the path analysis, which had become a standard estimation method in the literature, was applied. Blau and Duncan found for the United States that the effect of parents' socioeconomic status on children's edu-cational attainment was positive but had no significant effect on chil-dren's occupational attainment, since the effect of children's education was strong. Their study theorized a so-called meritocracy regarding the role of education, which will be argued later.

In Tachibanaki (1988a, b), I extend the path analysis approach to ac-count for children' income and job rank or hierarchy as additional vari-ables. I had earlier applied a similar model, although is not entirely equivalent to the Japanese one, for a number of other countries, focus-ing on France, in Tachibanaki (1980), and subsequently, on the United Kingdom in Tachibanaki (1998). Interested readers can refer to these studies for international comparisons. In figure 5.2 the essential recur-sive model is shown. The principal chain of effects goes in the fol-lowing direction: parents' socioeconomic status affects children's education, which in turn affects their occupation, rank, and thus

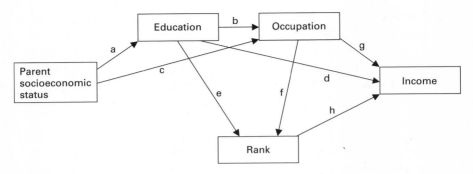

Figure 5.2
Recursive model of intergenerational occupational mobility and income in Japan.

income. The term rank is used to indicate the hierarchical position or managerial role in an organization and, of course, applies only to employees. In the case of the self-employed, this variable cannot be considered.

Among the trajectories shown in figure 5.2, economists are mostly interested in directions *a* and *d* while sociologists are mostly interested in directions *a*, *b*, and *c*. Here we consider first directions *e*, *f*, *g*, and *h*, and then directions *a*, *b*, *c*, and *d*. The novel feature of figure 5.2 is the introduction of rank in the model. (In Tachibanaki 1988a, b, I expand the number of hierarchical positions to five, each relating to the difference in responsibility and the number of subordinates.)

There are several arguments that can be used to explain the cause-effect relationships in the figure concerning directions *a* through *h*:

1. *Meritocracy claim.* Educational attainment is regarded as determining an individual's occupational attainment; the value can be close to zero for *c* and high positive for *b*.

2. *Mediatory claim.* Education facilitates the transmission of parents' socioeconomic status, and thus occupation, to children. The intermediation of education is represented by the positive values of both *a* and *b*. The difference between items 1 and 2 is as follows: meritocracy involves nearly zero value of *c* yielding large positive value of *b* whereas intermediation involves only modest values of both *a* and *b*.

3. *No social mobility claim.* Parents' socioeconomic status, in particular, their occupational attainment, determines children's occupational attainment. No social mobility is assumed by direction *c*, and this implies that *a* and/or *b* are negligible in value.

4. *Performance claim.* The effect of parents' socioeconomic status on children's educational attainment is weak, and at the same time the effect of parents' occupation on children's occupation is weak. In other words, the children are on their own, so their performance is crucial for occupational attainment. The values of both a and c are again negligible.

5. *Screening claim.* Education works to differentiate among individuals' capabilities and thus determines who should be promoted to higher rank or position. In this case the effect of e is positive and large.

6. *Human capital claim.* Education raises an individual's productivity and thus earnings power. So the effect of education on income is positive and strong, represented by the positive value of d. There is a huge literature in economics on human capital theory.

7. *Responsibility and leadership claim.* High rank or position in an organization demands high responsibility and leadership. These individuals must be able to manage subordinates with an eye toward raising an organization's productivity. It is natural to presume that high rewards are paid to individuals who occupy the higher ranks. The value of h is positive and large.

In Japan some of these claims have been explored in the sociological literature. For example, Hara and Seiyama (1999) observed that over time, with the development of industrialization, education has had a diminished effect on the determination of occupation. In the terminologies of the six claims above, there occurred a shift from the meritocracy effect to the intermediation effect of education early on, and ultimately a shift to zero social mobility. Thus today in Japan educational attainment has a minimal effect on occupational attainment. Grusky (1983) gave a similar finding for the United States.

What are the causes behind the declining effect of education in advancing an individual at the workplace? First, because of the high living standard in industrialized countries, a large number of people are able to obtain higher schooling. In Japan and in the United States, now about 50 percent of the work force has a four-year or at least junior college education. In European countries, for example, the United Kingdom, France, and Germany, these rates are 15 to 30 percent. From the high percentage of workers with higher education in Japan and in the United States there can be inferred that higher education at the college level is no longer a privilege of society's "elites." So we can rightly

expect college degrees and graduate degrees to not make a big difference in job promotions.

Second, there is a different regard for education in some countries.
The best-known studies of this issue are by Willis (1977) for the United
Kingdom and by Bourdieu (1979) for France. Willis found several successive generations of people staying in the working class and not showing any strong desire for the education that might improve their lot
because of a general contempt among the working class for educated
people. This evokes the sharp social distinction between UK working
and upper classes among which education is valued. Bourdieu found
a similar situation in France. In France, because of the small number of
elite schools, it is not possible students who do not come from professional and wealthy families to attend these schools. Bourdieu and Passeron (1970) called this a replication or reproduction system. Education
is the instrument of ensuring intergenerational replication.

The first and second studies yield thus two different interpretations
of the place of education in occupational rank as transmitted over generations. The first is on the perpetuation of working or lower class
mentality, and the second is on the perpetuation of upper class con-
duct and aspirations. In my opinion, the norm observed by Bourdieu
in France reflects that of the Japanese in the prewar years when the society was very closed, as I explained in chapter 2. Higher education
was available only to upper class and rich households; not even six
years of schooling was compulsory for the lower classes.

It is also the first study that helps us understand what is happening today, especially with the prestigious university education as will
be shown later. The situation observed by Willis is, of course, not
entirely applicable to Japan because today a large number of students
attend either junior colleges or four-year colleges regardless of their
socioeconomic backgrounds. Nevertheless, there is the issue of promotions being based on educational accomplishments.

Can we possibly infer native ability as supplementary to the factor of
education? In a situation where there is common educational attainment, say at the college level, the factor of native ability is likely to be
useful in differentiating the productivity of college graduates. Another
useful factor may be the quality of the college attended. We know that
schools differ considerably in quality at both high school and college
levels. Graduates of good schools often are more capable of doing
high-level work. A third factor is education beyond a four-year college
program. MA or PhD degrees may be helpful in making a further dif-

ferentiation when there are very many college graduates in the society. Graduate or professional schooling enables an individual to acquire the knowledge and specialization that is not possible in four-year college programs. Thus Japan has learned from the US professional schools in business, medicine, and law about the importance of ensuring high skills in these professions and is moving toward such graduate programs.

The main issue with prioritizing academic credentials from a quality school is, however, that all superior opportunities go to the already advantaged graduates of prestigious universities. This invites the emotional and valid argument that the entrance examinations to the few prestigious universities are very competitive, for the very reason that these graduates are known to have achieved top social class positions as executives in large firms, high bureaucratic officials in government, and so forth. The same is true in France and South Korea. It is, of course, academic credentialism that enables graduates of prestigious universities to be so successful.

There are several ways this discrimination is edged into hiring practices in Japan. First are the hiring tests whereby all candidates for the first-track career civil servant positions must face academic examinations in addition to interviews. Those who pass the exams are ensured a bright career in central bureaucratic organizations such as the Treasury and in foreign service. Most who pass the hiring tests are the graduates of prestigious universities. Among the most successful are graduates of the University of Tokyo, since every year about 400 University of Tokyo graduates pass the test. Next is the University of Kyoto, with about 200 annually passing the test. A few other reputed universities can boast of nearly 100. The presence of the University of Tokyo graduates among the top civil servants in the past is quite impressive. Among the many faculties at the University of Tokyo, the law faculty is the principal supplier of top civil servants. This is another clear case of academic credentialism.

A second way the prestige of the academic institution figures in hiring practices is in the backgrounds of executives at publicly listed firms. It is reputed that even at private firms graduates from prestigious universities are more advantaged in being promoted to executive positions. Particularly in corporations where the competition is keen, an individual's academic credentials provide the necessary competitive edge. Table 5.3 shows the number of graduates that occupy executive positions by college or university. Note that the University of Tokyo

Table 5.3
Number of graduates of prestigious universities holding executive positions at major firms

National and public universities		Private universities	
Top 10		Top 2	
Hokkaido	30	Waseda	164
Tohoku	54	Keio	138
Tokyo	184	*Subtotal*	302
Nagoya	40	Meiji	53
Kyoto	179	Chuo	42
Osaka	50	Rikkyo	16
Kyushu	57	Hosei	28
Hitotsubashi	67	Nihon	66
Tokyo Institute of Technology	26	Doshisha	66
Kobe	67	Ritsumeikan	27
Subtotal	754	Kansai	28
		Kansei-gakuin	32
		Subtotal	392
Other	318	*Other*	480
Total	2,246		

Source: Tachibanaki (1997).

has 184 and the University of Kyoto 179. Both are top national universities. The two top-level private universities are next in line: Waseda with 164 and Keio with 138.

As the table shows, graduates of the so-called top twelve national and private universities occupy about half of the executive positions at listed firms. Again, this is illustrative of the weight of academic credentials in the private sector, especially in large firms. Clearly, the probability of being promoted to an executive position at a large firm is higher for prestigious university graduates than for other universities provided that other qualifications such as job performances at the firm are at a higher level. However, it should be noted that graduates from other, nonprestigious universities do rise to executive positions by their impressive performances despite the stress on academic credentials in many social and economic circumstances. Notice in table 5.3 that graduates of nonprestigious universities indeed occupy nearly half the share of executive positions.

For reason of job performance and other issues it is probable that academic credentialism in both the public and private sectors will decline in the future. Today the central governmental offices are starting to see fewer applicants from prestigious universities, but this is due to a declining demand for government positions. Whereas in the past the position of top civil servant was viewed as socially prominent in bureaucratic countries like Japan and France, deregulation policies have eroded the importance of these positions, and the salaries of civil servants are now relatively low in comparison with those of corporations. So there are many more job opportunities for university graduates in other sectors than the central government. In the private sector most industry employers are recognizing that academic credentials as only a small part of the qualifications of a prospective employee; job performance is more crucial when candidates have similar schooling levels, namely the four-year college level. As a result the name of the university no longer carries weight in promotions to executive positions in corporations. It should nevertheless be emphasized that the value of a prestigious education is still operative in the screening of applicants for entrance level positions.

Class, Education, and Marriage
Besides the declining impact of prestigious university credentials in determining an individual's job promotions, and thus social mobility, there is the factor of marriage. Often today it is marriage between two individuals who have a common educational background. We have so far ignored the effect of the educated mother on the occupational attainment of children because it was important first to consider the traditional connection to the father with regard to the social mobility of sons through occupational changes. The probability of well-educated men and well-educated women getting married—and equivalently less-educated men and less-educated women getting married—is high in many societies. Japan is not an exception to this social phenomenon. It is just as probable that sons and daughters of well-educated couples are well educated, and that sons and daughters of less-educated couples are less educated. This is what lies at the core of a closed society, where fathers and sons are further expected to engage in the same occupations. Such a representation of married couples is today an exaggeration as much as the social immobility invoked by such a society. Nevertheless, human marriage is a factor in social immobility and often the social immobility associated with education is explained by marriage decisions.

Table 5.4 shows some interesting results from Shimizu (1990) relating social mobility to education and marriage. The combinations of

Table 5.4
Parents' social classes and children's educational levels at time of marriage

Generation	Total	Professional and managerial	White-collar	Blue-collar	Self-employed	Farming
A. Husband's social class and wife's social class						
1916–30	0.718	0.631	0.991	0.834	0.787	0.614
1931–45	0.819	0.819	0.987	0.861	0.912	0.664
1946–65	0.840	0.867	0.929	0.822	0.902	0.739
Total	0.794	0.798	0.951	0.844	0.878	0.646

Generation	Total	Elementary education	Middle education	Higher education
B. Husband's education and wife's education				
1916–30	0.496	0.266	0.633	0.436
1931–45	0.488	0.218	0.611	0.452
1946–65	0.586	0.497	0.664	0.573
Total	0.477	0.367	0.598	0.412

Source: Shimizu (1990).

both social class, represented by father's occupational attainment and educational attainment for both husbands and wives are shown for various cohorts. There are five occupational classes of father (professional and managerial, white-collars, blue-collars, self-employed and farmers), three educational attainments of husbands and wives (elementary, middle school, and higher), and three generations (births in 1916–30, births in 1931–45, and births in 1946–65).

Note in the table the rates of marriage that occur between husbands and wives with such features in common as occupations of their fathers and their own educational attainments. The closer the rates are to zero, the more common features the husbands and wives share; however, the rates closer to unity imply opposite features in husbands and wives. There are some other interesting observations we can make with regard to the data. First, the openness judged by fathers' occupations for all generations is 0.794, which signifies that the occupations of most married couples differ. This rate shows an increasing trend, which reflects the fact that marriages between different social classes are on the rise. It may be concluded that social class (father's occupation) does not matter in the marriage match. However, in terms of occupations, white-collar marriage matches are high while those of farmers are low.

In the case of educational attainment of husbands and wives, the table shows that the openness rate is slightly below 0.5, that is, 0.477. The marriage matches between spouses with common educational attainments is much higher than the marriage matches between spouses of different social classes. This is particularly evident for couples sharing low (elementary school) and high (college) education.

This observation confirms that education matters more than social class in marriage matches. Several comments can be made in this regard. First, because in modern Japan the choice of marriage partner is an entirely free human activity, it is ridiculous to criticize the existing practices. There is nothing negative to say about the high rate of marriages where the spouses have the same level of education. Such marriage matches can further be expected to be happier and more stable than those where the spouses have different educational levels, since marriages do occur between educated men (women) and less-educated women (men). The probability is, as was mentioned earlier, that couples with the same level of education will ensure that their children at least have that level of education, and thus reinforce the phenomenon of a closed society where the occupations of sons become the same, or nearly equivalent, to those of the parents. Education thus works as an instrument for social immobility in Japan, in contrast to the Blau and Duncan (1967) evaluation of effect of education on social mobility. This observation, however, may pertain only to Japan and not have any universal implications, such as for other industrialized countries.

Economics of Education

Among the cause–effect claims we listed earlier in this section, claims 4, 5, 6, and 7 are in the domain of sociology. Nevertheless, the economics literature has shown great interest in claim 6 on human capital. Some aspects of the human productivity implied in this claim have already been covered in chapters 1 and 3. Human capital theory relates an individual's productivity to formal education and job training. Because as a result the individual's productivity is raised, for example, as shown by Becker (1964), it is generally accepted that wages should be proportional to the level of formal schooling and job training.

From figure 5.2, however, claim 5, on the screening practices, is evidently more important than human capital theory if we consider the education required for positions of rank within organizations. This is the idea behind the theory of the economics of information as explored by Arrow (1973) and Spence (1973). Both Arrow and Spence found education to be the way some individuals are selected from among many candidates. Often the screening is of many job applicants for these positions, and the employer has only information on the educational backgrounds of the applicants. Job applicants who are freshly out of school also do not usually have anything but their education to show the employer to indicate their capability to perform higher jobs. Of course, job interviews may reveal an individual's capability, but most often not. So an employer must depend on level of schooling and the quality of the school in selecting which job candidate to hire.

Screening can also be a way to select workers from within a firm for promotion up the hierarchy. Because the jobs up the hierarchical ladder are generally few in number, there is keen competition among employees for selection to these jobs. Employers in Japan use information on employees' educational backgrounds as a criterion in the preliminary selections. Tachibanaki (1988a, b) found that in the preliminary selections most college and junior college graduates made the first cut (for promotion from ordinary employee to section head), but most high school graduates did not. Whether or not employees have a college diploma is an important criterion in the determination of promotions. This Japanese practice of screening as it relates to the effect of education on rank is given by direction e in figure 5.2.

A more complicated and difficult issue is that of the indirect effect of job performance (due to education combined with job training) in promotions in the combined directions b and f in figure 5.2. Tachibanaki (1988a, b) examined both the direct effect of education in higher jobs, direction e, and the indirect effect of job performance, directions b and f. Interested readers can refer to these studies. Only the conclusion is described here. Those hired to high positions directly, direction e, because of their education had more opportunity to move up the hierarchy than those moving in directions b and f combined. Consequently education prevails as the most determining factor in the screening of applicants for high-level jobs.

Finally we come to claim 7 on the responsibility inherent in positions of leadership. Since section heads, department heads, and directors have the high responsibility for the work quality of their subordinates, they must be good mentors as well as possess strong management skills that encourage productivity. The executives at the top of the hierarchy have the highest responsibility, and they must demonstrate in addition strong financial skills in order to run the firm efficiently.

Tachibanaki (1988a, b, 1998) observed that because of the importance of these skills, the earnings differentials are very large between ordinary workers and promoted workers. It is largest due to the influence of the other factors of education and/or accumulated levels of job training, shown as direction *h* in figure 5.2.

Recall from chapter 3 that despite the effect of education on occupation, the wage differentials are relatively small in Japan. The observations in this chapter have to do with higher-level positions. The earnings differentials up the job hierarchy are very large, and not at odds with the description in chapter 3. In Japan the high responsibility and leadership of those promoted to executive positions are appreciated and generously rewarded.

5.2 Changes in Work Attitudes and Equality of Opportunity

Changes in attitudes toward work and industrial relations, and equality of opportunity, are discussed. These subjects are important to the issue of inequality.

Changes in Industrial Relations

The Japanese industrial relation system is characterized by the following three features: (1) lifetime employment (more precisely, long duration of employment in a single firm), (2) a seniority system in the determination of wages and promotions, and (3) enterprise unionism. To these should be added the following two: (4) strong work incentive of employees and (5) cooperative industrial relations of employer with employees. Some of these characteristics have already been mentioned at various points in this book. In this section we take a look at some recent changes to these features.

First, there has been change made to the wage determination system. *Shunto* (Spring offensive) is the symbolic term used for wage determination because representatives of employers and trade unions gathered to negotiate wage payments every spring. The *Shunto* sessions were when equal wage increases could be negotiated for all union members. This system of centrally or semi-centrally oriented wage determination has eroded. Today most negotiations over wages take place in decentralized settings between individual employees and their employer. It is nevertheless too early to predict the demise of the central wage determination system or of the seniority wage and promotion system that is its core. All that can be said is that the wage determination system is undergoing a transition in the direction of a wider range of wages for employees.

Second, in connection to this change to the wage determination system, it should be pointed out that employers prefer a system whereby performance determines wages rather than seniority. Employers are starting to find that performance-based wages provide the incentive for skilled employees to work harder, which can raise productivity overall of a firm. As was pointed out in chapter 3, the seniority-based pay system has meant equal pay for employees of certain age groups and certain durations of employment regardless of the level of their skills. As more and more firms see the results of the recent initiative to reward work performance with higher pay, they will likely adopt this wage system.

Third, employees have not rejected the move toward performance-based pay because attitudes toward lifetime employment are changing among employees. Some individuals take pleasure in their work activities, whereas others prefer their leisure time. Figure 5.3 shows the shares of the Japanese people's preferences for only leisure time, lei-

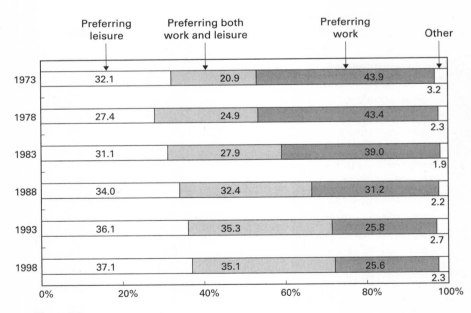

Figure 5.3
Preferences for work or leisure activities over time. Source: NHK Broadcasting and Culture Institute, *Conscientiousness of Japanese People*

sure together with work, and only working. Note that the preference for leisure time has been increasing over time. Most people want leisure or at least enough leisure to balance their work activities. These people are not interested in receiving higher earnings from hard work. Japan's considerably high economic prosperity enables these people to feel this way. During the postwar period when the Japanese economy was developing, having leisure time was unimaginable. Today the majority of people accept the wide earnings differentials between those who want to work harder to receive higher wages and those who do not mind receiving lower wages in order to enjoy their leisure activities.

A survey on attitudes toward work compensation reported by the cabinet office of the Japanese government in 1995 supports this claim. While the result is somewhat dated, it is nevertheless still relevant, and perhaps more appropriate today than in 1995. The survey, called "Survey on Attitudes toward Work in the Future," asked, "Is it necessary to change the principle of wage determination from seniority-based pay to performance-based pay, or capability-based pay?" Of the results, 63.0 percent answered positively and 19.6 percent negatively. Nearly two-thirds of the people preferred performance-based pay, that is, pay based on skill, to seniority-based pay. The large acceptance of change to the system suggests that wider wage differentials should be adopted.

Finally, the position of trade unions must be discussed. Historically trade unions have favored compressed wage distribution (i.e., equal distribution of wages) for their members, and also centrally negotiating wages. These are the practices in Sweden and Germany, where wages continue to be distributed fairly equally, and centralized decisions are made on wages (for the Swedish case, e.g., see Freeman, Swedenborg, and Topel 1998). The participation rate of workers in unions is very high in these countries. So it appears that high union participation rate is one of the necessary conditions for equal wage distribution.

The union participation rate in Japan was very high right after the Second World War. This was considered a sign of democratization, as was explained in chapter 2. Over time a gradual reduction in workers joining unions has resulted in the 20 percent membership evident today. Thus, with only a fifth of the work force being members, union power has declined. The decreasing dependence on unions in wage negotiations is further indicative of such declining power.

Why has the union membership declined so much? Tachibanaki and Noda (2000) examine the reasons for the decline as well as the efficacy of trade unions in these different economic circumstances concerning wages. Here is the summary. First, today the largest and increasing number of employees are part-timers and short-term contracted workers. Most unions do not admit these employees to their membership. Second, often regular employees who are qualified for union membership do not want to join, nor are not interested in becoming involved in union activities. The main reasons are, on the one hand, that these workers are just busy doing their jobs and are not interested in union activities, and on the other, that they know that union activities do not provide them with any significant benefits.

Third, there is the change in the structure of employment due to the increase in white-collar jobs along with the increase in college graduates ready to fill them. This segment of the work force has no need for union membership. In the past union members were mostly blue-collar workers with high school diplomas. This change has obviously worked to reduce union membership. Fourth, studies such as that by Tachibanaki and Noda (2000) show that for the most part, working conditions, including wages, are not so different in unionized firms as opposed to nonunionized firms, although there are several areas where union members receive higher benefits than nonunion members. This is, of course, more evidence in support of the second and third points noted above. Fifth, employees in small firms generally do not have the leaders among them eager to take on social issues and attempt to organize unions in these workplaces; at the same time some owners and executives of small firms can retaliate against such employees attempting to organize unions.

In short, changes to the industrial relations system are occurring because both employers and employees accept the wider differentials for the various reasons. In addition the production and sales systems of firms are changing from a principle of average productivity by all employers to a principle of productivity by a selected skillful few who become crucial to the firm's success. The former principle is nevertheless useful for firms that engage in mass production and mass sales activities for a smaller number of standardized products. The latter is useful for firms that engage in producing and selling certain expensive, high-quality products in small quantities. Japan's recent move from the former to the latter has been unavoidable.

A Change in Outlook on Equality

It is inevitable that wage inequality will increase with the consent of both employers and employees, due to the wage differentials being sought in Japan for performance-based wage pay in place of the dominant seniority-based pay system in the determination of wages. It appears thus that the Japanese peoples' evaluation of equality–inequality is undergoing change. The seniority-based pay system ensures that equal wages are attained for employees at certain ages and at certain lengths of employment in a firm. It is a means of ensuring equality of outcome in wages. A performance-based wage system does not necessarily result in equality of outcome; it presumes that people understand that it is fair when the wages are equal to each worker's contribution to the enterprise. In contrast, the seniority-based wage system does not pay each worker a wage that corresponds to his or her performance or contributes to the enterprise; it is centered on an individual's personal qualification of age and duration of employment and not on the contributions of that individual to the enterprise.

People today believe that performance-based pay is fairer than seniority-based pay because it reflect a degree of effort. The concept of equity, fairness or justice is appreciated, based on accepting the following principle: "Effort should be evaluated appropriately, and reward should be given in accord with one's effort." Even if wide wage differentials occur between employees who expend effort and thus contribute much to the enterprise and those who do not expend effort and contribute not much, all concerned employees should understand that they are being treated fairly. The extent of wage differentials is then determined by the majority rule of the concerned people, which has included both employers and employees.

Since wages are usually the major part of an individual's income, the consequences noted above should be presented to all concerned citizens to decide on the acceptable income differentials (i.e., primary income differentials). This would be consistent with the majority rule principle of citizens in a democratic society. Already both the tax and social security systems are committed to redistribution policies, so inequality of outcome is determined by the will of all citizens concerned with both primary incomes and redistributed policies. Majority rule appears to be the only way to determine the degree of income inequality, and we the citizens need to make some tough value judgments in this case. The similar process could be conceived for wealth distribution, but here the discussion is limited to inequality (or equality) of outcome.

Equality (or Inequality) of Opportunity

Equality of opportunity is a principle that stands in sharp contrast to equality (or inequality) of outcome (or consequence). In a democracy equality of opportunity is considered an initial condition of life–before all individuals begin their economic and social activities. The condition of equality (or inequality) of outcome comes after such economic and social activities have ended. This is observed, that is, expressed, before income is redistributed. Both the income tax and social security systems alter the condition of income distribution, and are thus instruments of redistributed income distribution. The effect of tax policies and social security programs on income redistribution will be examined later.

The general consensus in a democratic society, at least in principle, is that equality of opportunity should prevail. In other words, no one objects to the importance of equality of opportunity. In the real world, however, there are various kinds of inequalities of opportunity. Immediate examples in Japan are discrimination against women and educationally disadvantaged individuals in the screening of job candidates, as described earlier. Racial discrimination is observed in racially heterogeneous societies, and different treatments by religion and cultural background are common in some other societies. In the absence of such considerations of equality of opportunity, the advantaged individuals get better economic outcomes at the expense of the disadvantaged individuals.

Equality of opportunity is defined by the following two concepts: The first is a level playing field, to which a society must commit. This is a human basic principle of fairness in competition, and candidates for employment should be able to compete for positions. If institutional barriers are present, equality of opportunity is lost as a principle. The second is a nondiscriminatory principle that states that any individual with the relevant attributes and qualifications to perform a job well should be able to apply for an opening in that job. Therefore only the relevant attributes and qualifications should be used to select individuals for these jobs, and the other information such as age, sex, cultural background, religion, and race (in some countries) should not be used. Age is a difficult issue in Japan currently because there is a debate about mentioning age on job applications.

The Japanese Constitution and the various laws that uphold it assure equality of opportunity to be a basic human principle. The real world, however, does not guarantee equality of opportunity. A difficult example is provided. Say there are two high school students. Student A is intelligent and hardworking, while student B is less intelligent and lazy. Parents of student A are not well off financially, and hope that their son or daughter will work after graduation despite the child's desire to go to college. The parents of student B are wealthy, and hope that their son or daughter will go to college. If the society admits that equality of opportunity is a highly desired trait, financial aid for student A should be made available. However, Japan does not provide full financial aid to needy students. Therefore equality of opportunity is not perfect in Japan.

A delicate issue arises if we consider student C who is much less intelligent than students A and B. This individual may not finish college education in view of very low intellectual capability but nevertheless wants to go to college but has parents unable to pay the tuition. Is it necessary to prepare financial aids for student C if we commit to equality of opportunity? One answer may be that it is not necessary because financial aid for such a student C is not likely to be efficient. The money will be wasted. Another answer may be that it is necessary because we need to accept student C's aspiration despite its very high probability of failure.

Roemer (1996, 1998) gives strong justifications in support of the last argument. For Roemer, the capability or intelligence of a child is a circumstance beyond his or her control, and thus some compensation must be provided in order to sustain an equalizing opportunity for educational attainment. By this argument, he would likely agree to spend public money so that student C will have the opportunity for the college education along with some special effort. Special additional education may enable a learning disadvantaged child to attain sufficient strength academically to be admitted to college, and eventually to graduate from college. The Roemer's idea is that equality of opportunity requires compensating financial resources for the differences in their circumstances as long as those differences affect educational attainment. Roemer includes family background, cultural background, and more generally social milieu, in addition to native capability. The idea of native capability may sound unusual because some other people may find compensating it with money to be inefficient. In other words, consignment of public funds for educating incapable students is seen to be useless and thus not efficient. The issue of a trade-off between efficiency and equality will be argued later.

Relationship with Efficiency

The wrangle over the issue of inefficiency is evocative of a more sensitive argument associated with the racial heterogeneity of the United States. A small group of sociologists have argued that black children have limited capability to learn, and so have proposed reductions in provisions for the education of these children in order to spend public fund more efficiently (e.g., see Jensen 1969; Herrnstein and Murray 1994). In Japan we do not have use for the issue of black or racial heterogeneity, but we do have "less capable" children, as explained above. The common view on equality of opportunity assumes at least equal public educational expenditure on all children. The minority view, however, seeks less public educational expenditure on less capable students, as in the case of the US nonwhite children, because such payment may be frivolous and inefficient. Roemer (1998) proved the groundlessness of the minority view, and showed that more expenditure is desirable on the education of less capable children.

A clearly related systemic problem that goes against the principle of equality of opportunity is the importance placed on academic credentials in the screening of college graduates for employment. However, in addition to the screening practices described in section 5.1, Japanese corporations scout for prospective employees among students graduating from the handful of prestigious universities. They grant these students job interviews through so-called designated interviews, which are restricted to the name universities.

It is unlikely that students excluded from such partiality in the job market find the system fair and equal. But there are some good reasons why corporations do this. First, corporations can save considerably on hiring costs by limiting the number of candidates. Second, the small number of interview candidates allows corporations to be more precise and careful in the selecting the new employees. Third, corporations hire on the strength of past history, which often confirms that the employees selected from designated interviews do relatively well in their corporate careers. So the designated interview system is more efficient way for corporations to hire than opening their doors to all applicants.

In addition to this efficiency argument, it is possible to also see equality of opportunity being assured even in this designated interview system. In Japan all high school students have an equal opportunity to apply to the prestigious colleges and universities. Those high school students desiring a future in one of the corporations know they must expend extra effort in their academic work to be admitted by the prestigious universities. College entrance examinations are tough in Japan because of the importance of academic credentials from the prestigious universities. High school students can apply to any university, but they face tough entrance examinations to the prestigious universities. In this sense, equality of opportunity exists for all high school students who desire corporate careers and thus will be privileged by the designated interview system if they are admitted to the prestigious universities. Of course, it is unrealistic to expect high school students to recognize the importance of the designated interview system. In Japan equality of opportunity is not easy to implement; it is difficult to agree on at what place, in what period, and to whom equality of opportunity should be assured.

In principle, equality of opportunity for all citizens is a respectable objective in our society. Equality of opportunity should be the initial state in any competitive situation. After that, an individual's effort is what should mostly determine the course of that individual's life. Educational opportunity, job opportunity, employment opportunity, promotion opportunity, and many other opportunities are accessed through hard work. It is inevitable that there are winners and losers once the course of economic life is begun and that the differences between winners and losers are measured by income and wealth, as inequalities of outcome. The extent to which inequality of outcome can be accepted will be argued later.

Three Criteria That Determine Equality and Justice

Next important after equality of opportunity are the criteria of contribution, need, and effort. To some extent these criteria have already been present in the discussion, and here we attempt to ground them conceptually. In a firm and in society in general these are conflicting criteria, but they are related because they each require some value judgment.

Contribution relates to the productivity of each individual in a firm or organization. For example, suppose that a manufacturing firm employs a number of workers with different outputs. It is difficult to measure how much each individual contributes to the final product, but it is possible to measure it at least theoretically. A simple but not good way to measure the individual output is to take a simple average. This is relatively easy when individuals are responsible for the sales activity of a firm. Say it is car dealers. The average is based on the number of cars sold. When such a precise method is not possible, the manager must frequently depend on using some subjective measure. Employers must find a way to measure each individual's productivity where employees demand that payments or rewards be determined on the basis of each employee's contribution.

Need has to do with the income all individuals, except children, have to have in order to support their economic lives. Nearly all adults work to earn wages. This is true even for retired people, which is in the form of pension payments. Need is understood by the individual or number of individuals of a household that require income in order to support their economic lives. If one household has five children with no working activity of his or her spouse, the need is certainly high, while it is low in the case of one household with no children and with working activity of the two spouses. It is desirable to take into account the difference in living standards caused by the difference in need, and to adjust household incomes so that extremely dissimilar economic conditions among households are avoided. The arrangements in many countries include spouse allowances, child allowances and benefits, and subsidies to child-care systems paid by the tax and social security systems. These arrangements are generally successful in lowering large differences in living standards due to the differences in need.

A number of delicate issues arise in regard to need. In the case of women, in Japan a certain amount of spouse allowance in the calculation of taxable income is admitted for the household where the married women do not work outside the home. Married women with jobs find this arrangement to be unfair because they are unable to use any such allowance but must pay income taxes. Another example comes from couples with no children and single individuals who find child allowances and benefits unfair because they have to pay extra taxes. Couples with children may say that their children will contribute to society in the future labor force and thus financially to social insurance. However, there are no universal and justifiable theories that can convince all concerned individuals of the appropriate solution. One way is to rely on the majority rule in democratic societies. Yet the majority rule does not necessarily produce the best policy. Of course, concerned individuals can use information from economic studies in their voting behavior.

A further reason why need is important is that most everyone wants to survive. Societies were originally formed to guarantee minimum subsistence for their members. Ideally, if an individual is incapable of receiving an income above the subsistence level, economic assistance is provided to keep that individual from starvation. This is a support system that has been prepared in almost all industrialized countries. It is unfortunate that all developing countries have not prepared such systems. Nevertheless, even in developed countries including Japan to a lesser extent, there are a large number of hungry adults and children whose living conditions do not satisfy the condition of need, meaning the minimum subsistence level.

Effort is a concept that has already been discussed at various places in this book. Workers who consistently put high effort into their jobs contribute a lot to a firm. Normally, if the wages are proportional to an individual's contribution, as was mentioned for this first concept above, it is also proportional to the effort expended on the job. Therefore a high correlation exists among effort, contribution, and wage, and many individuals do not object to this correlation, at least nowadays.

The difficult and sensitive problem regarding effort arises when an individual is observed not to have contributed much. Say this individual failed to accomplish a certain project despite enormous effort. This is not uncommon, and of course, the contribution is zero. Should the employer pay a higher wages to the individual to compensate for the expended great effort but with nothing in return? The employer's decision then depends on the difficulty of the job assignment, the frequency of failure, the preparation involved, and so forth. Again, it is difficult to present more than a general direction in which the concerned individuals might act in resolving the problem. The problem is, nevertheless, an intriguing one to investigate both theoretically and empirically.

The next important area associated with effort is that of bequests from parents to children. Children, or offspring, do not make an effort in the same sense as productive or sales activity for them to receive bequests from the preceding generation, except where an exchange (or strategic) motive is made. Children who received bequests without any effort are truly advantaged because they start higher in their economic lives. If we regard the concept of effort as important for determining payments, or the state of income and wealth distribution, the 100 percent bequest tax rate is relevant because no effort has been made. This tax rate, however, is often judged to be too high, so we might think about a lower bequest tax rate. My own preference is for a very high bequest tax because it supports the principle of equality of opportunity. At the other extreme there are enough people who argue against any bequest tax rate. So opinions differ on the importance of effort in the relation of justification to taxes on bequests.

Taken together, therefore, the three criteria of contribution, need, and effort determine rewards in the form of income. Income distribution should be based on a balance of these criteria and the prevalent social ideology. The main difficulty here is to create a single policy that embraces all concerns. I will examine later the relevant ideology. A second difficulty is that it is not easy to convert the three criteria into some quantitative measures. Economics and public policy theory have attempted to apply measurements in these criteria but not convincingly. Again, it is a question of value judgments. To be feasible, the measurements should show a way to resolve the inherent conflicts among contribution, need, and effort, and democratically by the majority rule.

Inequality (or Equality) of Outcome (or Consequence)

In the ideal society where equality of opportunity is assured, all individuals commit to economic activity, and then earn income. Already we have seen that how each individual's income is determined is fairly detailed. Ability, education, training, effort, contribution, need, and many other factors influence an individual's income level. One factor that has not been mentioned is luck, or uncertainty. If we conceive of economic life as a series of gambles, such as in horse racing, football "toto," and the lottery, it is not hard to accept this idea for why some people earn a lot while others earn little or nothing at all. The real world is full of successes that can be attributed to luck. To become the president or the prime minister of one country is a phenomenon connected with luck. Many occupational achievements are attained with some luck. Some immediate examples are huge numbers of sales by a single sales person, accidental new inventions, and new R&D arising from thorny research questions at institutes and factories.

The concept of luck has also been applied indirectly to the determination of individual incomes. Jencks (1972), for example, considered luck as behind most income inequality in the United States where income distribution varies across states. In other words, some of the visible income differentials from US state to US state can be explained by luck.

Technically different outcomes (or consequences), understood as income inequality, appear after all individuals commit themselves to economic activity. This is the first stage of economic life. From the start some individuals may find the outcome to be unequally distributed; others may understand it to be equally distributed. It all has to do with personal tastes, value judgments, understandings of fairness, and so forth. When the second stage of economic life arrives, the income taxes and social security systems should ably redistribute income from the rich to the poor (or the young to the old). If all concerned individuals had outcomes that were equally distributed, no redistribution policies in the form of income taxes and social security payments would be necessary. That is to say, a proportional income tax rate should be sufficient to finance public goods expenditures and social security benefits, and no additional social security programs with redistribution purposes would be necessary.

Worldwide, however, the majority of people have learned that the first-stage income distribution is unequal, and thus redistribution policies are often adopted. In a few countries the governments have understood, instead, that it is not necessary to adopt any redistribution programs through taxes and social security payments, and have therefore introduced a flat (i.e., proportional) income tax rate. The rationale here is that if the first-stage income distribution is already equal, it is against basic human economic freedom for a society to levy heavy tax burdens on some individuals (often the rich) and light burdens on some others (the poor).

However, this policy disregards a crucial element that calls for redistribution policy. This is the *inexistence* in the real world of equality of opportunity. As was noted previously, equality of opportunity must be assured; otherwise, it is natural to observe the condition of income inequality, and even a huge gap in income distribution. Because most people agree that the violation of equality of opportunity is unfair, the good society responds and adopts income redistribution policy for the purpose of compensating the unfairness.

In what areas might the government respond to the inequalities of opportunity evident in Japan? I have already mentioned the discriminatory treatment of women in the workplace. The low wages they are paid could be compensated. Any number of less educated individuals might claim that they should be compensated because they were unable to complete their education because of their parents' poor economic circumstances. This could be judged to be a violation of equality of opportunity. Most of the populace would agree that physically and mentally handicapped persons should be compensated.

Then there are the important selected industries such as financing industries, public utilities like electricity, gas, and water industries, medical and pharmaceutical industries, and so forth, regulated by government. Employees in these industries receive higher wages than the market wages because the regulated industries enjoy so-called regulation rents. Since deregulation policies have set in, the degree of regulation has been decreasing. However, the wages remain high, so employees in these industries are still advantaged. In contrast, other groups of employees, namely in small sized firms and in part-time jobs, are drastically underpaid. For these workers some compensation programs could be introduced.

A last, but somewhat controversial, area of inequality of opportunity is the advantageous initial condition of receiving a bequests at the starting stage of one's economic life, as discussed in chapters 3 and 4. Whether or not this is regarded as contributing to inequality of opportunity depends largely on individual value judgments. Nevertheless, it is useful to review the several ways bequests can be regarded this way. First, the individual receiving the financial and/or real assets could be additionally receiving financial resources for human capital investment—meaning educational opportunity. The reasoning is the since the capital market is imperfect—imperfect, meaning that there are some liquidity constraints for younger individuals by which they are unable to borrow funds from financial sectors—those young individuals who receive bequests, or who expect to receive them, do not face these liquidity constraints. Consequently they are able to invest their human capital. (For the useful theoretical discussions, see Galor and Zeira 1993 and Banerjee and Newman 1993.)

Second, bequests often take the form of occupational transfers from parents to offspring. We can conceive of several such arrangements among farmers, retail traders, industrialists, politicians, and artisans. Individuals not able to benefit this way may resent these arrangements because they must instead make risky occupational choices. Further it is possible that individuals outside these occupational transfer areas do not have open access to the occupations. Therefore some people have proposed that intergenerational occupational transfers should be

restricted because they go against human freedom and altruistic behavior. This effect of bequests is more controversial.

If in the real world a majority finds the presence of inequality of opportunity, there should be no objection against policy decisions to redistribute the income differentials. For a society there is a more basic
reason for a redistribution policy if income inequality or distribution
of income is deemed to be "excessively" unequal. It is the ethic of a social contract incumbent in income redistribution policies through taxes
and social security payments. The problem, of course, is how to determine adequately what is an excessive condition of unequal income
distribution. This is because a possible consequence of income redistribution is a sacrifice of efficiency, in particular, economic growth, if
redistribution policies go too far. So there is a trade-off to regard
between equality and efficiency, as was argued in chapter 1. The next
chapter is dedicated to a way this dilemma might be resolved.

6

Policy Recommendations
for Some Efficiency and
Equity Trade-Offs

6.1 Efficiency and Equity (or Equality)

Trade-off between Efficiency and Equity

The main goal of economic policy is to manage the economy efficiently. There are many subgoals associated with economic efficiency: increasing the gross national product, allocating limited resources (capital, labor, natural resources, government fund, etc.), raising gross domestic product and thus income revenues, lowering the cost of production in firms, lowering the unemployment rate, lowering the inflation rate, and so forth. In some government administrations, lowering the budget deficit, lowering the trade or balance-of-payments deficit, and stabilizing the exchange rate are additionally desirable. If all or most of these subgoals are achieved, we can say that economic efficiency has been achieved. It is, of course, impossible to achieve all such objectives simultaneously. Therefore there are priorities assigned to the subgoals, and these can differ by country, state of economic conditions, preference of people, and so forth.

Equity can be regarded as nearly the same as equality, as is argued at many places in this book. Some authors distinguish between equity and fairness in the following way: equity (or equality) is concerned with minimizing the differences in individual incomes, and in social and economic opportunities; fairness is concerned with just decision rules, without barriers and discriminations, and with just allocation of economic resources regardless of an individual's interests and desires. Fairness has already been covered to a certain extent in this book.

Economics emphasizes the importance of the Pareto optimum when efficiency is argued. The Pareto optimum is used to appraise the efficient allocation of limited resources that improve the economic life of the social majority. Economic policy that succeeds in raising one individual's welfare without worsening all remaining individuals' welfare is called Pareto-improving. It is known that perfect competition is the Pareto optimum for an economy, since there is no possibility then of Pareto-improving the economy. There are many examples of resource allocations that satisfy Pareto optimums. Unless a certain condition is given, it is impossible to determine the best-case resource allocation among many Pareto optimums. One criterion for this condition is the concept of equity, or equality. If a desirable degree of income inequality (or income distribution) is given, then the economy can determine the best resource allocation.

The next concern is addressed to equity, or equality. Here we undertake a more formal consideration of equity than that of the general public. Equity is defined formally by the situation where no concerned individual feels "envy." Economic theoreticians prefer such a definition. The simple case is that of two individuals, A and B, in a society. Individual A's income is higher, and as a result consumes more than individual B. If individual B feels envy toward individual A, economists often say that equity is not satisfied. Of course, there would be no individuals who do not feel any envy in this circumstance. However, if ability and/or effort differ between individuals A and B, then individual B's envy should be lessened to some extent. Thus it is the positive value of envy that calls for income redistribution policy to narrow the income differential between these two hypothetical individuals. In reality the extreme case of no envy, which is equal to perfect equity, is impossible to achieve.

What is the trade-off between efficiency and equity? Above and beyond any formal or mathematical definitions, we have an appealing intuitive example provided by Pazner and Schmeidler (1974). Suppose that we have a production economy with two individual workers. Worker A is more productive than worker B. Assume that the Pareto optimum for the production process provides the economy with unequal resource allocations. The efficient way to carry out production in this economy is to have only worker A to do the job and to allocate the outcome to the two workers later. Because leisure is a homogeneous good, worker A feels envy toward worker B who did not work. In other words, equity is not satisfied because of envy. This is an illustration then of a case where efficiency is achieved but equity is not satisfied. A trade-off must be made between efficiency and equity.

This is the trade-off considered in personal income tax. Say that a very high income tax rate is levied to high income earners and a low rate to low income earners. Such a tax system is desirable if the objective is to achieve high equity. Perfect equity or equality here is defined by equal after-tax incomes between the two types of earners. However, the high income earners may be then motivated to lessen their productivity, or lessen their work intensity, because their after-tax incomes are greatly lowered by this tax policy. In such a case efficiency is reduced along with productivity. The similar case can be made for imposing a high tax rate on interest income, as it is likely to reduce personal savings. Whereas a high tax rate on interest income can help lower income inequality, a reduction in savings has a negative effect on capital accumulation, and thus economic growth. Although either way equality is reinforced, the negative consequences of lower labor productivity (or intensity) and lower personal savings are detrimental to efficiency. Again, a trade-off must be made between efficiency and equity.

There are nevertheless two historical examples of successful trade-offs between efficiency and equity. These are the two economic reforms of the 1980s in Britain by Mrs. Thatcher and in the United States by Mr. Reagan. In both cases deregulation policies were adopted and encouraged competition, and tax reductions worked to revitalize the two economies. As a result both countries gained economic strength throughout the 1980s and 1990s. However, we know well that this emphasis on economic efficiency was at the expense of equity to a certain extent. Income inequality rose as a consequence in both the United Kingdom and the United States. So efficiency came at the expense of equity.

A different attempt at the trade-off between efficiency and equity occurred in Scandinavia in the 1980s. The economic conditions in these countries were at an all time low, as indicated by high unemployment and worsening balances of payment. Criticism was hurled at the welfare systems of these countries with their very high welfare provisions financed by very high tax and social security contributions. The ruling social democratic parties were ousted in favor of the conservative parties that advocated welfare reform. Welfare provisions found to be detrimental to economic efficiency were reduced until the economies recovered in the 1990s. Then the people in these countries restored their social democratic governments, with the exception of Denmark. The Danes have recently reinstated their conservative government. The Scandinavian experience shows that people recognize the importance of the trade-off between efficiency and equity, and adjust their governments accordingly. Efficiency is emphasized in years when the economy is weak, and equity in years when the economy is strong.

It should be added that despite the need for these Scandinavian countries to make the small trade-off between efficiency and equity, their high living standards were not compromised. The prosperous economies of Scandinavian countries in recent years indicate that a high degree of efficiency is possible without sacrificing equality in both opportunity and outcome (i.e., income distribution). The trade-off between efficiency and equity in these countries was not long term but a pragmatic solution to a short-term crisis.

Philosophy and Ethics
The trade-off between efficiency and equity can be argued philosophically in line with several schools of thought. It is primarily moral principle that drives economic policies and causes a people to favor certain policies among many policy alternatives. If the majority of people see equity as more important, their economic policy will adopt equal distribution of income, and something similar will be observed for efficiency. However, the political philosophies come with different thoughts on what is moral political behavior. There are four major schools of thought that are important for understanding the different philosophical positions to which an economy can be redirected through policy initiatives. I choose to discuss here four doctrines from among many philosophical doctrines because they relate to contemporary instead of the classical ideas, and to the issue of the welfare state. These are (1) libertarianism, (2) communitarianism, (3) liberalism, and (4) (analytical) Marxism.

Libertarianism   Libertarianism is sometimes called ultra-liberalism or classical-liberalism. It emphasizes the importance of human liberty or freedom, and is against any outside interference in human activities. It is therefore a doctrine that opposes the idea of a welfare state for the following reasons: First, economic inequality is not the first priority. Second, government welfare policies are claimed to deter the incentive to work, and thus removing all government intervention is desirable. Third, social welfare is not endorsed, but the right to life is. Fourth, the role of the state should be minimal. Hayek (1960), Friedman (1962), and Nozick (1974) are among the scholars associated with this school. They all see economic freedom is the most important principle, with no government intervention. Such a system can significantly raise economic growth. It is possible to describe the political and economic policies of Mrs. Thatcher and Mr. Reagan as subscribing to this view.

Communitarianism   The communitarianist school promotes the just distribution of social goods, and such just distribution is among people who are bound together by some commonality such as culture, religion, language, or race, and/or are living in a community. In other words, community members help each other. Sandel (1982) and Waltzer (1983) expound on the main ideas behind this school. Both social justice and welfare provision are promoted. This is mainly how communitarianism differs not only from libertarianism but also from liberalism à la Rawls, although like liberalism, communitarianism accepts provisions of welfare. On social welfare, Communitarianism, however, differs from liberalism. Its method and policy of welfare is within the large or small community where the people are supposed to have common interests. There is no provision for universal welfare by a central government. Therefore it excludes the services provided by a bureaucratic authority, but encourages nonprofit organizations and/or associations to give decentralized and mutual welfare services. Communitarianism is also open to the possibility of different welfare provisions among different groups or communities, which is inconsistent with universalism.

Liberalism   Liberalism is an idea made popular by Rawls (1971), and it is a school of thought that has influenced my ideas. Liberalism, of course, is not a new idea; it has been interpreted variously over history in the works of Hagel, Stein, Bentham, and Pigou, for example. I do not discuss these writers because Rawls gives the most contemporary interpretation. Rawls is sometimes severely criticized, however, because in his 1993 and 2001 books he altered the original propositions he made in his 1971 book. I will not go into the fine details of these propositions because this book is not on his philosophy.

Rawls reputed human moral activity to be organized around two principals: the first is the liberty principle by which humans express political thought and opinion, plot their lives, evade violence and psychological pressures, for example. The second is the difference principle by which humans attempt to maximize the welfare of the least advantaged individual even when equity of opportunity is assured.

The latter, difference principle derives from the so-called utilitarian principle of Jeremy Bentham and John Stuart Mill, and became known as the max-min principle.

Rawls's difference principle generated some criticism. Two were serious. The first, by Harsanyi (1975), called the max-min principle immoral, and suggested instead the maximization of the average utility principle. The second, by Hare (1989), imagined in his criticism the max-min principle to be a sort of insurance strategy that assures a social minimum for all citizens. Both criticisms may be explained by the mix of concepts that forms the modern version of the utilitarian doctrine, by which the society is expected to assure a minimum social welfare level for all citizens and limit the principle of the average utility to citizens below a social minimum level. Rawls in turn called the modified version of Harsanyi and Hare the principle of restricted utility. It depends on an individual person's preference whether the original difference principle due to Rawls or the principle of restricted utility due to Harsanyi and Hare is the desired welfare state.

In his later work Rawls criticized the traditional welfare state because it produces an alienated underclass of people that relies on endless government help and is thus without an incentive to work or to participate in society. Rawls promoted an idea of a property-owning democracy instead of welfare-state capitalism. This is a bold idea because it mediates against the welfare state, which can produce a large number of people who cannot survive without help from the state. Participation and work are essential for all individuals who are able to do so both physically and mentally. This idea corresponds to that of workfare ("welfare though work") and the idea of participation income due to Atkinson (1995).

Rawls has presented some path-breaking conceptions of equity, liberty, and democracy. In my view, his propositions also have value for the discussion they have generated. The most important contribution of Rawls, in my view, is the attention to persons who are the least advantaged, or who are below the minimum level in a society. There are differing opinions on the treatment of these least advantaged persons. Because Rawls is a philosopher and not an economist who can make policy recommendations on the treatment of the least advantaged individuals, it is up to us economists to carry on in the spirit of Rawls's ideas.

It would be a mistake to ignore Sen when we talk about liberalism. Sen (1992, 1995), an economist, was not happy with the traditional measurements of welfare according to income in economics and/or with utility theory. So he developed his own view on well-being. Happiness as a part of human nature cannot be measured only by economic variables such as income and/or utility, and it should be measured by the degree of human "capability" that utilizes one's native ability fully. If one can utilize his capability highly, happiness is higher. Sen, who is a native in India, was concerned with poverty in Asia, and thought that it would be difficult to evaluate welfare of people in developing countries only by income and/or utility. The degree of illiteracy, availability of medical care, and so forth, is more important in this setting, so capability is measured by these indexes.

Sen's idea is valuable, and the differences he points out between developing countries and developed countries are also captured in this book in our welfare comparisons. Sen's work can even have application to developed and advanced countries including Japan, and there are some attempts in these countries to measure welfare using his indexes. Nevertheless, income and/or utility are better measures at least in developed countries, so the index data are merely redundant. We will end the discussion of Sen's idea here, but it is not without some value.

(Analytical) Marxism   Marxism is a fairly well-known idea, so Marxist thought requires no special discussion. There were many countries where Marxism has served as the main doctrine behind their political and economic systems. The Marxist influence has declined considerably in those countries where the economies have been transformed from socialist to market economies. It is nevertheless important not to forget the Marxian emphasis on workers' human rights and care of the weakest people. In this regard there has arisen an analytical Marxian school, representatively given by Cohen (1995) and Roemer (1996, 1998), that considers the importance of distributive justice and equal opportunity. The contributions to the literature are in their scientific and mathematical evaluations of various theories without strong prior bias or prejudice. Of course, there exist some ideas and thoughts in their propositions that are influenced by the traditional Marxian doctrines such as class conflicts between capitalists and workers, or landowners and tenants, and the exploitation theory. Nevertheless, it is hard even for a non-Marxian like myself not to feel some sympathy with their propositions, in particular, with distributive justice and equality of opportunity.

In sum, I believe that the idea of liberalism, in particular, Rawls's propositions regarding philosophical and ethical backgrounds for the welfare state or the role of income redistribution policies, is crucial to consider for Japan and the much needed change to the after-tax income inequalities.

6.2   Tax Policies and Social Security Reform

Effects of Tax Policies in Support of Social Security Programs

There are two different views on the effects of tax policies and social security programs. One is that the taxes used to finance social security programs have a negative effect on labor and on the savings incentive, and thus are detrimental to efficiency. The other is that there is no observed evidence of any negative effect. Often people in Japan who are opposed to the welfare state profess the first view. I do not subscribe to the negative view, as neither do many Japanese economists.

The tax and social security policies in Japan further do not seem to have had a negative effect on the labor supply, particularly that of the young working-age males. If, as reported by some studies, older people and married females have felt the pinch, it is very small and thus negligible overall. The same can be said for the effect on the savings rate. Even taken together, the minor effects on labor supply and savings due to taxation and social security programs are nearly negligible (see Tachibanaki 1992, 1996b for the details behind this conclusion). Consequently, at least in Japan, the taxes and social security contributions have not had a detrimental effect on economic efficiency.

However, we need to address the strong objections in Japan to the perceived burden of the taxes and social security contributions. As we saw in chapter 1, while the Japanese people may complain about their income tax payments, the ratio of tax and social security revenue over the GDP (or national income) is actually very low. The statistics therefore show the complaints about high burden to be groundless. Nevertheless, people already talk about the taxes and social security contributions as if they live in one of the welfare states despite the unexceptional tax and social security outlays.

Still there is some value to exploring why people continue to harbor misconceptions about taxes and social security contributions that amount to very low rates. In my opinion, it is due to the high public spending being witnessed on various public goods such as roads, bridges, harbors, airports, and railroads. Some of the spending on pub-

lic goods has recently proved to be redundant and understood to benefit only the construction and civil engineering companies involved, not
the ordinary people. Of course, people are quick to associate high government spending with too much collected tax revenue. There is the inevitable impression that the government is being overpaid and that,
likewise, the government has a huge store of funds for welfare provisions despite the fact that the taxes do not contribute enough to welfare
services, as we saw in chapter 1. Simply put, people do not recognize
the difference in allocation of funds between public goods and welfare
provisions.

Additionally the Japanese people perceive their government to be already too large, and see the idea of providing people with more welfare services as unnecessarily enlarging the size of the government.
This cynicism is encumbered by the worry about the negative effects
of taxes and social security contributions among a people that do not
consider themselves to be living in a welfare state, as was described
previously.

The task is the economists' to provide the crucial facts to correct the
misconceptions of the Japanese people. Economists therefore must get
hold of reliable elasticity values on the employment and savings activities in order to convince the people that the taxes and social security
contributions are not undermining the people's incentives to work and
save. The elasticity values are useful for observing more precisely how
the effect of tax policies on the economy and for computing the extent
of that effect.

For guidance we have an extremely large number of US and other
country studies of elasticity values. Although, unfortunately, Japan
lacks data on individual observations of economic variables, including
tax and social security variables, by which economists estimate the
elasticity values, there are some estimates currently. So far the estimates indicate that the elasticities are small, as was noted previously
(for the details, see Tachibanaki 1992, 1996b). However, the computations were performed using imperfect data. As the database is
improved, economists should have more reliable and perfect elasticity
values with which to evaluate the effect of social security taxes on the
economy.

In sum, there exist some strong reservations against the welfare state
in Japan. However, this appears to be due to some misunderstanding.
First, Japan is not today a welfare state. Second, from the scant data
now available, employment and savings activities do not appear to be

affected by taxation and contributions to social security programs, so this is an unnecessary worry over loss of economic efficiency. Third, as was emphasized in chapter 1, the time is now for people to decide whether or not families and large enterprises can still be the main welfare providers as in the past. My feeling is, as I've said from the start of this book, that Japan is destined to move toward a welfare state, willingly or unwillingly, because of the already high inequality getting higher.

Tax Policies

There are different policies for different taxes. In this book we are interested only in income taxes, corporate taxes, and consumption (or value-added) taxes because these are the taxes connected with income redistribution. In this section we review how these tax policies have worked over the past two decades because the general opinion is that recent tax policies have failed to redistribute income. On the contrary, they have worked to widen the after-tax income inequality.

The few recent tax reforms have mostly benefited rich households. For example, a value-added tax was introduced in 1988. The rate was 3 percent, so it was not so regressive. It also was neither neutral nor progressive. Recently the rate was raised to 5 percent. This strengthened its regressive function. The year 1988 was also when the large tax payments on interest and dividend income were abolished, and a proportional 20 percent tax rate was levied on this income separate from the income tax base. Both reforms have been advantageous for households with large financial assets and disadvantageous for those without, meaning the poor. Additionally the income tax rate has been decreasing since 1988. The highest income tax rate was once over 70 percent, and today it is 37 percent. The progressive income tax is clearly in a significantly decreasing trend. See table 3.12 for the recent tax rate.

Alone, these three tax reforms are enough to show that the tax system is contributing to the after-tax income inequality that has been steadily growing over nearly two decades. But there are some additional concerns with income taxation that should be mentioned, at least briefly. First are the tax avoidance and evasion practices among the different occupational groups. It is said that farmers report only 30 percent of their income to tax bureaus, self-employed 50 percent, and employees 100 percent. Another source claims 40 percent, farmers; 60

percent, self-employed; and 90 percent, employees. Underreporting of income has remained a problem because the punishment for tax evasion is rather weak. The only reason employees report all their income is not because of their honesty but because their tax payments are withheld from their wages. In other words, the withholding system makes it difficult for employees to underreport and evade taxes. While employees regard the tax evasions by other occupational groups as unfair, tax officials are not so eager to reduce the unfairness because the great majority of farmers and self-employed business people support the current ruling political party.

Second is the gradual shift of the tax base from direct taxation (i.e., personal income tax and corporate tax) to indirect taxation (i.e., consumption tax and commodity tax). As a result tax revenues from the consumption tax (i.e., value-added tax) are expected to increase in coming years. This shift is not unfavorable, since the adverse effect of indirect taxation on resource allocations, labor supply and work incentive, savings incentive, and so forth, is smaller than that of direct taxation. Value-added taxes also work to lower the disparities in the reporting of earnings by the various occupational groups. However, there is some efficiency loss, since the revenue from indirect taxation is smaller than that from direct taxation.

Third is the equity issue of the value-added tax becoming a smaller proportion of high-income households but a larger proportion of low-income households. Although increasing the rate of the value-added tax is desirable from the economic efficiency point of view, it is undesirable from equity point of view. Because Japan is moving toward higher income inequality, the increasing value-added tax can seriously deplete the means of low-income households. It is therefore important to control the rate of the value-added tax, or to reduce such taxes in order to ensure a stronger income redistribution policy. Based on these three factors, let us consider a way to reform the tax system.

The Proposed Progressive Expenditure Tax or Consumption Tax

Suppose that the tax base consists of consumption spending by a household. In the current system a consumption tax is formally called a value-added tax. Then the principal tax base is the cost of a good, and a proportional tax rate (currently 5 percent) is levied on that good. Let us introduce a tax rate that differentiates each good by the degree of luxury implicit in the cost of the good. So higher tax rates are to be levied on more luxurious goods, and lower rates are to be levied on ordinary goods. In the case of foods, drinks, medical drugs and supplies, and educational supplies, the tax rates can be zero. The different consumption tax rates on different goods classified by luxury should make the tax more progressive because it would be levied proportionately on all goods. The regressive tax in effect could be changed to a progressive tax.

The above is but the first stage of implementation of a new tax system. At the second stage we introduce a progressive expenditure tax. This tax base is an application and modification of a famous tax proposal by Kaldor (1955). The following is the actual method of the implementation. Tax bureaus collect information on each household's expenditures. The expenditures of households are measured by household income minus household savings. The method of collecting income figures is based on the current method, as many countries rely on reported household incomes to tax bureaus. Savings data are collected through reports from all financial institutions that manage savings deposits, bonds, equities, life insurance premiums, and so forth, for households. If in Japan every household is provided with a tax number (like the social security number in the United States, or the national insurance number card in the United Kingdom), then a computer system could calculate every household's total savings and thus expenditures. Once the household expenditures are available for all households, different expenditure tax rates are levied using the different expenditure figures. A higher expenditure tax rate is levied on higher expenditures, and a lower rate is levied on lower expenditures.

Such a progressive expenditure system could work well provided that a tax number is available for every household, and also a powerful computer system to do the massive computations. A political office could easily issue the tax numbers, but the computer technology may take some years to develop. Therefore such a progressive expenditure tax can take years to perfect. Nevertheless, the principal motivation behind this proposal is that a progressive expenditure tax can satisfy the need for both efficiency and equity in Japan. The fact that neither efficiency nor equity is compromised, at least conceptually, can be supported by a numerical simulation analysis (see Okamoto and Tachibanaki 2002 for such an analysis). The introduction of a progressive expenditure tax appears at this time to be the best solution, although its implementation has to wait for some distant moment in the future.

Tax Reforms in Immediate Future

If it takes many years, even a decade, to implement a progressive consumption tax, or progressive expenditure tax in Japan, there has to be a way to make some immediate tax reforms. The arguments here are fairly brief because these reforms are not complicated. First is the need to prevent reductions in the progressivity of the income tax rate. This is an important because there are people calling for still more reductions in the progressive income tax. This issue was addressed in Atoda and Tachibanaki (2001), where it was found that the Japanese progressivity of the income tax is almost at the optimal level in both efficiency and equity. Any further reductions in the progressive income tax will violate the present balance.

Second is the average income tax rate in Japan. The tax burden in Japan is considerably lower than that in other advanced countries. Therefore it should no longer be necessary to lower the average income tax rate except for very short-term reductions of income tax in accordance with policy adjustments to plumb faltering business cycles. If an increase in the share of indirect tax over direct tax is a goal, a reduction in the income tax burden should be accepted. Third is a very marginal decrease in the amount of the minimum taxable income. In Japan this is at a considerably high level by international standards; it has to do with the number of income tax payers. The income tax rate, however, can be kept at a minimum level such as 5 percent for the lowest income class. Currently it is 10 percent. Fourth is the separate tax base for financial assets income should be changed to a comprehensive income tax base. The same tax rate should be levied on the sum of taxable incomes.

Last, an argument can be made for raising the bequest tax rate. Recall from chapter 4 that bequests, or intergenerational wealth transfers, play an important role in transmitting wealth inequality from generation to generation. Contrary to the majority opinion in contemporary Japan, which calls for a decrease in the bequest tax burden, I feel that to uphold the principle of equality of opportunity, the bequest tax rate must be raised. The main reasons for bequests are noted in chapter 4. In the main, they enable intergenerational wealth transfers as well as occupational transfers. Often it is difficult to separate between wealth transfers and occupation transfers. Further there are a nonnegligible number of people who receive only small bequests, and they too are opposed to any increase in the bequest tax rate.

Although the altruistic bequest motive cannot be strongly criticized because many people believe that it is a human virtue, the principle of equality of opportunity is as important to humans. Everyone should start his or her economic life with a common endowment. If an individual has an enormous amount of initial wealth from bequests, he or she has an advantageous starting line. If an individual has no initial wealth, he or she has an enormously handicap compared with the other individual with the initial wealth. Then again, an individual who is able to receive an enormous bequest may become lazy. This is not good for the individual, or for society as a whole.

The Relationship between Bequests and Ability

The delicate problem in proposing a higher bequest tax rate to ensure equality of opportunity is that where the native ability of an individual is the bequest. In life it is often the more capable individuals who receive higher earnings, while less capable individuals receive lower earnings. There are, of course, different kinds of individual abilities: the usual among these are academic, physical, mental, entrepreneurial, and artistic abilities. Some of these abilities predispose the individual to higher income circumstances. They may become professional sports players, artists, musicians, or business executives, all of whom earn very high incomes. Some people may say that the talented individuals are very lucky because they inherited their marketable talents and abilities from their parents. If a higher bequest tax were to become a norm in society, it should be possible to levy a high tax rate on ability potential, as would lead to high income. In other words, taxing bequests in the form of physical assets and/or financial assets, and taxing abilities and capabilities in the form of nontangible assets can be treated analogously because both are inherited from the preceding generation.

By this argument, then, equality of opportunity is not satisfied unless we see capable and talented individuals with the potential to earn a lot taxed more than less capable and less talented individuals not able to earn a lot. Some individuals even talk as if they inherited their talents from their parents as if these talents were bequests. So a higher tax rate on high capability could be justified so long as a higher tax rate is levied on all bequests. Of course, there are those few individuals who talk as if a capable individual is just "lucky," meaning that a superior capability is due to a gift from God. In that case is it possible to tax the individual for a decision made by God? A high tax rate is then not likely to be justified.

I do not have any precise answers to the delicate issue of whether or not ability or talent should be taxed like a bequest tax on intergenerational tangible wealth transfers. This is because it is almost impossible to identify whether ability or talent is an inherited good. I am hesitant to say whether an extremely capable and talented individual who earns an exorbitant income should have only a very high income tax levied on his or her income. There is some unfairness in a system where there is zero tax rate levied on ability or talent but a positive tax rate on tangible bequests. Consequently it does make sense that some tax rate should be levied on ability or talent. In the real world such a tax on ability is transformed into an income tax on a high income, which is due to higher ability or talent. In other words, because it is difficult to levy a tax on the intangible asset of ability or talent directly, the society levies a tax on tangible income indirectly.

Economists pay attention to academic ability as defined by IQ and mathematical skill in identifying the effects of native ability on earnings differentials. One good reason is that data on these variables are available, whereas it is hard to measure other native abilities such as artistic, physical, and entrepreneurial skills. Even if data on these latter abilities were available, it would not be easy to isolate their actual effects on earnings. The same can really be said for the effect of native academic ability on earnings, but economists and statisticians have found a way to study the effect of IQ on earnings differentials by using cases of twins, who are presumed to have the same native abilities, separated by adoption and reared in different family environments and with different education. The results, at least for US twins, indicate that overall an individual's IQ has relatively minor, and even negligible, impact in the determination of earnings (see Taulman 1975 and Griliches 1977). There are no such studies of native academic ability in Japan. Consequently it is not possible to relate any scientific results on native ability and earnings differentials in Japan.

I'd like to add nevertheless that academic ability, namely IQ, is being given too much emphasis. My feeling is that physical, artistic, and entrepreneurial abilities are better determinants of earnings differentials; there may be even something said for attractive physical appearance, that is, the role of beautiful face and body in earnings differentials, as has been attempted recently. Unfortunately, we do not have enough solid information accumulated on these effects.

In sum, except for the case of a measured IQ, it is not possible to make any definitive statement on the ways various native abilities have made a difference in an individual's earnings. Further, although native academic ability is important for success in school, and in particular, in Japan for attending a prestigious university, we do not know its effect on earnings differentials well enough. These questions suggest that it is too early to make any policy recommendations on taxing inherited native abilities.

Social Security Reforms
There are different ways that social security or social insurance systems work. The representative examples are old-age pension, medical care, poverty relief, unemployment compensation, and child benefits. Some benefits are financed by social insurance, and thus by social insurance contributions, and some others are financed by taxes. There are some systems that are financed by both social security contributions and tax revenue. To argue each system separately and in depth would mean to go beyond the scope of this book. Interested readers can refer to Tachibanaki (2002, 2003b). Here we will be concerned only with the general features associated with income redistribution.

First, social security benefits are intended mainly to compensate for chance events affecting employment. Medical insurance exists for the ill and bedridden, and unemployment insurance for the jobless. In contrast, the public pension exists for the aged, who usually retire at a predicted time. In general, the principal idea behind social security is to ensure that individuals or groups of individuals that suffer loss of wages from some chance event receive income support. This is similar to the car insurance and hazard insurance sold by private insurance companies. Public authorities, of course, administer the social security and social insurance systems.

Because social security benefits are doled out by the public sector, some people believe that this is income redistribution. However, technically social security was instituted as nothing more than a safety net for people in uncertain circumstances. It is not a system that was intended to redistribute income from the rich to the poor or from younger to older generations.

Nevertheless, income redistribution does occur from the rich to the poor and from the younger to the older generations whenever income uncertainties occur within the population. The following example should illustrate this more precisely. Say that there are two individuals A and B. Individual A survives until the age of 100, while individual B dies at the age of 61. Therefore an enormous amount of income is transferred from individual B to individual A. This is not only due to the death age differences between individuals A and B but also to what was intended by the public pension system a priori. This is the most common system of income redistribution, and many people find it to be a just system.

Tax systems are not associated with any uncertainty. Thus no unpredictable event can cause a redistribution of income as in the social security system. Nevertheless, there are ways that tax policies have a function of income redistribution. So it is possible to set up income redistribution through tax policy.

As we saw in chapters 1 and 3, in Japan, despite the appropriateness of taxation for income redistribution, social security has been increasingly thrust in this role. As I noted above, in allowing government to adopt this role, we are disregarding the two basic concepts that led to the creation of social security: support in times of uncertainty and the insurance against hazard inherent in the system.

Here the national minimum, or civil minimum, is an important principle that should be regarded for social security systems. It says that all individuals have a human right to a minimum level to a decent living standard. No one should be below the national minimum, and the social security system should be organized to satisfy this condition. Public sectors are expected to set up their social security systems to maintain the agreed-upon living standard.

In this regard some social security systems can conceivably initiate income redistribution policies. However, they are limited to such programs as unemployment insurance and poverty relief. Unemployment compensation is for able people with zero wages, and poverty relief is for helpless people whose incomes are below the certain level due to various reasons, including illness, mental and physical handicaps, and widowed women with very young children. In both cases the social security system is designed to give economic support to the most unfortunate in a population. In this sense, strong income support or strong income redistribution is accepted as a sound goal.

There are some officials who have called for the privatization of the public pension system and public health insurance system in order to enhance the productivity and efficiency of these systems. They regard the public sector as being inefficient in managing such systems. It is true that the private sector is often more efficient than the public sector in economic activities. However, in my view, welfare provisions must continue to be managed by the public sector, partly because there will always be some individuals whose welfare service levels fall below the national minimum under private sector management and partly because private sectors tend to seek the highest returns to their economic programs. The very high returns that the private sector hopes to seek do not seem to be possible for the welfare provisions of pension, health care, and unemployment compensation. This is not to say that the public sector can ignore economic efficiency in managing welfare provisions. It is in fact desirable for the public sector to raise its management efficiency in dealing with welfare provisions.

Last is a reform that should be made in the welfare programs of firms. I believe that the provision of welfare is a duty of government. Welfare provision is implicit in the contract between the individual citizen and government. In the past Japanese firms took charge of the welfare provisions for their employees. Today many firms still finance welfare programs for their employees, as we saw in chapter 3, but there is change in industrial relations that has affected the relationship between employer and employees. I believe that it is no longer necessary for firms to take responsibility for welfare provisions to their employees; they would do better to concentrate on business profits and on maintaining reasonable employment levels (see Tachibanaki 2003a and 2005 for a discussion of Japanese firms' welfare programs).

Below are some suggestions for different policy reforms to the various components of the social security system. These are based on the principles noted above. For more detail, the interested readers can refer to Tachibanaki (2000, 2002, 2003b).

Public Pension   Currently there are two parts to the public pension program. One is a basic to all individuals. The sum paid to individuals who contributed fully over their economic lives is about 65,000 yen per month; it is smaller for those who had shorter economic lives. One-third of this amount comes from tax revenues, and the rest from social security contributions. The other part is paid out proportionally and is financed by a pay-as-you-go scheme and defined by a benefit formula.

In my opinion, the public sector should administer only the basic part of the public pension. Further the monthly payments should be increased to about 170,000 yen for a couple and 90,000 yen for a single person, and these increases should be financed by progressive consumption taxes. This can be done if, as my simulations show, the tax rate is raised to 15 percent from the current 5 percent rate. The other, proportional part could be privatized or modified to a funded scheme with a defined contribution formula.

The main impetus for this suggestion is that the universal payment scheme, which is supposed to support all retired people at a minimum living standard, should reflect the national or civil minimum standard. Tax revenues are more appropriate than social security contributions for subsistence payments to citizens. The very serious size of the aging population in today's Japan has led the young population to object to paying social security contributions because they are fearful of the very low reserve left by the time they are ready to retire. The expected huge deficit in the public pension system has put the social insurance system in a crisis. The only way to extend the reserve fund for future retirees appears to be by higher taxation. In the privatized part of the current public pension scheme might be expected to grow through the merit of the market mechanism and the investment choices of the participants. Thus a private fund with defined contributions would be desirable for this type of pension.

Health Care   The medical insurance system is burdened by a large number of different medical insurance programs. The system categorizes participants by age (retired, or working), occupation (employee, or self-employed), employer (public or private), employer's size, and so forth. The benefits and contributions so differ among the many programs that some people get good medical treatments and others do not. Also costs of the medical programs vary considerably. In my view, all the various health care programs could be integrated into one universal medical insurance system. The national health services in the United Kingdom is the model I am looking for, and the basic financing source for such an integrated system is tax revenues rather than health insurance premiums. Thus it could be set up the same way as I described the public pension program above, with an additional fund for medical care relating to chronic diseases.

I recognize that universal health care is not easy to implement for two reasons. First, if different programs are combined, many attractive features that make some programs more desirable than others will be compromised, so many people will be reluctant to accept the reform. There are nevertheless some people who will benefit from such integrated health care. Second, it is not easy to define what is minimum medical care. While it may not be difficult for an economist to define the minimum level of income for retired people, such as the 170,000 yen per month for a couple suggested above, which is based on consumption and expenditure data, the feasible minimum expenditure on medical care calls for a joint effort of medical doctors and economists.

Unemployment Compensation   The unemployment insurance system has been left relatively untouched since the 1950s because of the very low unemployment rate in Japan. Recently unemployment did jump to about 5 percent. So there is today a sizable population of the unemployed with very low incomes. It is time to consider serious reform to the system in order to improve the safety net for the unemployed. I will focus on some ways to make improvements, but these are only a few out of many possible reforms to the unemployment insurance system.

First, a large number of employees are excluded from unemployment compensation because they were employed part-time (less than twenty working hours a week), had less than one-year contracts, and were employed in extremely small firms, and were civil servants and thus did not participate in the system. Statistics show that about half of the employed population of Japan does not belong to the unemployment insurance system. Clearly, it is important to enlarge the reach of membership.

Second, both the duration of benefit payments and the amount are considerably less generous compared with European nations. The government, people, and economists worry about the moral hazard problem, in the sense that the unemployed might lose incentive to search for jobs if the system is more generous. This is not likely because the Japanese system was too far from generous to approach moral hazard. I do not say that unemployment compensation should be very generous, but that it should be close to that of most European countries. The level should be just short of encouraging moral hazard.

Third, both employers and employees need to recognize that an increase in unemployment insurance premiums is unavoidable to ensure a sufficient economic safety net for the unemployed.

Poverty Relief   Poverty relief is the ultimate reserve for people who suffer from serious illnesses or who have no possibility of employment because of mental and/or physical handicaps. The poverty relief system in Japan is, however, the most difficult program in the social security system for individuals to access despite its definitive function to provide financial means to extremely troubled individuals. Why is this so? First, by law, families and relatives are supposed to help the unfortunate among them before the poverty relief program is considered and applied for. Second, there is a stringent means test that is too indifferent in the screening of applicants. Third, most needy people are ashamed to apply because there is stigma to receiving poverty relief in Japan.

These are three explanations why, despite the large majority of people in Japan with falling living standards due to unemployment and old age, only about 10 percent of the population collects poverty relief, and this is at a far lower rate than in other advanced countries. Because since the 1950s there has been no major reform in the poverty relief program, the time is now to take the initiative and make the reforms, instead of just contemplating about doing so.

6.3   Policy Reforms in Education and Enterprises

Equality of Opportunity in Education

In chapter 2 we saw that educational opportunity in Japan was unequal before the Second World War, and continued to be unequal until the period of rapid economic growth. Only sons of fairly rich households could receive higher education. Sons of poor households as well as nearly all daughters were excluded from higher education. The rapid economic growth that ensued in the late 1950s and the subsequent stable economy greatly raised household incomes, and sons and daughters were able to attend junior colleges and four-year universities. Currently, about 50 percent of 18-year-olds go to college, and over 90 percent of 15-year-olds go to senior high schools. Consequently it is not an exaggeration to say that family backgrounds or economic conditions are no longer barriers to the education of their young, although some financial barriers exist for a small number of youths.

For these financially strapped students Japan still lacks fellowship programs that are comparable to those in Europe, where in addition most universities do not charge tuition, and North America, where in addition there a flourishing government loan program. Much effort is thus needed in Japan to achieve equality of opportunity in higher education. In my view, a government loan program is preferable to a stipend program because some financial responsibility is demanded of the beneficiary students, who are bound to recover the costs of higher education through economic gains made after entering the workforce.

In the more sensitive area of equality of opportunity in higher education is the number of prestigious universities that are the source of bright future careers, as was described in chapters 4 and 5. As was noted, the students able to pass the entrance examinations for these universities come from well-to-do families. Although a student's intelligence and diligence are crucial for these examinations, a number of studies show that only the children from upper-income households are able to pass the difficult entrance examinations (e.g., see Kariya 1995, 2001; Takeuchi 1995). It is thought that students of these households have better opportunity to prepare for the examinations because they attend preparatory high schools that succeed in sending many students to these universities. To qualify for entering these preparatory high schools, these households enroll their children tutorial sessions at special private night schools and/or Saturday or Sunday schools. Because it costs more money to go to preparatory high schools, or to attend the special tutorial schools, only upper-income families can afford send their children to these schools. This is Japanese-style replication of social rank through education, which is considerably similar in spirit to the finding by the Coleman Report (1996) for the United States, and that by Bourdieu (1979) for France.

Besides the economic conditions of households there is a so-called incentive divide proposed by Kariya (2001) that should not be ignored. That is, pupils from upper-income households are encouraged to keep on learning, and they are provided with many incentives to learn in their playtime activities. Everyday life within upper-income families is planned to be conducive toward their children's learning and diligent study. This environment builds a child's self-esteem and fills the child with aspiration for attending the prestigious schools and universities. The self-esteem and a sense of accomplishment promoted in the upper-income environment are important incentives in educational psychology.

The other extreme is the children of lower-income households. These children lack in self-esteem at school, and tend to deny any success at school because their parents are not very interested in their children's school life or academic achievements. The immediate response of the children is to have fun and not to think about any future plans. Thus they do not put in the necessary effort to do well in school. This is the attitude also found among the UK working classes as shown, for example, by Willis (1977).

The divide in the incentive toward learning between the two income groups may be more serious than the actual economic conditions in the inequality of opportunity attributed to prestigious academic credentials. Economists can offer numerous ideas about financial help to lower income students such as fellowship systems, loan systems, and voucher systems in order to support equality of opportunity in education. It is, however, difficult if not impossible for any of these ideas to reduce the incentive divide between the different income groups. For effective policy suggestions we need the assistance of educational psychologists on this incentive divide.

Finally, briefly, there are three policy reforms in education that, I think, may help reduce the significance of academic credentialism, since it is the entrance examinations' competition that eventually results in the severe discrimination university graduates encounter in employment opportunities. First, the most important reform, which will be argued again below, is to eliminate the screening by name of university in hiring practices. Second, the screening of candidates should be shifted instead to academic achievement. In other words, attention should be paid to what was studied at the university instead of what university the candidate graduated from. Third, universities should use other criteria than the entrance examination in selecting their students from among many applicants. Fourth, students should have the flexibility to transfer from one university to another.

Reforms in Firms and Public Offices

Equality of opportunity should be the aim of employers in both the public and private sectors. The following proposals are fairly brief because they reflect the recommendations on removing wide wage differentials that have been discussed at length throughout this book.

First and foremost, employers are urged to do their best in disregarding both years of schooling and college and university names when they screen candidates for employment and when these employees seek promotions. This is a basic first step in attempting equality of opportunity. Although educational achievements and school and college reputations do provide useful information for entry-level jobs, and thus cannot be entirely overlooked, once an applicant is hired, it is better to erase these credentials from the employee's career qualifications. The only criteria that count should be ability, diligence, contribution, and productivity in achieving job assignments. These are the qualities that must be used in job allocations and promotions to higher positions within any organization. It is a merit system for the work place, and it also benefits the organization by raising the productivity average.

Second, it is necessary to prepare a fair performance assessment program for each employee. If the performance assessment is perceived to be unfair and fallacious by most employees, it will lower the work incentive and, worse, compel work sabotage. Productivity will decline in any case.

Third, the seniority system in the determination of wages and promotions must be changed, as discussed in chapter 3. A strong merit system as is recommended above, of course, can displace the seniority system. Thus this reform is likely to be the result of the other and to affect the distribution of wages. By the seniority system, younger workers receive lower wages; by the merit system, these workers can aspire to raise their wages and thus their living standards by their performance and productivity. The merit system can work in this way to reduce the wage differentials between younger and older workers.

Of course, the differences in performance and productivity could increase the wage differentials in a strict application of the merit system, where those that do not perform well are not rewarded. This is the dilemma in replacing wage inequality due to seniority by wage inequality due to merit. In my view, a merit system has more positive results than a seniority system despite any increase of wage inequality. A merit system has the potential for raising efficiency in the work place.

Fourth, most industries should be deregulated. Regulated industries must pay wages to employees who oversee compliance with regulations. Such regulation-rents cannot be justified in productivity terms and should be eliminated. Deregulation enables both public and private firms to be more competitive. The more successful firms can then pay higher wages, and this is a fair outcome as long as the competition is fair. In sum, I see the wide wage differentials due to fair competition among businesses as preferable to regulation-rents.

Fifth, in chapter 3 we saw that the wage differentials by firm size have been increasing. This is in part a natural outcome of large firms being more productive than small firms in general. Thus it is not easy to alter the balance unless some strong anti-free-market forces are institutes such as subsidies to or favorable tax treatment of small firms. Of course, these policies are not desirable in a free market economy. So we have to expect small firms to commit to other instruments such as concentrating on a few attractive products, investing in innovative products, and introducing cost-saving technologies. Case studies show this formula to have worked for a number of successful small businesses, and these businesses have consistently paid higher wages to their employees.

Sixth, wage differentials between men and women must be eliminated. There are two ways to do this. The first is legally, to enforce law that prohibits discrimination against women in hiring, wages, share of work, promotion, and so forth. The Japanese society does not recognize the seriousness of the gender discrimination problem, and likely only legal measures will rid the work place of discrimination against women. The second is to require men to freely surrender male privileges, including higher wages, to women. In the same spirit, the transfer or sharing of work by full-timers and part-timers can be considered as it applies to discrimination of mostly women part-timers; in this case such advantageous treatment of part-timers may not be feasible if it is left entirely to male willingness to make the change. Unfortunately, men are often reluctant to share their economic rents with women. So in some businesses it may take a decade or more for all such changes to be made. Nevertheless, the elimination of wage differentials between men and women should be a priority.

Summary

The various policy recommendations presented in this chapter require trade-offs between efficiency and equity, and thought about the ethics that justify making such reforms. Changes to tax and social security programs, education, business practices, market, and so forth, are thus all offered in the spirit of efficiency, equity, and human decency. We saw that policy reform that aims at rewards and work incentives can increase wage inequalities but create more economic efficiency as a result. By contrast, the criterion of equity is given more importance in evaluating income and wealth distributions. Equality of outcome should be the aim of reforms to taxation of income and wealth, and value judgments are necessary to determine the extent to which society should strive to equalize income distribution. Again, in my view, a more equal distribution is preferable because Japan has gone too far in the direction of inequality, but it is up to the democratic majority to move society in this direction.

7   Concluding Remarks

Japan is no longer an equal country. The income inequality in Japan is noticeable everywhere in the inequality of outcome (or consequence). If we look closely, we see that the inequality in Japan is even moving to higher inequality. In this book we saw that the unequal income distribution in Japan is due to a historic change and that it is high internationally. The same is true in Japan for the inequality in wealth distribution, although the gap is not as serious as that in income distribution. The evidence therefore contradicts the strong belief both in Japan and internationally that Japanese society is an equality-oriented society. It is necessary to discard this myth.

Over the past one hundred years, both income and wealth distributions changed remarkably in Japan. Historically after the Meiji Restoration Japan was a very unequal country in both its social and economic structures until the Second World War. The social and economic reforms after the war helped modernize and democratize Japan, and to develop in the Japanese people an equality-oriented consciousness.

However, we also saw how recently income distribution has come to move toward high inequality. Over the last two decades the gradual modest increases in wage inequalities, the aging trend, the increase in single member households, the increase in the number of income earners within a household, the increase in imputed rents, the increase in nonwage incomes for wealth holders, the weak influences of tax and social security income redistribution policies, have all combined to produce the high inequality in Japan. A plausible way to conceive of an end to the income inequality problem is by applying the cubic-curve hypothesis.

The attention to wage distribution is by factors such as gender, age, job tenure, education, and size of firm. We saw that some factors work to increase total wage inequality and other factors decrease wage inequality. A similar examination was made of wealth distribution. The bubble economy of the late 1980s was discussed in regard to spreading wealth inequality, as were intergenerational wealth transfers, in the form of bequests.

We considered two subjects at length: the balance between equality of opportunity and equality (or inequality) of outcome (or consequence), and the balance between economic efficiency and equity. The discussions of the principle of equality of opportunity and the economics of efficiency and equity ranged to concepts from ethics, philosophy, political science, and sociology.

The conclusion we drew suggests that equality of opportunity is endangered in Japan. In some areas equality of opportunity has yet to be observed such as in the treatment of women in the workforce, in intergenerational wealth transfers, and in the educational and occupational attainments of children from low-income households. In effect, in recent times the many favorable social and economic reforms adopted after the Second World War have reached a state of regression. To revert the trend toward inequality of opportunity, Japan needs to adopt strong measures and policies.

Equality of outcome, however, is a delicate and sensitive issue because just about everyone cannot escape from making value judgments. Some people prefer a highly equal distribution of income and wealth, whereas some other people do not care about a highly unequal distribution of income and wealth. Economic efficiency is an important factor in this dispute, and it offers some information on which choice is better between the two alternatives: equal distribution and unequal distribution. One way to solve this issue is by a trade-off between efficiency and equity. However, at least in Japan, there is no need to worry about the consequence of loss of efficiency because so far there is no sign of such a trade-off being considered. In other words, Japan could adopt an economic program through both tax and social security policies that aims at achieving more equality of outcome in income and wealth distribution, but no such attempt has been undertaken because of the possible loss of economic efficiency.

One sure way to equalize the spread of income and wealth is for Japan to become a welfare state. Like the United States, Japan has never been a welfare state. A welfare state, however, presents many disadvantages as well as advantages. Nevertheless, Japan is at risk of moving in the direction of a welfare state willingly or unwillingly if it does not act now to avert the growing impoverishment of its people. Therefore, alternatively, there are the policy suggestions made in this book that might work to strengthen the Japanese economy today. These are the introduction of a progressive value-added tax or a progressive expenditure tax, deregulation of the industries, and reforms in the industrial relations systems.

In sum, the time is now to stop the ever-higher increases in inequality in Japan. Because the inequalities are largely in the areas of unreasonable and unjustified gains, policy changes can still be undertaken without compromising economic efficiency. The critical changes are those recommended in this book.

References

Aaberge, A. et al. 2002. Income inequality and income mobility in the Scandinavian countries compared to the United States. *Review of Income and Wealth* 48: 443–71.

Acemoglu, D. 1997. Matching, heterogeneity, and the evolution of income distribution. *Journal of Economic Growth* 2: 61–92.

Aghion, P., and P. Bolton. 1992. Distribution and growth in models of imperfect capital markets. *European Economic Review* 36: 603–11.

Aghion, P., and P. Howitt. 1998. *Endogenous Growth Theory*. Cambridge: MIT Press.

Ahlwalia, M. S. 1976. Inequality, Poverty and Development. *Journal of Economic Development* 3: 307–42.

Anand, S., and R. Kanbur. 1993a. The Kuznets process and the inequality-development relationship. *Journal of Development Economics* 40: 25–52.

Anand, S., and R. Kanbur. 1993b. Inequality and development: A critique. *Journal of Development Economics* 41: 19–43.

Arrow, K. J. 1973. Higher education as a filter. *Journal of Public Economics* 2: 193–216.

Asano, S., and T. Tachibanaki. 1992. Testing constancy of relative risk aversion: An analysis of the Japanese household financial data. *Journal of the Japanese and International Economies* 6: 52–70.

Asano, S., and T. Tachibanaki. 1994. Relative risk aversion once more: An analysis of Japanese households' financial asset holding pattern. *Finanacial Engineering and the Japanese Markets* 1: 137–54.

Atkinson, A. B. 1995. *Incomes and the Welfare State*. Cambridge: Cambridge University Press.

Atkinson, A. B. 1997. Bringing income distribution in from the cold. *Economic Journal* 107: 297–321.

Atoda, N., and T. Tachibanaki. 1985. Decomposition of income inequality by income sources. *Quarterly of Social Security Research* 20: 330–41 (in Japanese).

Atoda, N., and T. Tachibanaki. 2001. Optimal nonlinear income taxation and heterogenous preferences. *Japanese Economic Review* 52: 198–207.

Banerjee, A., and A. Newman. 1993. Occupational choice and the process of development. *Journal of Political Economy* 101: 211–35.

Benabou, R. 1996a. Inequality and growth. In B. S. Bernanke and J. Rotemberg, eds., *NBER Macroeconomics Annual 11*. Cambridge: MIT Press.

Benabou, R. 1996b. Heterogeneity, stratification, and growth: Macroeconomic implications of community structure and school finance. *American Economic Review* 86: 584–609.

Blau, F. D., and L. M. Kahn. 2000. Gender differences in pay. *Journal of Economic Perspective* 14: 75–100.

Blau, P. M., and O. D. Duncan. 1967. *The American Occupational Structure*. New York: Wiley.

Bourdieu, P. 1979. *La Distinction: Critique Sociale du Judgement*. Paris: Éditions de Minuit.

Bourdieu, P., and J.-C. Passeron. 1970. *La Reproduction: Éléments pour une Theorie du Systéme d' Enseignement*. Paris: Éditions de Minuit.

Bourguignon, F. 1990. Growth and inequality in the dual model of development: The role of demand factors. *Review of Economic Studies* 57: 215–28.

Bowles, S., and H. Gintis. 1976. *Schooling in Capitalist America*. New York: Basic Books.

Brown, C., and J. Medoff. 1989. The employer size-wage effect. *Journal of Political Economy* 97: 1027–59.

Cohen, G. A. 1995. *Self-ownership, Freedom, and Equality*. Cambridge: Cambridge University Press.

Cohen, D., T. Piketty, and G. Saint-Paul. 2002. *The Economics of Rising Inequalities*. Oxford: Oxford University Press.

De Janury, A., and E. Sadoulet. 1983. Social articulation as a condition for equitable growth. *Journal of Development Economics* 13: 275–303.

Deere, D. R. 2001. Trends in wage inequality in the United States. In F. Welch, ed., *The Causes and Consequences of Increasing Inequality*. Chicago: University of Chicago Press, pp. 9–36.

Doyle, C. 1996. The distributional consequences during the early stages of Russian's transition. *Review of Income and Wealth* 42: 493–506.

Esping-Andersen, G. 1990. *The Three Worlds of Welfare Capitalism*. London: Polity Press.

Eswarm, M., and A. Kotwal. 1993. A theory of real wage growth in LDC. *Journal of Development Economics* 42: 243–69.

Featherman, D. L., R. M. Hauser, and F. L. Jones. 1975. Assumption of social mobility research in the U.S.: The case of occupational status. *Social Science Research* 4: 329–60.

Förster, M., and M. Pearson. 2002. Income distribution and poverty in the OECD area: Trends and driving forces. *OECD Economic Studies* (34): 7–39.

Fortin, N. M., and T. Lemieux. 1997. Institutional changes and rising wage inequality: Is there a linkage? *Journal of Economic Perspectives* 11: 75–96.

Freeman, R., B. Swedenborg, and R. H. Topel, eds. 1998. *The Welfare State in Transition*. Chicago: University of Chicago Press.

Friedman, M. 1962. *Capitalism and Freedom*. Chicago: University of Chicago Press.

Galor, O., and J. Zeira. 1993. Income distribution and macroeconomics. *Review of Economic Studies* 60: 35–52.

Genda, Y. 1998. Japan: Wage differentials and changes since the 1980s. In T. Tachibanaki, ed., *Wage Differentials: An International Comparison*. London: Macmillan Press, pp. 35–71.

Glomm, G., and B. Ravikumar. 1992. Public versus private investment in human capital: Endogenous growth and income inequality. *Journal of Political Economy* 100: 818–34.

Goldin, C., and L. F. Katz. 2001. Decreasing (and then increasing) inequality in America: A tale of two half-centuries. In F. Welch, ed., *The Causes and Consequences of Increasing Inequality*. Chicago: University of Chicago Press, pp. 36–82.

Gottschalk, P. 1997. Inequality, income growth, and mobility: The basic facts. *Journal of Economic Perspectives* 11: 21–40.

Gottschalk, P., and T. M. Smeeding. 1997. Cross-national comparisons of earnings and income inequality. *Journal of Economic Literature* 35: 633–81.

Gottschalk, P., B. Gustafsson, and E. Palmer, eds. 1997. *Changing Patterns in the Distribution of Economic Welfare*. Cambridge: Cambridge University Press.

Griliches, Z. 1977. Estimating the returns to schooling: Some econometric problems. *Econometrica* 45: 1–22.

Grusky, D. B. 1983. Industrialization and the status attainment process: The thesis of industrialism reconsidered. *American Sociological Journal* 48: 494–606.

Hadley, E. M. 1970. *Antitrust in Japan*. Princeton: Princeton University Press.

Hara, J., and K. Seiyama. 1999. *Social Stratification: Inequality in Affluent Society*. Tokyo: University of Tokyo Press (in Japanese).

Hare, R. M. 1989. Rawls' theory of justice. In N. Daniels, ed., *Reading Rawls: Critical Studies on Rawls' "A Theory of Justice."* Stanford: Stanford University Press.

Harrison, B., and B. Blueston. 1988. *The Grate U-Turn: Corporate Restructuring and the Polarizing of America*. New York: Basic Books.

Harsanyi, J. C. 1975. Can the maximin principle serve as a basic for morality? A critique of John Rawls's theory. *American Political Science Review* 69 (2): 594–606.

Hayashi, F. 1997. *Understanding Saving: Evidence from the United State and Japan*. Cambridge: MIT Press.

Hayek, F. A. 1960. *The Constitution of Liberty*. London and Chicago: Routledge and Kegan Paul, and University of Chicago Press.

Herrnstein, R. J., and C. Murray. 1994. *The Bell Curve*. New York: Free Press.

Horioka, C. Y. 1996. Economics of savings, bequests and inheritances. In N. Takayama, C. Y. Horioka, and K. Ohta, eds., *Savings, Bequests and Inheritances in Aging Society*. Tokyo: Nihon-hyoronsha, pp. 2–8.

Hutton, W. 1996. *The State We Are In*, rev. ed. London: Vintage.

Idson, T. L., and D. J. Feaster. 1990. A selectivity model of employer-size wage differentials. *Journal of Labor Economics* 8: 99–122.

Ishi, H. 1993. *The Japanese Tax System*. Oxford: Clarendon Press.

Ishida, H. 2002. State of differentials based on social mobility. In H. Miyajima, ed., *Income Distribution and Difference*. Tokyo: Toyo-keizai-shinposha, pp. 65–100 (in Japanese).

Itaba, Y., and T. Tachibanaki. 1987. Measurement of tax progressivity when the forms of both income distribution and tax functions are given. *Economie Studies Quarterly* 38: 97–108.

Jacobi, S. M. 1997. *Modern Manors: Welfare Capitalism since the New Deal*. Princeton: Princeton University Press.

Jencks, C. 1972. *Inequality*. New York: Basic Books.

Jensen, A. R. 1969. How much can we boost IQ and scholastic achievement. *Harvard Educational Review* 39: 1–123.

Johnson, G. E. 1997. Changes in earnings inequality: The role of demand shifts. *Journal of Economic Perspectives* 11: 41–54.

Kaldor, N. 1955. *An Expenditure Tax*. London: Allen and Unwin.

Kalsay, J. 1997. *The New Zealand Experiment: A World Model for Structual Adjustment*, new ed. Aukland: Aukland University Press.

Kanomata, N. 2001. *Inequality of Both Opportunity and Outcome*. Kyoto: Minerva Press (in Japanese).

Kariya, T. 1995. *Future Course of Mass Education*. Tokyo: Chuokoronshinsha (in Japanese).

Kariya, T. 2001. *Class Society in Japan and Education Crisis*. Tokyo: Yushindo (in Japanese).

Kasters, M. H. 2001. Government policy and wage inequality: Regulation, incentives, and opportunities. In F. Welch, ed., *The Causes and Consequences of Increasing Inequality*. Chicago: University of Chicago Press, pp. 201–40.

Katz, L. R., and K. M. Murphy. 1992. Changes in relative wages, 1963–1984: Supply and demand factors. *Quarterly Journal of Economics* 107: 35–78.

Kawaguchi, A. 1997. Economic theory of male-female wage differentials. In H. Chuma and T. Suruga, eds., *Changing Employment Practices and Female Labor Force*. Tokyo: University of Tokyo Press, pp. 207–42 (in Japanese).

Klasen, S. 1994. Growth and well-being: Introducing distribution weighted growth rates to reevaluated U.S. post-war economic performance. *Review of Income and Wealth* 40: 99, 251–72.

Kosai, Y. 1983. *The Period of Economic Growth*. Tokyo: Nihon-hyoronsha (in Japanese).

Kotlikoff, L. H., and L. H. Summers. 1988. Intergenerational transfers and savings. *Journal of Economic Perspectives* 2: 41–59.

Kotlikoff, L. J., and L. H. Summers. 1981. The role of intergenerational transfers in aggregate capital accumulation. *Journal of Political Economy* 90: 706–32.

Kuznets, S. 1955. Economic growth and income inequality. *American Economic Review* 45: 1–28.

Levy, F., and R. J. Murnane. 1992. U.S. earnings levels and earnings inequality: Review of recent trends and proposed explanations. *Journal of Economic Literature* 30: 1333–81.

Lipset, S. 1996. *American Exceptionalism*. New York: Norton.

Lipset, S., and G. Markets. 2000. *It Didn't Happen Here: Why Socialism Failed in the United States*. New York: Norton.

Lipset, S. M., and H. Zetterberg. 1959. Social mobility in industrial societies. In S. M. Lipset and R. Bendix, eds., *Social Mobility in Industrial Society*. Berkeley: University of California Press, pp. 11–76.

Lucas, R. E. 1988. On the mechanics of economic development. *Journal of Monetary Economics* 22: 3–42.

Luttwak, E. 1999. *Turbo-Capiralism: Winners and Losers in the Global Economy*. New York: Harper Collins.

Maki, A. 1998. *Consumption Behavior of Japanese People*. Tokyo: Chikuma-shinsho (in Japanese).

Minami, S., and A. Ono. 1987. Income distribution in pre-war Japan. *Economic Review* 38: 333–52 (in Japanese).

Mirrlees, J. A. 1971. An exploration in the theory of optimum income taxation. *Review of Economic Studies* 38 (2): 175–208.

Mizoguchi, T. 1986. Long-run fluctuations in income distribution in Japan. *Economic Review* 37: 152–58 (in Japanese).

Mizoguchi, T., and Y. Matsuda, eds. 1997. *Analysis on Income Distribution and Poverty in Asia*. Tokyo: Taga-shuppan (in Japanese).

Mizoguchi, T., N. Takayama, and T. Terasaki. 1978. Income distribution in post-war Japan. *Economic Review* 37: 44–60 (in Japanese).

Modigliani, F. 1988. The role of intergenerational transfers and life cycle savings in accumulation of wealth. *Journal of Economic Perspectives* 2: 15–40.

Muramatsu, M., and M. Okuno, eds. 2002. *A Study of the Heisei Bubble*. Tokyo: Toyo-keizai-shinposha (in Japanese).

Murphy, K. M., A. Shleifer, and R. Vishny. 1989. Income distribution, market size, and industrialization. *Quarterly Journal of Economics* 104: 537–68.

Nakamura, R. 1978. *Japanese Economy*. Tokyo: University of Tokyo Press (in Japanese).

Nakata, Y. 1997. Factors which explain male-female wages differentials in Japan. In H. Chuma and T. Suruga, eds., *Changing Employment Practices and Female Labor Force*. Tokyo: University of Tokyo Press, pp. 173–99 (in Japanese).

Nishizaki, B., Y. Yamada, and E. Ando. 1998. *Income Differentials in Japan*. Tokyo: Economic Planning Agency Report (in Japanese).

Nozick, R. 1974. *Anarchy, State and Utopia*. New York: Basic Books.

Ogwang, T. 1994. Economic development and income inequality: A non-parametric investigation of Kuznets' U-curve hypothesis. *Journal of Quantitative Economics* 10: 139–53.

Okun, A. M. 1975. *Equality and Efficiency: The Big Trade-Off*. Washington, DC: Brookings Institution.

Ohtake, F. 1991. Bequest motives of aged households in Japan. *Richerche Economiche* 45: 283–306.

Ohtsuki, T., and N. Takamatsu. 1982. On the measurement and trend of income inequality in pre-war Japan. *Papers and Proceedings of the Conference on Japan Historical Development Experience and the Contemporary Developing Countries.* Tokyo: International Development Center of Japan.

Okazaki, T., and M. Okuno, eds. 1993. *Historical Origins of the Modern Japanese Economic Systems.* Tokyo: Nihon-keizai-Shinbunsha (in Japanese).

Oxley, H., J. M. Burniaux, T. T. Dang, and M. Mira D'Ercole. 1999. Income distribution and poverty in 13 OECD countries. *OECD Economic Studies* (29): 55–94.

Pazner, E. A., and D. Schmeidler. 1974. A difficulty in the concept of fairness. *Review of Economic Studies* 41 (3): 441–43.

Peracchi, F. 2001. Earnings inequality in international perspective. In F. Welch, ed., *The Causes and Consequences of Increasing Inequality.* Chicago: University of Chicago Press, pp. 117–52.

Perrotti, R. 1993. Political equilibrium, income distribution, and growth. *Review of Economic Studies* 60: 755–76.

Person, T., and G. Tabellini. 1994. Is inequality harmful for growth? *American Economic Review* 84: 600–21.

Psacharopolos et al. 1995. Poverty and income inequality in Latin America during the 1980's. *Review of Income and Wealth* 41: 245–64.

Rawls, J. 1971. *A Theory of Justice.* Cambridge: Harvard University Press.

Rawls, J. 1993. *Political Liberalism.* New York: Columbia University Press.

Rawls, J. 2001. *Justice as Fairness: A Restatement.* Cambridge: Harvard University Press.

Reich, R. B. 2000. *The Future of Success.* New York: Random House.

Roemer, J. E. 1996. *Theories of Disributive Justice.* Cambridge: Harvard University Press.

Roemer, J. E. 1998. *Equality of Opportunity.* Cambridge: Harvard University Press.

Romer, P. M. 1986. Increasing returns and long-run growth. *Journal of Political Economy* 94: 1002–37.

Sandel, M. 1982. *Liberalism and Limits of Justice.* Cambridge: Cambridge University Press.

Sato, H. 2002. *An Unequal Country, Japan.* Tokyo: Chuo-koronshinsha (in Japanese).

Sawyer, M. 1976. Income distribution in OECD countries. *OECD Economic Outlook.* Paris: OECD.

Schor, J. 1991. *The Overworked American.* New York: Basic Books.

Seiyama, K., and M. Naoi. 1990. Class structure in Japan and its changes. In M. Naoi and K. Seiyama, eds., *Social Class and Process.* Tokyo: University of Tokyo Press, pp. 15–50.

Sen, A. 1992. *Inequality Reexamined.* Oxford: Oxford University Press.

Sen, A. 1995. *Commodities and Capabilities.* Amsterdam: North-Holland.

Shimizu, K. 1990. Schooling, marriage and class reproduction. In S. Kikuchi, ed., *Education and Social Mobility.* Tokyo: University of Tokyo Press, pp. 107–26 (in Japanese).

Shirahase, S. 2001. Trends and current states in Japan's income differentials based on international comparison. Internal report. Ministry of Welfare and Labor (in Japanese).

Spence, M. 1973. Job market signaling. *Quarterly Journal of Economics* 87: 355–74.

Tachibanaki, T. 1975. Wage determinations in Japanese manufacturing industries: Structural change and wage differentials. *International Economic Review* 16: 562–86.

Tachibanaki, T. 1980. Education, occupation and earnings: A recursive approach for France. *European Economic Review* 13: 103–27.

Tachibanaki, T. 1982. Further results on Japanese wage differentials: Nenko wages, hierarchical position, bonuses, and working hours. *International Economic Review* 23: 447–61.

Tachibanaki, T. 1987. Labour market flexibility in Japan in comparison with Europe and the U.S. *European Economic Review* 31: 647–84. Reprinted in G. deMenil and R. J. Gordon, eds. *International Volatility and Economic Growth*. Amsterdam: North-Holland, pp. 115–152.

Tachibanaki, T. 1988a. The determination of the promotion process in organizations and the earnings differentials. *Journal of Economic Behavior and Organization* 8: 603–16.

Tachibanaki, T. 1988b. Education, occupation, hierarchy and earnings. *Economics of Education Review* 9: 221–30.

Tachibanaki, T. 1989. Changes in wealth values and inequality in wealth distribution. *Japanese Economic Review* 18: 79–91 (in Japanese).

Tachibanaki, T. 1992. Japanese tax reform: Efficiency versus equity. *Public Finance* 47 (suppl.): 271–88.

Tachibanaki, T. 1996a. *Wage Determination and Distribution in Japan*. Oxford: Oxford University Press.

Tachibanaki, T. 1996b. *Public Policies and the Japanese Economy: Saving, Investment, Unemployment, Inequality*. London: Macmillan Press.

Tachibanaki, T. 1997. *Structure of Promotion*. Tokyo: Toyo-keizai-Shinposha (in Japanese).

Tachibanaki, T., ed. 1998a. *Who Runs Japanese Business?* London: Edward Elgar.

Tachibanaki, T. 1998b. The United Kingdom. In T. Tachibanaki, ed., *Wage Differentials: An international Comparison*. London: Macmillan, pp. 210–38.

Tachibanaki, T. 2000. *Economics of Safety Nets*. Tokyo: Nihon-keizai-shinnbunsha (in Japanese).

Tachibanaki, T. 2000. Japan was not a welfare state, but . . . . In R. T. Griffiths and T. Tachibanaki, eds., *From Austerity to Affluence*. London: Macmillan, pp. 188–208.

Tachibanaki, T. 2002. *Economics of Mind in Safety*. Tokyo: Iwanami-shoten (in Japanese).

Tachibanaki, T. 2003a. The role of firms in welfare provisions. In S. Ogura, T. Tachibanaki, and D. Wise, eds., *Labor Markets and Firm Benefit Policies in Japan and the United States*. Chicago: University of Chicago Press, ch. 12.

Tachibanaki, T. 2003b. Social security reform in Japan in the 21st century. In T. Tachibanaki, ed., *Social Security in Japan*. London: Edward Elgar.

Tachibanaki, T., ed. 2003c. *Examination of the Post-war Japanese Economy*. Tokyo: University of Tokyo Press (in Japanese).

Tachibanaki, T., ed. 2003d. *Social Security in Japan*. London: Edward Elgar.

Tachibanaki, T. 2005. *End of Enterprise Welfare Provisions*. Tokyo: Chuo-koron (in Japanese).

Tachibanaki, T., and T. Mori. 2005. *Who Are the Rich in Japan?* Tokyo: Nihon-keizai-shinbunsha (in Japanese).

Tachibanaki, T., and K. Shimono. 1991. Wealth accumulation process by income class. *Journal of the Japanese and International Economies* 32: 239–60.

Tachibanaki, T., and S. Takata. 1994. Bequests and asset distribution: Human capital investment and intergenerational wealth transfers. In T. Tachibanaki, ed., *Savings and Bequests*. Ann Albor: University of Michigan Press, pp. 197–229.

Tachibanaki, T., and T. Noda. 2000. *The Economic Effects of Trade Unions in Japan*. London: Macmillan.

Tachibanaki, T., and T. Yagi. 1997. Distribution of economic well-being in Japan: Toward a more unequal society. In P. Gottschalk, B. Gustafsson, and E. Palmer, eds., *Changing Patters in the Distribution of Economic Welfare*. Cambridge: Cambridge University Press, pp. 108–32.

Tachibanaki, T., and T. Yagi. 2003. Welfare improvement caused by changes in income distribution, needs, and labor supply. Mimeo.

Taira, K. 1970. *Economic Development and the Labor Market in Japan*. New York: Colombia University Press.

Takayama, T., and F. Arita. 1996. *Savings and Asset Accumulation*. Tokyo: Iwanami-shoten (in Japanese).

Takeuchi, H. 1995. *Meritocracy in Japan*. Tokyo: University of Tokyo Pres (in Japanese).

Taubman, P. 1975. *Generating Inquality: Mechanisms of Distribution in the US Economy*. New York: Basic Books.

Therborn, G. 1987. Welfare state and capitalist markets. *Acta Sociologica* 30: 237–54.

Tocqueville, A. de. 1835. *Democracy in America*. London: Saunders and Otley.

Topel, R. E. 1997. Factor proportions and relative wages: The supply-side determinants of wage inequality. *Journal of Economic Perspectives* 11: 55–74.

Treiman, D. J. 1970. Industrialization and social stratification. E. O. Laumann, ed., *Social Stratification: Research and Theory for the 1970s*. Indianapolis: Bobbs-Merrill, pp. 207–34.

Wada, R. O. 1975. Impact of economic growth on the size distribution of income: The post-war experience of Japan. In Japan Economic Research Center and Council for Asian Manpower Studies, ed., *Income Distribution, Employment, and Economic Development in Southeast and East Asia*. Tokyo: Japan Economic Research Center and Council for Asian Manpower Studies.

Waltzer, M. 1983. *Spheres of Justice: A Defense of Pluralism and Equality*. New York: Basic Books.

Willis, P. 1997. *Learning to Labor: How Working Class Kids Get Working Class Jobs.* Westmead: Saxon House.

Wolff, E. 1996. International Comparisons of Inequality. *Review of Income and Wealth* 42: 433–51.

Wright, E. O. 1978. *Class, Crisis and the State.* London: New Left Books.

Wright, E. O. 1997. *Class Counts: Comparative Studies in Class Analysis.* Cambridge: Cambridge University Press.

Yagi, T., and T. Tachibanaki. 1996. An estimation of equivalent scale and re-evaluation of Japanese income inequality. *Quarterly of Social Security Research* 32: 178–90 (in Japanese).

Yazawa, H. 1992. A comparison between pre-war and post-war on extremely wealthy families. *Japan Economic Review* 23: 146–85 (in Japanese).

Yoshida, T. 1997. Income distribution in the world and Asia's positions. In T. Mizoguchi and Y. Matsuda, eds., *Analysis on Income Distribution and Poverty in Asia.* Tokyo: Tagashuppan, pp. 21–49 (in Japanese).

Yoshikawa, H. 1997. *Rapid Economic Growth.* Tokyo: Yomiuri-shinbunsha (in Japanese).

Index

Abilities, bequests as, 204–206
Academic credentialism, 169, 170, 171,
   213
Advanced countries vs. developing
   countries, income inequalities in, 12–14
After-tax income, 93
Age
 and elderly poor, 76
 and employment, 180
 and source of income (pensions vs.
   wages), 91
American dream, 33
Americas, income inequality in, 13
Anti-monopoly law, 49–50
Asian countries, and income inequality,
   12–13
Asset income, 65–66
 and aging population, 116
 and income inequality, 95
Assets
 real and financial, 127 (*see also* Financial
   assets; Real assets)
 value of, 129–30
Atkinson index, 77
Australia
 income inequality in, 26
 poverty relief payments in, 121–22
 wage differentials by sex in, 101

Baby boom, postwar, 59–60
Banking system, Japanese
 in Japan's rapid growth, 56
 in postwar reforms, 44
 regulation of, 139–40
 safe financial assets in, 132, 133–34
Bentham, Jeremy, 196
Bequest motive, 138, 146–47, 149

Bequests, 146–50, 218
 abilities as, 204–206
 and effort, 185
 and inequality of opportunity, 188–89
 policies on, 153–55
 as savings, 138
 taxation of, 185–86, 203–204 (*see also*
   Inheritance taxes)
 and wealth distribution, 150–53, 154–55
Beveridge Report, 35
Blair, Tony, 36
Bonus payments, 137
Bowles, S., 32
Britain. See United Kingdom
Bubble economy in Japan, 64–66, 127,
   142–43, 218
 cause and effects of, 66
 collapse of, 17, 66
 inequality from, 26–27
 and landholding, 51
 and wealth distribution, 15–16, 143–45

Canada, 26, 101
Capitalist world vs. socialist world, in
   income distribution, 9–12
Capital market
 and educational inequality, 28, 188
 for home buying, 137–38
 and income inequality, 74
Causes of income inequality in Japan. *See*
   Income inequality in Japan, causes of
Child care
 and household welfare vs. income, 117
 subsidies to, 184
China, communist market economy in,
   11–12
Class (stratum), 157–59

and inheritance tax, 154, 155
and intergenerational social mobility, 160–65
and outcome, 183
Equality (or inequality) of outcome, 186–89, 218
in comparison of Japan and other countries, 2
vs. equality of opportunity, viii, 32–34, 180
and performance-based wage system (Japan), 179
as policy aim (Japan), 215
and wealth distribution (Japan), 179–80
Equity, 191
and performance-based pay, 179
Equity-efficiency trade-off. *See* Efficiency-equity trade-off
Equity holdings, 144
Equivalent scale, 77, 77–79
Export-led economy, and industrialization, 22

Fairness, 191
and performance-based pay, 179
Fair wage hypothesis, 34
Families
change in composition of, 57–58, 112–18
and international income comparisons, 76, 77
in Japanese economic support, 37
and need criterion, 184
Family Expenditure Survey, 67–70, 81, 88
Family Savings Survey, 141
Featherman-Jones-Hauser hypothesis, 160
Feudal characteristics of Japanese society (pre-WWII), 44
Financial assets, 128–29
as bequests, 152
safe, 132–35
Financial market, and educational inequality, 28. *See also* Capital market
Finland, education of workers in, 28
Firms, reforms in, 213–15
France
and class differences, 158
education and occupation in, 167, 168
income distribution in, 82
and income-inequality report, 80
top civil servants in, 171

Gender, and wage distribution, 47–48, 52, 100–104, 215. *See also* Women

Germany
East vs. West, 10, 11
education and occupation in, 167
and inequality, 124
and Kuznets hypothesis, 72
wage determination in, 177
Gini coefficient, 4–5, 77
and adjustments, 78, 79
and bubble economy, 143, 145
for income inequality (1900 to 2000), 70
increase in, 5
in international comparison, 7, 12–13, 83
prewar and postwar, 45, 46, 58
for primary incomes and before-tax incomes, 68
and redistribution effects of tax and social security, 123, 125
for Russia, 11
for US and UK, 26
and wealth distribution, 14, 15, 16
Globalization, and wage disparities in advanced countries, 27–28
Great Britain. *See* United Kingdom
Growth. *See* Economic growth

Happiness
economic prosperity as measure of, 88
Sen's analysis of, 197
Harrod-Dowar growth theory, 135
Health care, reform of, 209–10
Homeownership, 130–32
Households Expenditure Survey, 3
Household structure, changes in, 112–18
Housekeepers, and household welfare vs. income, 117
Human capital theory, 109
and education, 173, 188
and occupational mobility, 167

Imputed rents, 64–65, 66, 77, 131
Incentive divide, 212–13
Income, 93–94
after-tax, 93
as indicator of economic condition, 3
primary, 5, 93
redistributed, 5
uncertainties in measurement of, 90–91
Income distribution
in capitalist vs. socialist world, 9–12
and economic growth, 21–24
Income distribution in postwar Japan. *See* Postwar Japan's income distribution